PEOPLE WITHOUT POWER

Thomas Frank is the author of *Listen, Liberal*; *Pity the Billionaire*; *The Wrecking Crew*; and *What's the Matter with Kansas?* A former columnist for *The Wall Street Journal* and *Harper's*, Frank was also the founding editor of *The Baffler*. He lives outside Washington, D.C.

PEOPLE WITHOUT POWER

the war on populism
and the fight for
democracy

THOMAS FRANK

SCRIBE
Melbourne • London

Scribe Publications
2 John St, Clerkenwell, London WC1N 2ES, United Kingdom
18–20 Edward St, Brunswick, Victoria 3056, Australia

Published by Scribe 2020

People Without Power began as an essay that appeared in *The Guardian* in May 2018; pieces from that original essay are incorporated into the introduction and chapter one. Fragments from a *Guardian* essay I wrote in February 2017 appear in chapter seven. "The Utopia of Scolding" is an idea I first rolled out in *Harper's Magazine* in April 2018; chunks of that essay are incorporated into chapters four and eight. I wrote an introduction to everything that follows for *The Baffler* #42; hope I can live up to it.

Text design by Designed by Kelly S. Too
Printed and bound in the UK by CPI Group (UK) Ltd, Croydon CR0 4YY

Scribe Publications is committed to the sustainable use of natural resources and the use of paper products made responsibly from those resources.

9781912854226 (UK edition)
9781925849288 (Australian edition)
9781925938173 (ebook)

Catalogue records for this book are available from the National Library of Australia and the British Library.

scribepublications.co.uk
scribepublications.com.au

Who shall speak for the people?
Who knows the works from A to Z
      so he can say, "I know what the
      people want"? Who is this phenom?
      where did he come from?
When have the people been half as rotten
      as what the panderers to the people
      dangle before crowds?

—from "The People, Yes" by Carl Sandburg

CONTENTS

The Cure for the Common Man

Just a few short years ago we Americans knew what we were doing in the world. We were going to make the planet into one big likeness of ourselves. We had the experts; we knew how it was done. Our policy operatives would de-radicalize here and regime-change there; our economists would float billions to the good guys and slap sanctions on the bad; and pretty soon the whole world was going to be stately and neat, a place that was safe for debt instruments and empowerment seminars; for hors d'oeuvres in the embassy garden and taxis we hailed with our smartphone. Democracy! Of thee we sang.

Now we stand chastened, humiliated, bewildered. Democracy? We tremble to think of what it might do next.

"Government of the people"? When we open the door to ordinary people—let them actually influence what goes on— they will insist we make bigotry and persecution into our great national causes.

"Government by the people"? When we let the people have

their say—unmanaged, uncurated—some large part of them will choose the biggest blowhard on TV to be our leader. And then they will cheer for him as he destroys the environment and cracks down on migrant families.

Heed the voice of the plain people and all the levees of taste and learning will immediately be swamped. Half of them will demand that minorities be consigned to the back of the bus; the other half will try to confiscate the hard-won wealth of society's greatest innovators.

SO GOES THE wail of the American leadership class as they endure another year of panic over where our system is dragging them. They know on some level that what has happened in Washington isn't due to majority rule at all, but to money and gerrymandering and the electoral college and decades of TV programming decisions. But the anxiety cannot be dislodged; it is beyond the reach of reason: the people are out of control.

"Populism" is the word that comes to the lips of the respectable and the highly educated when they perceive the global system going haywire like this. Populism is the name they give to the avalanche crashing over the Alpine wonderland of Davos. Populism is what they call the mutiny that may well turn the supercarrier *America* into a foundering wreck. Populism, for them, is a one-word evocation of the logic of the mob; it is the people as a great rampaging beast.

What has happened, the thinkers of the Beltway and the C-Suite tell us, is that the common folk have declared independence from experts and along the way from reality itself. And so they have come together to rescue civilization: political scientists, policy advisers, economists, technologists, CEOs, joining as one to save our social order. To save it from populism.

This imagined struggle of expert versus populist has a fundamental, almost biblical flavor to it. It is a battle of order against chaos, education against ignorance, mind against appetite, enlightenment against bigotry, health against disease. From TED talk and red carpet, the call rings forth: democracy must be controlled . . . before it ruins our democratic way of life.

In attacking populism, the object is not merely to resist President Donald Trump, the nation's thinkers say. Nor is the conflict of our times some grand showdown of Left and Right. Questions like that, they tell us, were settled long ago when the Soviet Union collapsed. No, the political face-off of today is something different: it pits the center against the periphery, the competent insider against the disgruntled sorehead. In this conflict, the side of right is supposed to be obvious. Ordinary people are agitated, everyone knows this, but the ones whose well-being must concern us most are the elites whom the people threaten to topple.

This is the core assumption of what I call the Democracy Scare. If the people have lost faith in the ones in charge, it can only be because something has gone wrong with the people themselves. As Jonathan Rauch, a senior fellow at Brookings and a contributing editor to the *Atlantic*, put it in the summer of 2016: "Our most pressing political problem today is that the country abandoned the establishment, not the other way around."[1]

DENUNCIATIONS OF POPULISM have been commonplace for years; they only flowered into a full-blown panic in 2016, when commentators identified populism as the secret weapon behind the unlikely presidential bid of the TV billionaire Donald Trump. Populism was also said to be the mysterious force that had permitted the self-identified "outsider" Bernie Sanders to do so well in the Democratic primaries. Populism was *also* the name of the mass delusion that had foisted Brexit on the United Kingdom. Indeed, once you started looking, unauthorized troublemakers could be seen trouncing ruling classes in countries all around the world. Populists were misleading people about globalization. Populists were saying mean things about elites. Populists were subverting traditional institutions of government. And populists were winning.

In basing our civilization on the consent of the plain people, it suddenly seemed that our ancestors had built on a foundation of sand. "Democracies End When They Are Too Democratic" blared the title of a much-discussed 2016 essay by Andrew Sullivan. An article in *Foreign Policy* expressed it more archly: "It's Time for the Elites to Rise Up Against the Ignorant Masses."

Then came the unthinkable: the ignorant demagogue Trump was elected to the most powerful office in the world. Trump's victory that November only happened thanks to the Electoral College, an anti-populist instrument from long ago, but that irony quickly receded into the background. Instead, the Democracy Scare developed into a kind of hysteria. Across the world there were panels and convenings and academic projects dedicated to analyzing and theorizing and worrying about this thing called populism.

The 2017 "global report" for Human Rights Watch was titled, simply, "The Dangerous Rise of Populism."[2] In March of that year, former British prime minister Tony Blair rang the alarm with a *New York Times* essay titled, "How to Stop

Populism's Carnage." At about the same time he founded the Tony Blair Institute for Global Change, an organization whose website announces that populists "can pose a real threat to democracy itself."

Sober citizens were worrying about populism at the Aspen Ideas Festival. Scholarly types were moaning about it at the annual Prague Populism Conference. High-net-worth individuals reviled it at the World Economic Forum in Switzerland. The cool kids deplored it on the plains of Texas—at SXSW, a festival that originated as a punk rock gathering. In the Netherlands, the Friedrich Naumann Foundation sponsored another convening on the subject; the proceedings were described like this:

> Populism has become a wide spread phenomenon throughout the world. The danger of their backward-looking nostalgia for an idealized past, half-truths and fake news stories pose a threat for free and open societies.

At Brigham Young University a squad of experts on this dangerous phenomenon were ready to go even before 2016; "Team Populism" (as it called itself) swung into action with a flurry of policy memos and innovative statistical techniques. At Stanford, the "Global Populisms Project," which is co-chaired by a prominent former member of the Obama administration, declared as follows on its website: "Populist parties are a threat to liberal democracy."

The Democracy Scare was impressively pan-partisan. The liberal Center for American Progress came together in 2018 with its Beltway nemesis, the conservative American Enterprise Institute, to issue a report on "the threat of authoritarian populism" and to outline "the task facing America's political elites" as they went about beating it down.

The National Endowment for Democracy, supposedly a nonpartisan foundation, hosted a launch party for two books dedicated to pumping up the fear. *Anti-Pluralism: The Populist Threat to Liberal Democracy* was one of them; in it political scientist William Galston announced that "Populists damage democracy as such." *The People vs. Democracy* was the other; in it political scientist Yascha Mounk wrote that populism is a "disease."

And the disease was spreading; it was in fact an epidemic. "There can no longer be any doubt that we are going through a populist moment," Mounk continued. "The question now is whether this populist moment will turn into a populist age—and cast the very survival of liberal democracy in doubt."

DEPLORING POPULISM MIGHT seem like a peculiar thing to do in a land whose most treasured historical utterance concerns a government that is "of the people, by the people, for the people"; in a tradition where visiting the Iowa State Fair is a religious pilgrimage for politicians of every sort; in a culture that regards anyone who is less than enthusiastic about Burger King or the Batman franchise as some kind of sickening snob.

The anti-populist war effort ignores facile contradictions such as these, however. Populism works, we are told, by summoning up the worst features of democracy. It puts the common man on a pedestal, it promises him the strong leaders he craves, and it assaults the multiculturalism he hates. When populism gets in power, it ignores norms and attacks institutions that protect basic rights like free speech and innocence-till-proven-guilty. Populism is simply another word for mob rule, a headlong collapse into the tyranny of the majority that our Founding Fathers so dreaded.

"Populism arrays the people against the intelligentsia, natives against foreigners, and dominant ethnic, religious, and racial groups against minorities," charges the Berkeley economist Barry Eichengreen. "It is divisive by nature. It can be dangerously conducive to bellicose nationalism."[3]

"Populist parties" are "particularly prone to internal authoritarianism," says yet another political scientist, since they believe there can only be one way of representing the people. For the same reason populists are said to be suspicious of the media. They are would-be tyrants and dictators, claiming "that no action of a populist government can be questioned" because, of course, it's really the action of the people. And populists are always hinting at a "massive disenfranchisement" of those parts of the population of which they don't approve.[4]

Prizing the will of the people as it does, populism is also said to be unavoidably hostile to intellectuals. Indeed, as we shall see, this is often said to be its most critical failing. "The voice of ordinary citizens," one 2019 book about populism tells us, "is regarded as the only 'genuine' form of democratic governance even when at odds with expert judgments—including those of elected representatives and judges, scientists, and scholars, journalists and commentators."[5]

Thus the tragic flaw in the populist approach: its ideal of government of, by, and for the people doesn't take into account the ignorance of the actual, existing people. The people can't find Syria on a map, they think God created humans one day in their existing form, and if you give them half a chance, they will go out and vote for a charlatan like Donald Trump.

This is what made the election of 2016 a veritable "dance of the dunces," according to Georgetown political philosopher Jason Brennan's book, *Against Democracy*, an accounting of the ignorance of the average American that even includes suggestions for how an enlightened modern government might, in effect, disenfranchise the stupid and thus deal with the problem of democratic error.[6]

THIS IS THE diagnosis. The patient's condition is said to be critical. But before we succumb to the hysteria of the Democracy Scare, allow me to point out some curious aspects of this controversy.

The backlash against populism typically comes down to us from the citadels of higher learning—from think tanks, university presses, and academic conferences—but it is not a disinterested literature of social science. Although they don't like to acknowledge it, the anti-populists are combatants in this war, defending themselves against a perceived assault on their authority. Which is to say that anti-populism is an adversary proceeding. Our thought leaders relate to populism not so much as scholars but as a privileged class putting down a challenge to itself.[7]

Another peculiarity: The English language has a great many solid choices when someone wishes to describe mob psychology or racial intolerance. "Demagogue" is an obvious one, but there are others—"nationalist," "nativist," "racist," or "fascist," to name a few. They are serviceable words, all of them. In the feverish climate of the Democracy Scare, however, none of those will work: "populist" is the word we are instructed to use. "Populists" are the ones we must suppress.

Let's find out why.

FOR ALL THE trouble and confusion surrounding populism, the word's origins are unusually clear. We know where this word comes from; we know why it was invented; and we know the time and the place that it was born.

As it happens, the birthplace is a locale familiar to me: the countryside between Kansas City and Topeka. Drive the highway between those two cities today and you will pass through a landscape of peaceful rolling hills and occasional violent tornado damage. In the fertile valley of the Kansas River the farms are raising corn and soybeans; through the fields run the tracks of the old Atchison, Topeka and Santa Fe railroad.

It was somewhere in this bucolic setting that the controversial word "populist" was invented. There are no historical markers to indicate exactly where the blessed event took place, but nevertheless it happened—in this stretch of blank, green countryside, on a train traveling from K.C. to Topeka, one day in May 1891.

Could they have peeked into the future, that group of Topeka-bound passengers would have been astonished by the international reach and malign interpretations of their deed. That they were inventing a noun signifying "mob-minded hater of all things decent" would have come as a complete surprise to them. By coining the word "populist," they intended to christen a movement that was brave and noble and fair—that would stand up to the narrow-minded and the intolerant.

Oh, they meant to cause a certain amount of trouble, all right.

In so naming themselves, the original Populists were consecrating a brand-new third-party movement that aimed to break the grip of conventional politicians and conventional ideas. The organization's formal name was the "People's Party"; it was mainly composed of angry farmers, insurgent agrarians who, in an enormous electoral surprise, had upended the political system in Kansas some six months previously. The farmers' revolt against the existing two-party system had quickly spread to other states, and in the month when our story begins, a delegation of Kansans attended a convention in Cincinnati, Ohio, and launched their People's Party at the national level. By the time those reformers boarded the train home to Topeka, their movement looked to have a promising future: they had a platform, a cause, millions of potential constituents, and the ringing Jeffersonian slogan, "Equal rights to all, special privileges to none."

One thing the insurgent movement did not have, however, was a catchy word to describe its adherents, and so on that fateful train ride—and in conversation with a local Democrat who knew some Latin—this bunch of Kansans came up with one: "Populist," derived from *populus*, meaning "people."[8]

The word's debut in print followed immediately. The *American Nonconformist and Kansas Industrial Liberator*, a radical newspaper out of Winfield, Kansas, used the new word as part of its excited coverage of the Cincinnati proceedings. The date was May 28, 1891.

There must be some short and easy way of designating a member of the third party. To say, "he is a member of the People's party" would take too much time. Henceforth a follower and affiliator of the People's Party is a "Populist"; for a new party needs and deserves a new term.[9]

A new party needs a new term. And how that term caught on.

For the two brothers who ran the *American Nonconformist*, "Populist" was a term without ambiguity. It referred to economic radicals like them. Populists were those who supported a specific list of reforms designed to take power away from "the plutocrats" while advancing what the brothers called "the rights and needs, the interests and welfare of the *people*." In the same issue of the paper that premiered the word, the *Nonconformist* spelled out the grievances of the People's Party—it protested poverty, unbearable debt, monopoly, and corruption—and it looked forward to the day when these were ended by the political actions of the people themselves. "The industrial forces have made a stand," the paper declared of the events in Cincinnati. "The demands of the toilers for right and justice were crystallized into a strong new party."[10]

In fact, the Populist revolt against the two major parties would turn out to be even more momentous than that grandiose passage implied. Populism was one of the first of the great political efforts to tame the capitalist system. Up until then, mainstream politicians in America had by and large taken the virtues of that system for granted—society's winners won, those politicians believed, because they were better people; because they had prevailed in a rational and supremely fair contest called free enterprise. The Populists were the people who blasted those smug assumptions to pieces, forcing the country to acknowledge that ordinary Americans who were just as worthy as bankers or railroad barons were being ruined by an economic system that in fact answered to no moral laws.

. . .

NOT EVERYBODY THOUGHT Populism was such a wonderful invention, however. Kansas Republicans—whose complacent rule over the state had been interrupted by the People's Party— insisted that a better term for their foes was "Calamityites," because they complained all the time.[11] The *Kansas City Star*, an influential regional paper, surveyed the Cincinnati convention where the third party was born and sneered that it "bore a much closer semblance to a mob than to a deliberative assembly." What's more, the *Star*'s editorialist continued, "The conference, from beginning to end, was distinguished for its intolerance and extreme bigotry," words the paper used to describe the way a heavy-handed leadership faction steered the proceedings according to its own preferences.[12]

The judgment of the *Topeka Capital*, the leading voice of Republican rectitude in Kansas, was even harsher than that. The paper's lively page 1 news story on the gathering of reformers in Cincinnati was headed as follows:

THIRD PARTY!

Cincinnati Rapidly Filling Up with the Disgruntled
Ravelings of the Old Parties

KANSANS TO THE FORE

In Large Numbers and Making Themselves
Ridiculously Conspicuous by Their Gab

. . .

HAYSEED IN THEIR HAIR

Kansas Alliancers Proclaim Their Politics by
the Uncouthness of Their Personal Attire[13]

This is how the establishment welcomed the Populist revolt
into the world, and this is pretty much how the establishment
thinks about populism still.

From the very beginning, then, populism had two meanings.
There was Populism as its proponents understood it, meaning
a movement in which ordinary citizens demanded democratic
economic reforms. And there was Populism as its enemies characterized it: a dangerous movement of groundless resentment in
which demagogues led the disreputable.

The specific reforms for which the People's Party stood are
largely forgotten today. But the insults and accusations with
which Populism was received in 1891 are alive and well. You
can read them in best-selling books, watch them flashed on the
PowerPoint at prestigious foundation conferences, hear the
words of the *Kansas City Star* and the *Topeka Capital* mouthed
by people who have never heard of Topeka, Kansas: Populist
movements, they will tell you, are mob actions; reformers are
bigots; their leaders are blatherskites; their followers are mentally ill, or ignorant, or uncouth at the very least. They are
cranks; they are troublemakers; they are deplorables. And, yes,
they still have hayseed in their hair.

DO THE ORIGINS of words matter? Does it make any difference
who invented the word "populist" and what they meant by it?
After all, the meaning of words evolves all the time. Mutability is part of the nature of language. Merely figuring out the

intentions of the people who coined a given word doesn't tell us a whole lot.

In this case I think it does matter. For one thing, "populist" is not a word that fell conveniently from the sky, empty of signification and ready for pundits to use however they want: it was consciously invented to denote a particular group with a particular purpose. And though the People's Party is no more, the political philosophy that the Populists embodied did not die. The idea of working people coming together against economic privilege lives on; you might say it constitutes one of the main streams of our democratic tradition.

The populist impulse has in fact been a presence in American life since the country's beginning. Populism triumphed in the 1930s and 1940s, when the people overwhelmingly endorsed a regulatory welfare state. Populist uprisings occur all the time in American life, always with the same enemies—monopolies, banks, and corruption—and always with the same salt-of-the-earth heroes.

When we use the word to describe demagogues and would-be dictators, we are inverting that historic meaning. Populism was profoundly, achingly democratic. The Kansans who invented the term were referring to something that by the standards of the time was anti-demagogic; that was pro-enlightenment and pro-equality. In its heyday, and alone among American political parties of the time, Populism stood strong for human rights. Populism had prominent women leaders. Populists despised tyrants and imperialism. Populism defied the poisonous idea of southern white solidarity.

In these days of feverish anti-populism my mind often goes back to a 1900 speech by one of the very last Populists in Congress, a Nebraska lawyer named William Neville. His subject was America's then-new policy of imperial rule over the Philippines, and the Populist spelled out his party's opposition. But first he deplored Southern Democrats for trying to "exclude the black man from the right of suffrage," and he denounced Republicans for "shooting salvation and submission into the brown man because he wants to be free." And then Neville said this:

> Nations should have the same right among nations that men have among men. The right to life, liberty, and the pursuit of happiness is as dear to the black and brown man as to the white; as precious to the poor as to the rich; as just to the ignorant as to the educated; as sacred to the weak as to the strong, and as applicable to nations as to individuals, and the nation which subverts such right by force is no better governed than the man who takes the law in his own hands.[14]

Of course, scholars and journalists have a right to ignore such statements and to divorce any word they choose from its original meaning. It's legitimate for them to take this particular word back to its Latin root and to start all over again from there, to pretend that the train from Kansas City never arrived and the farmer's revolt never happened and to define "populist" just however they please.

But why would someone do that? Why use such a fine, democratic word to mean "racist," to mean "dictator," to mean "anti-intellectual"?

Before we begin on that story, let me make clear that I strongly approve of studying racist, right-wing demagogues and figuring out what can be done to defeat them. I have spent my adult life engaged in exactly this project. Calling such figures "populists," however, is a mistake if defeating them is really our purpose. Opponents of the Right should be claiming the high ground of populism, not ceding it to guys like Donald Trump. Indeed, this is so obvious to me that I am flabbergasted anew every time I see the word abused in this way. How does it help reformers, I wonder, to deliberately devalue the coinage of the American reform tradition?

It is my argument that reversing the meaning of "populist" tells us something important about the people who reversed it: denunciations of populism like the ones we hear so frequently nowadays arise from a long tradition of pessimism about popular sovereignty and democratic participation. And it is that pessimism—that tradition of quasi-aristocratic scorn—that has allowed the paranoid right to flower so abundantly.

The name I give to that pessimistic tradition is "anti-populism," and as we investigate its history, we will find it using the same rhetoric over and over again—in 1896, in 1936, and today. Whether it is defending the gold standard or our system of healthcare-for-a-few, anti-populism mobilizes the same sentiments and draws the same stereotypes; it sometimes even speaks to us from the same prestigious institutions. Its most toxic ingredient—a highbrow contempt for ordinary Americans—is as poisonous today as it was in the Victorian era or in the Great Depression.

ONE NAME SCHOLARS have applied to this tradition is the "elitist theory of democracy." It holds that public policy should be made by a "consensus of elites" rather than by the emotional and deluded people. It regards mass protest movements as outbreaks of irrationality. Marginalized people, it assumes, are marginalized for a reason. The critical thing in a system like ours, it maintains, is to allow members of the professional political class to find consensus quietly, harmoniously, and without too much interference from subaltern groups.[15]

The obvious, objective fact that the professional political class fails quite frequently is regarded in this philosophy as uninteresting if not impossible. When anti-populists have occasion to mention the elite failures of recent years—deindustrialization, financial crisis, opioid epidemic, everything related to the 2016 election—they almost always dismiss them as inevitable or unpredictable, episodes no one could possibly have foreseen or managed more successfully.[16]

On the subject of elite failure, there is no international program of inquiry as there is with populism. There are no calls for papers, no generous foundation grant program, no Stanford global elitisms project, no incentives at all to discover why experts keep blundering. Indeed, anti-populists find it harder to criticize their colleagues for fouling things up than they do to deride the voting public of America for being angry over those foul-ups. If the choice is between admitting that professionals often fail or determining that popular democracy must be reined in, anti-populists will choose the latter every time.

If only it were possible, they sigh, to dissolve the people and elect another.

1

What Was Populism?

Populism was the first of America's great economic uprisings, a roar of outrage from people in the lower half of the country's social order. It was a quintessential mass movement, in which rank-and-file Americans came to think of the country's inequitable system as a thing they might change by common effort. It was a glimpse of how citizens of a democracy, born with a faith in equality, can sometimes react when the brutal hierarchy of conventional arrangements is no longer tolerable to them.

Populism was also our country's final serious third-party effort, the last one to stand a decent chance of breaking the duopoly of the Republicans and Democrats. In the 1890s the two main parties were still basically regional organizations, relics of the Civil War; Populism transcended that system by making an appeal based on class solidarity, aiming to bring together farmers in the South and the West with factory workers in northern cities. "The interests of rural and civic labor are the same," proclaimed the famous 1892 Omaha Platform of the People's Party, and "their enemies are identical." By which the Pops meant those who prospered while producing nothing: bankers, railroad barons, and commodity traders, along with their hirelings—corrupt politicians who served wealth instead of "the people."

This was, of course, a time of unregulated corporate monopolies, of in-your-face corruption, and of crushing currency deflation—and it was also a time when everyone agreed that government's role was to provide a framework conducive to business and otherwise to get out of the way. That was the formal ideal; the execution was slightly uglier, a matter of smoke and exploitation, bankruptcy and foreclosure, of cabinet seats for sale and entire state legislatures bought with free-ride railroad passes.

Against this backdrop came the Populist revolt. The rightful subject of the government's ministrations, populism insisted, was not business at all but the People.

It all began in the 1880s when farmers started signing up by the thousands for a cooperative movement called the Farmers' Alliance. America was still largely an agricultural nation, and in the places where Populism eventually took root farmers made up overwhelming majorities of the population.

They were not particularly affluent majorities, however. In the South, farmers tended to be desperately poor, borrowing against future crops to buy food and necessities. The merchants from whom they borrowed took pains to ensure not only that the farmers never got out of debt but that they took the merchants' dictation on what to grow and how to grow it. What to grow always turned out to be cotton, and as the southern farmers produced crop after bumper crop of the stuff, the price only sank.

Farmers in the West, meanwhile, found themselves at the mercy of a different set of middlemen—local railroad monopolies and far-off commodity speculators. Like their brethren in the South, they worked and borrowed and grew and harvested; they watched as what they produced was sold in Chicago and New York for good prices; and yet what they themselves earned from their labors fell and fell and fell. In 1870, farmers received forty-three cents a bushel for corn; twenty years later in eastern Kansas it sold for ten cents a bushel, far less than what it cost to grow. Accounts from the period describe corn lying around on the ground with no takers; corn burned in stoves for heat.[1]

To such people the Farmer's Alliance made a simple proposition: Let's find out why we are being ruined, and then let's get together and do something about it. Education was the first order of business, and the movement conceived of itself as a sort of "national university," employing an army of traveling lecturers. Chapters of the movement ran lending libraries; radical rural newspapers (of which there were many) sold cheap books about agriculture and political reform.[2]

The movement also promised real results for farmers, by means of rural cooperatives and political pressure. And the Farmers' Alliance spread like a wildfire. By the end of the 1880s it had millions of members, mainly in the South; the Colored Farmers' Alliance (the southern Alliances were segregated) represented a million more; similar farm groups in the northern states brought additional millions into the radical fold. News reports marveled at the enormous audiences that would turn out to hear Alliance speakers—crowds of the size typically found at modern-day football games, gathering in a pasture somewhere. A novel published at the time describes the way American minds began to change:

People commenced to think who had never thought before, and people talked who had seldom spoken. . . . Little by little they commenced to theorize upon their condition. Despite the poverty of the country, the books of Henry George, [Edward] Bellamy, and other economic writers were bought to be read greedily; and nourished by the fascination of novelty and the zeal of enthusiasm, thoughts and theories sprouted like weeds after a May shower. . . . They discussed income tax and single tax; they talked of government ownership and the abolition of private property; fiat money, and the unity of labor; . . . and a thousand conflicting theories.[3]

At first, the political program of the Farmers' Alliance focused on a handful of big issues: the regulation of railroads, federal loans to farmers, and currency reform of a kind that would help debtors. The Alliance developed positions on a whole host of other matters as well: it supported free trade, for example, and votes for women, and secret ballots on Election Day. Thanks to the movement's vast numbers, conventional politicians in every farm state began to pay attention, promising to act on the farmers' demands.

But somehow the politicians never delivered. The power of business over the state legislatures always turned out to be too great to overcome. The same thing on a larger scale was obviously true of Congress in Washington, D.C. And while the politicians triangulated, the farmers' position worsened.

Something profound had taken place, however. The farmers—men and women of society's commonest rank—had figured out that being exploited was not the natural order of things. So members of the Farmers' Alliance began taking matters into their own hands. In Kansas and a few other western states they went into politics directly, styling themselves as the People's Party, a new organization with a new agenda. In the fall of 1890 they challenged and in places overthrew the dominant local Republicans, turning out old-school senators and representatives and replacing them with leaders from their own movement.

Over the next few years, the party organized itself nationally, and at their gathering in Omaha in the summer of 1892 they formally announced their program to the world. By this time the Knights of Labor and a number of other unions were on board, along with most of the reform-minded farm groups of the era, and so the People's Party declared itself to be "the first great labor conference of the United States and of the world," bringing together "the producers of the nation" from both the country and the city. They denounced "capitalists, corporations, national banks, rings, trusts," and they declared that "the time has come when the railroad corporations will either own the people or the people must own the railroads." In that heyday of American inequality, that golden age of Vanderbilt and Rockefeller, the Populists alone saw things clearly:

> The fruits of the toil of millions are boldly stolen to build up colossal fortunes for a few, unprecedented in the history of mankind; and the possessors of these, in turn, despise the republic and endanger liberty. From the same prolific womb of governmental injustice we breed the two great classes— tramps and millionaires.[4]

In 1892 the Populist presidential candidate, a Civil War general from Iowa named James B. Weaver, won 22 electoral votes, and by following a strategy of "fusion" or coordination with local Democrats, the party managed to elect governors in several western states ordinarily controlled by the Republicans.

In the South, where the dominant group was the conservative "Bourbon" Democrats, the Populist revolt met with disaster. The party of white supremacy casually cheated the Pops out of victories that should have been theirs. The only southern state where the third party prevailed was North Carolina, where fusion with the local Republicans brought Populism into power in the middle of the decade. To this subject we shall return anon.

SOCIAL CLASS WAS essential to how the Populists understood their situation, and they talked often about what they called "the producing class." But the phrase they favored above all others when speaking of the toilers was "the people." As in: "We the People." As in: "Of the people, by the people, for the people." That was the struggle as they saw it: the "plain people" versus the power.

It is common to cast Populism as the end of something, as the farmer's last political stand or the terminus of nineteenth-century radicalism. With a slightly wider focus, the arrival of Populism looks a lot more like the shock of the new. "A new way of looking at things," in the words of historian Lawrence Goodwyn; "a mass expression of a new political vision."[5] This was the first movement in American politics that demanded far-reaching government intervention in the economy in order to benefit working people, and contemporaneous accounts of the movement often describe its arrival as a sort of epiphany, a "Pentecost of politics," a moment of sudden, mass enlightenment. Consider this description of a gathering of Texas Populists:

For a whole week they literally lived and breathed Reform: by day and by night they sang of Populism, they prayed for

Populism, they read Populist literature and discussed Populist principles with their brethren in the faith, and they heard Populist orators loose their destructive thunderbolts in the name of the People's Party.[6]

In truth, that vision was manifesting all over the world in those days. The Pops won the support of a significant chunk of the emerging American labor movement, and in some places the People's Party was basically a labor party. As such, Populism was part of a great wave of working-class political movements then rising up in the industrialized countries. The British Labour Party was founded at about the same time, and Populists on occasion looked to it for inspiration. The Australian Labor Party, for its part, actually considered adopting the name "People's Party" in homage to what then looked like a powerful new force in the United States.[7]

Like these other groups, the Pops concentrated their efforts on economic issues and the closely related matter of electoral reform. By and large, they stayed away from the culture-war issues of the day. This surprises the modern-day student of the movement: the Populists may have had a churchly way of speaking, but for the most part they refrained from denouncing ordinary people for their bad values. Questions like prohibition, for example, threatened to break the Populist coalition apart and therefore had to be avoided despite the distaste of many Pops for liquor and saloons. With their singular focus on economics, they regarded many of the controversies of the day as traps or distractions.

Populist rhetoric oscillated between passionate denunciations of injustice and methodical, even boring exegeses on complicated economic problems. "Starvation stalks abroad amid an overproduction of food," roared a typical Populist *j'accuse* of 1891; within a few sentences, however, it had gone from hot to cold, calling on readers to

> calmly and dispassionately examine the facts which we are prepared to submit in support of our claims. . . . [I]f the facts and arguments we present can be refuted we neither ask nor expect your support.

These were peculiarly math-minded reformers. Look over introductions to the reform cause like the 1895 pamphlet *What Is Populism?*, and you will find a detailed, plank-by-plank exposition of the party's economic program: its demands for a government-controlled currency, for government control of the railroads, for rooting out political corruption . . . and precious little else.[8]

Many of Populism's causes are familiar to us today: the regulation of monopolies, the income tax, the initiative and referendum, the direct election of senators,* and so on. They are familiar because they have largely been achieved.

One item on the list of Populist grievances requires a lengthier explanation today, however. For many Americans of the late nineteenth century, currency deflation was the single greatest issue facing the nation. At that time, the worth of the dollar was fixed to the value of gold: the "gold standard." As a result, the amount of dollars in circulation could not increase unless

---

* Before the adoption of the Seventeenth Amendment to the Constitution (1913), senators were chosen by state legislatures.

the government's reserves of gold—a scarce metal—increased as well.

One consequence of the gold standard was painful, constant *deflation*. Since the population and the economy were both growing explosively, and since the number of dollars in circulation could not grow with them, dollars became scarcer every year and constantly increased in value. If you were a banker, this was a fantastic situation. If you were a debtor—and farmers were debtors—the gold standard was dreadful. It meant you had to repay what you had borrowed using dollars that were now far more valuable than they had been when you took out your loan. Debt of this kind was not something you paid off easily; it was a condition in which you struggled all your days, a form of servitude, almost.

"Fiat currency" was the hard-core Populists' proposal for solving this problem. It would have authorized the government simply to print the nation's medium of exchange however it chose and then to establish its value by administrative pronouncement, without any reference to precious metals. (This is the system we have today, incidentally.) The other remedy Populists embraced was "free silver": simply replacing the limited reserves of gold with a more plentiful supply of silver. Since silver was being mined all the time in America, the money in circulation under a silver standard would stand a better chance of keeping up with the economy's growth.

"Free silver" proceeded to catch the imagination of certain classes of Americans in a way that is difficult to understand today. Silver became the object of a sort of crusade in the 1890s, a symbol that made everything fit together. Silver would not only solve the problem of deflation, people thought; it would humanize capitalism. Silver would bring back fairness. Silver represented democratic virtue and workerist authenticity. Gold, meanwhile, came to stand for aristocratic privilege and deathly inequality. As the silver craze swept America, the Populists saw their fortunes ascend with it—ascend so rapidly that eventually free silver came to crowd out everything else the party stood for.

IN 1893 THE national economy went into one of its periodic recessions—this time it was sharp and painful. Banks and businesses failed all over America and especially in the West. Unemployment came close to 20 percent, with millions thrown out of work. Homeless people roamed the country. There were of course no federal programs in place for relief or stimulus or recovery; the crisis response of the Grover Cleveland administration in Washington consisted of an aggressive campaign of . . . buying gold.

The plight of the unemployed was of little concern to the country's economic authorities. But the confidence of bankers and investors was a different matter: such people had to be assuaged. They had to be convinced of the government's unswerving devotion to economic orthodoxy, meaning the gold standard. And this the Democrat Cleveland set out to do. To stave off a panicked run on the nation's gold supply, he stockpiled gold and then he stockpiled more gold. He made deals with bankers, keeping them happy with guaranteed profits, so that they wouldn't withdraw that precious yellow stuff. He worked hard to restore their confidence. Above all, he stockpiled that gold.

Before long, outrage was no longer confined to farm country; all over America working people were learning what the Populists had figured out a few years previously. In the summer of 1894, a local strike at the Pullman passenger-car plant in

Chicago blew up into a vast national conflagration. In solidarity with the workers at Pullman, the American Railway Union, led by Eugene Debs, refused to handle trains with Pullman cars attached. Rail traffic throughout the country quickly came to a standstill. President Cleveland took a break from stockpiling gold to order the U.S. Army into Chicago; his Justice Department tossed Debs in jail for obstructing the mail.

An even more spectacular event occurred that same year when one Jacob Coxey, a Populist from Ohio, conceived of the idea of "a petition in boots"—an army of unemployed men that would march to Washington, D.C., to make plain the miserable economic conditions in the hinterlands. From all over the country, jobless people joined up with Coxey's Army and, several weeks and a few borrowed train rides later, they arrived in the nation's capital: the first-ever mass protest march on Washington. Their demand was that the government hire unemployed people to build roads and other infrastructure, paying for it with deficit spending. Respectable Washingtonians laughed at the cockeyed suggestion and at the dirty tramps who supported it: what a bunch of cranks! D.C. police tossed Coxey in jail for walking on the Capitol lawn.

The Populists seemed perfectly positioned to take advantage of these dreadful developments. They were, after all, the self-proclaimed party of working people and economic grievance. They loudly deplored the methods used by the Cleveland administration to smash the Pullman strike in the streets of Chicago, and after the strike was over the Pops embraced Eugene Debs as their newest hero.[9]

Meanwhile, as the hard times deepened and the Democratic administration did its grotesque favors for the banking community, the mania for silver grew and grew. Both of the old parties remained committed to the gold standard, leaving only the Populists standing outside this tidy consensus of the orthodox and the comfortable. Never before had the reformers' charge that the two parties ignored the real issues seemed more obvious, more self-evident. Populism was going to ride the silver escalator to the top. Reform was on the march; Populism was unstoppable.

Then something crazy happened. As the recession deepened, the Democratic Party began to turn against its sitting president, the banker-coddling Grover Cleveland. When the Democrats gathered for their convention in Chicago in the summer of 1896, pandemonium broke loose. Not only did the party denounce its own president, but it declared its intention to toss the gold standard itself overboard. Then they nominated for the presidency the virtually unknown William Jennings Bryan, a thirty-six-year-old free-silver advocate from Nebraska who talked as much like a Populist as did anyone from the Cornhusker state.

Eastern respectability reeled as it beheld one of the country's two traditional parties apparently captured by radicalism. The actual radicals in the People's Party, meanwhile, reckoned with the very different problem of seeing a powerful rival swipe the idea upon which they had strategically placed all their hopes. Meeting right after the shocking Democratic convention, the Populists felt they had little choice but to throw in their lot with Bryan. Fusion had been a successful strategy for the party at the state level, and now Populist leaders hoped to follow it into the executive branch in Washington.

The gamble was a painful one for certain Populists, however. Not only did it mean selling out their far-reaching reform program in favor of one issue, but many among the party's southern and black contingents had risked their lives to make a stand against the Democratic Party. For them to come crawling back because their colleagues wanted to endorse Bryan was a humiliating prospect.[10]

Still, the wager was done. The crusade was launched. It was free silver against the gold standard, with Populists and Democrats standing more or less united to defeat the plutocracy. When Bryan proceeded to lose to Republican William McKinley, Populism fell mortally wounded.

The People's Party struggled on for a few more years, but after the catastrophe of the 1896 election its fate was sealed. The party immediately broke into squabbling factions. Its conventions, scheduled for large auditoriums, were attended by embarrassingly small crowds. At length the economy recovered, even for farmers. Agricultural prices rose and, thanks to various technological advances, the global production of gold increased enormously, finally erasing the problems of deflation.

Meanwhile, the two big parties slowly came around to the Populist innovations. Populist voters gradually made their way back to their previous partisan homes, while a chunk of the leadership joined the Socialist Party. By the first few years of the twentieth century, the third party's grievances and its evangelical style seemed dated and easy to forget.

POPULISM'S LIST OF demands, however, did not perish. It lived on and met with success. The direct election of U.S. senators, for example, was secured through the Seventeenth Amendment to the Constitution in 1913. Railroads were regulated and so was the telephone system. Other monopolies were broken up. Women got the vote. Rich people got the income tax. Beginning in the 1910s, farmers got a whole host of programs designed to protect them from speculators and middlemen and the ups and downs of the market. Putting unemployed people to work on infrastructure eventually became a standard element of economic policy.

In monetary policy, Populism also won in the end. The country finally came off the gold standard in 1933. Ultimately the United States moved to adopt the most radical Populist demand of them all, a managed or "fiat" currency—although we didn't do it fully until 1971, some eighty years after Populism first came thundering over the prairies.

These items make up "The Populist Contribution," a phrase that a long-ago historian used to describe this list of belated triumphs.[11] For scholars of that generation, Populism was a chapter in the story of democracy's advance, part of a long-running drama in which the American people faced off against aristocratic financial interests. The movement aimed "to make of America a land of democratic equality and opportunity," wrote historian Vernon L. Parrington in 1930—"to make government in America serve man rather than property." Populism showed that egalitarian aspirations lived and were capable of prevailing even in the country's most corrupt, most plutocratic period.[12]

The ideology of Populism was not a difficult thing for historians in 1930 to identify. Its signature ideas—equality, hostility to privilege, anti-monopoly—were part of a radical nineteenth-century tradition that could be traced to Thomas Paine and Thomas Jefferson. One reason that historians knew this was because the Populists said so all the time. The Jefferson the Pops admired is easy to pinpoint—it was the Jefferson who declared that banks were "more dangerous than standing armies," who believed that the natural divide between political factions fell between "aristocrats and democrats," who once urged a friend not to be intimidated by "the croakings of wealth against the ascendency of the people."

Understood in this way, Populism is not only a radical tradition, it is *our* radical tradition, a homegrown Left that spoke our American vernacular and worshipped at the shrines of Jefferson and Paine rather than Marx. We may have lost sight of the specific demands of the Populists' Omaha Platform, but the populist instinct stays with us; it is close to who we are as a people. We may gag at political correctness, but populism endures; populism is what ensures that, even though we bridle against the latest crazy radical doings on campus, we also hate snobs and privilege with the core of our collective democratic being.

OVER THE LAST century, observers called countless movements and politicians "populist" because they were reminiscent in some way of the original. The People's Party, however, was one of very few movements to apply that word to itself, to proudly call itself "Populist." For decades after its brief flowering, it remained virtually the only example of the species, the number one definition of the word in English-language dictionaries.

It is therefore surprising that modern-day thinkers who assail what they call populism only rarely bother to consider the movement that invented the word. Of the contemporary anti-populists I describe in this book, almost every single one is employed by an American news outlet, university, or think tank, and yet they attach the term far more frequently to the deeds of the Le Pen family in France or the rhetoric of South American politicians than to the group that revolutionized U.S. politics in the 1890s. Some of these experts seem unaware that the People's Party existed.* Others mention it only casually and in passing.†

Still, in their characterization of populism as a threat to democracy—an "ism" as insidious in its own way as communism used to be—these present-day thinkers are doing far more than calling into question various racist demagogues: they are also attacking the American radical tradition. That is ultimately what's in the crosshairs when such commentators insist that populism is a "threat to liberal democracy"; when they announce that populism "is almost inherently antidemocratic"; when they declare that "all people of goodwill must come together to defend liberal democracy from the populist threat."[13]

These are strong, urgent statements, obviously intended to frighten us away from a particular set of views. Millions of

---

* Yascha Mounk, in *The People vs. Democracy*, suggests that "one of the earliest populists to rise to prominence" was Jörg Haider, an Austrian rightist whose heyday was in the 1980s and '90s (p. 114). Similarly, the home page of the Stanford Global Populisms Project tells us that populism was "initially associated with Latin America in the 1990s" before migrating to the United States and giving us President Donald Trump. This seems like the place to mention that the founder of Stanford University, California senator Leland Stanford, was briefly considered as a Populist presidential candidate in 1892 (Hicks, *The Populist Revolt: A History of the Farmer's Alliance and the People's Party* [University of Nebraska Press, 1959 (1931)], p. 234).

† The saga of the People's Party is related briefly in *Populism: A Very Short Introduction* by Cas Mudde and Cristobal Rovira Kaltwasser (Oxford University Press, 2017), but the details of the movement are weirdly garbled. For example, the authors explain the rise of Populism by pointing out that "economic changes, such as the coining of silver, affected the rural areas particularly hard." As we have seen, Populists actually supported the coining of silver as a way of relieving rural hardship.

foundation dollars have been invested to put scary pronounce-
ments like these before the public. Media outlets have incorporated them into the thought feeds of the world. They are
everywhere now: your daily newspaper, if your town still has
one, almost certainly throws the word "populist" at racist demagogues and pro-labor liberals alike.

When we fact-check the claims of this anti-populist onslaught,
however, we find that they miss the reality of the original Populist movement as well as the many subsequent expressions
of the populist credo. Again and again, upon investigation,
the hateful tendencies that we are told make up this frightful
worldview are either absent from genuine populism, or are the
opposite of what it stood and stands for, or else more accurately
describe the people who hated populism and who have opposed
it since back in the 1890s.*

I do not point all this out merely as a historical corrective;
that is just the starting point. This book has larger ambitions.
As we shall see, anti-populism always serves as a tool for justify-
ing unaccountable power. As such, it is a doctrine worth exploring in its own right. But the immediate and urgent task before

---

* Only one of the present-day populism experts openly acknowledges that
the 1890s Populists do not fit the current, voguish definition. This is Jan-
Werner Müller of Princeton University, who writes that "the one party in
US history that explicitly called itself 'populist' was in fact not populist,"
by which he means, the people who invented the word were not the racist,
authoritarian demagogues Müller wishes to associate with the word (*What
Is Populism?* [University of Pennsylvania Press, 2016], p. 85). This is admirably forthright of Müller, to be sure, but it somehow doesn't lead him to
do the obvious thing—stop using the word "populist" to describe racist,
authoritarian demagogues. Instead he gives us an entire book doing exactly
that and then exempts the 1890s Pops from his critique. If historical reality
conflicts with fashionable political theory, I guess, it is reality that must
give way.

us is to rescue from the anti-populists the one radical tradition
that has a chance of undoing the right-wing turn.

THE FIRST ITEM in the bill of charges against populism is that it
is nostalgic or backward-looking in a way that is both futile and
unhealthy. Among the many public figures who have seconded
this familiar accusation is none other than the president of the
United States, Barack Obama, who in 2016 criticized unnamed
politicians for having "embraced a crude populism that promises a return to a past that is not possible to restore." What he
was taking aim at was obviously Trump's slogan: "Make America Great Again," which implied that the country's best days
lay in the past.[14]

Obama's understanding of "populism" as a politics of point-
less pining for bygone glories is unremarkable, but a more
accurate noun for this sentiment would be "conservatism"—the
political philosophy that defends traditional ways. The agrarian
radicals of the late nineteenth century did no such thing. Populism called for radical reforms that would have put this country
on an entirely different trajectory from the finance-capital road
we followed.

Indeed, the Populists believed in progress and modernity as
emphatically as did any big-city architect or engineer of their
day. Their newspapers and magazines loved to publicize scientific advances in farming techniques; one of their favorites was
a paper called the *Progressive Farmer*. For all their gloom about
the plutocratic 1890s, the Populists' rhetoric could be surprisingly optimistic about the potential of ordinary people and the
society they thought they were building.[15] This did not mean,
however, that the Pops simply welcomed whatever happened as

an improvement on what had happened the day before. It was not a step forward to pack the nation's wealth into the bank accounts of a handful of people who contributed nothing; real progress meant economic democracy as well as technological innovation.

Anti-populism is similarly misleading on the crucial matter of international trade. In a 2017 paper about the "populist backlash of the late nineteenth century," the Hoover Institution historian Niall Ferguson tells us flatly that hostility to free trade has always been one of the signature issues that define populism, because populism, as he puts it, is always a "backlash against globalization." Lots of other scholars say the same thing: William Galston of the Brookings Institution, for example, tells us that populism has always been "protectionist in the broad sense of the term"; that all forms of populism stand "against foreign goods, foreign immigrants, and foreign ideas."[16]

When applied to Gilded Age America, these arguments are almost entirely upside-down. If you look up where the parties stood on the then-important issue of tariffs, you find that the great champions of protectionism were in fact big business and the Republicans. The man responsible for crushing Populism first rose to fame as the author of the "McKinley Tariff," the very definition of a backlash against free trade. It was William Jennings Bryan's Democrats who were the true-believing free-traders of the period.*

---

* For the record, here is the statement on trade from the Democratic Platform of 1896, on which Bryan ran for the presidency: "We denounce as disturbing to business the Republican threat to restore the McKinley law, which has twice been condemned by the people in National elections and which, enacted under the false plea of protection to home industry, proved a prolific breeder of trusts and monopolies, enriched the few at the expense

It's also worth remembering that agrarian organizations in America have nearly always supported free trade, for the simple reason that American farmers export huge amounts of food and because many of the things that farmers consume can be purchased more cheaply overseas. And sure enough, among the various manifestos of the Farmers' Alliance is found the following: "We further demand a removal of the existing heavy tariff tax from the necessities of life, that the poor of our land must have." Indeed, the Populists were so passionate about encouraging trade that a number of their legislators enlisted in a scheme to build a publicly owned railroad running from the Great Plains to the Texas Gulf Coast, which would theoretically allow farmers to export directly to the world without having to pay the high freight rates imposed by private railways. That's how actual Populists regarded protectionism—in precisely the opposite way from what modern scholars assure us populism always does.[17]

CONTEMPORARY EXPERTS FURTHER inform us that populists feel an "instinctual antagonism" to government agencies, particularly of the sort that are insulated from politics.[18] While this is certainly true of modern-day conservative Republicans (who despise regulation of business) and of Brexit supporters in the United Kingdom (who fear the unaccountable bureaucracy of the European Union), it is almost precisely the opposite of the viewpoint of American Populists.

In point of fact, the Pops came out of the reform tradition

---

of the many, restricted trade and deprived the producers of the great American staples of access to their natural markets." See more at https://www.presidency.ucsb.edu/documents/1896-democratic-party-platform.

that *invented* the modern independent regulatory agency,* and historians generally acknowledge that the People's Party was the first to call for large-scale government intervention in the economy—by which I mean, intervention on behalf of ordinary people, not corporations. Their 1892 Omaha Platform spelled it out clearly: "We believe that the powers of government—in other words, of the people—should be expanded . . . as rapidly and as far as the good sense of an intelligent people and the teachings of experience shall justify, to the end that oppression, injustice, and poverty shall eventually cease in the land."

The Populists wanted the government to own and operate the nation's railroads, to manage the currency, to take possession of land owned by speculators, to set up postal savings banks, and a dizzying list of other interventions. The third party's hopes for government assistance were one of the things that made Populism seem so sick and twisted to men of respectability at the time. "The Populist faith in the 'Gover'ment' is supreme," observed one of the earliest students of the movement, in 1893.

> The Government is all-powerful and it ought to be all-willing. When a Populist debtor is approached by a creditor his reply is actually often in these words: "I can't pay the debt until the Government gives me relief." This intervention or saving grace of the Government is a personal influence to

* The world's first modern independent regulatory agencies were midwestern state railroad commissions, set up at the behest of the Granger movement in the 1870s. The Grangers were the direct ancestors of the Farmers' Alliance, which became the People's Party. See Chester McArthur Destler, *American Radicalism, 1865–1901* (Quadrangle, 1966 [1946]), p. 10.

him, a thing of life. What shall minister to a mind diseased like the Populist's? Only constitutional remedies.[19]

Yes, ordinary, working-class people once demanded that government get bigger and take over vast chunks of the economy. That was what American liberalism was all about, once upon a time, and it started with Populism.

AUTHORITARIANISM IS A grave danger that always attends the rise of populism, modern-day scholars assure us. The menace of "authoritarian populists" is one of the important themes in Yascha Mounk's book, *The People vs. Democracy*. Harvard political scientist Steven Levitsky, meanwhile, argues that populists "weaken" democracies by "undermining the norms that sustain them," thus raising the specter of authoritarianism. "When populists win elections, they often assault democratic institutions," he warns in his best-selling book, *How Democracies Die*.[20]

Now, there is no doubt that Donald Trump is a norm-violating, would-be autocrat. And attributing his authoritarianism to his "populism" draws on the long-running scholarly tendency to find that virtually all working-class movements are tyrannies-in-waiting.[21]

If the original 1890s Populists were authoritarians, however, they were some of history's most ineffectual tyrants. Discipline was always poor in the People's Party: the organization could never shake what the historian Charles Postel calls its "nonpartisan and anti-party origins"; it started splitting into factions soon after it got going. The Pops were even lousy at selling out.

After endorsing the Democratic presidential candidate in 1896, they were unable to convince the Democrats to reciprocate and accept the Populist choice for the vice presidency.

Then: the Pops and their Sunday-school hero William Jennings Bryan were torn to pieces in one of the most brutal demonstrations of military-style politics ever seen in this country, a coldly efficient electoral massacre organized by William McKinley and Mark Hanna, the tycoon warlord of the Republican Party. The GOP is estimated to have outspent the Democrat/Populist campaign by twenty or thirty to one that year. To this day, by one standard of measurement, the Republican effort of 1896 still holds the record for the most expensive presidential campaign of all time.[22] To study that famous contest and announce that the Populists were the authoritarian team in the match would be a pants-on-fire outrage.

IN ONE OF the more distorted charges, virtually everyone who writes on the subject nowadays agrees that populism is "anti-pluralist," by which they mean that it is racist or sexist or discriminatory in some other way. The source of this sin is said to be populism's love of "the people," a concept that always supposedly excludes big parts of the population for being inauthentic or ethnically different. Populism's hatred for "the elite," meanwhile, is thought to be merely a fig leaf for this ugly intolerance.[23]

Something like this is true in today's world: The leader of the Republican Party denounces elitists in what he calls the "global power structure" and also sets nativist hearts a-thumping with his promises of a wall along the Mexican border. And so, liberal intellectuals conclude, the two must be connected. Movements that criticize elites in the name of the people are by definition opposed to the colorful mosaic of complex modern societies; intolerance is encoded in populism's very DNA.

It's a funny thing, though: the example of Populism once inspired intellectuals as they went about *attacking* racism. C. Vann Woodward, the legendary historian of the American South, writes in his memoirs that he was drawn to the subject of Populism as a young man because it "compelled reconsideration" of the racist shibboleths of the South's Democratic Party elite: "progress, prosperity, peace, consensus, white solidarity, black contentment. . . ." The young Woodward meant to shatter these stupid, stifling complacencies, and when he discovered the South's Populist past as a graduate student in the 1930s, he thought he had found the weapon with which to do so.[24]

This is because attacking racist shibboleths was something that certain Populist leaders famously did during the movement's brief career. The South in the 1890s was filled with poor farmers both white and black, and keeping these two groups at each other's throats was virtually the entire point of the region's traditional politics. "A generation of white-solidarity indoctrination," as Woodward called it in his classic *Origins of the New South*, ensured poverty for both groups but unchallenged power for the "Bourbon" Democratic elite.

Populism's strategy for taking on the region's one-party system, as Woodward described it, was to organize "a political union" between white and "Negro farmers and laborers within the South," a shocking affront both to racist tradition and to the interests of the local moneyed class.[25] The Pops, Woodward continued, "ridiculed the clichés of Reconciliation and White Solidarity."

The bolder among them challenged the cult of racism with the doctrine of common action among farmers and workers of both races. The very existence of the third party was, of course, a challenge to the one-party system as well as to white solidarity.[26]

In 1892, the Populist leader Tom Watson of Georgia declared in a national magazine that "the People's Party will settle the race question" by addressing the common economic interests of black and white farmers. Watson then spoke to those farmers directly: "You are kept apart that you may be separately fleeced of your earnings. You are made to hate each other because upon that hatred is rested the keystone of the arch of financial despotism which enslaves you both. You are deceived and blinded that you may not see how this race antagonism perpetuates a monetary system which beggars both."[27]

This is not to say that white southern Populists were racial liberals or that they practiced what they preached; they weren't and they didn't. What they did do, however, was defy the Bourbon Democrats of the South, for whom white solidarity and the suppression of African Americans were the monolithic first principles of political consciousness. Populism's very existence was an attack on these doctrines.

At times, the People's Party appeared to be making progress toward its stated ideal of class-based political action across the color line. Charles Postel reminds us that the marchers of Coxey's Army deliberately violated segregated norms and that they were often helped along the road to Washington by black churches. In some southern states, the Pops struck fusion deals with local Republicans, the party to which many blacks were still loyal. By this device, for example, the Pops and the Republicans were able to defeat the Democratic Party of North Carolina and take over the government of that state for several years.[28]

"Poverty has few distinctions among its victims," observed Hamlin Garland in an 1897 novel set amidst the rise of Populism. Describing a protest of Kansas farmers, he wrote, "The negro stood close beside his white brother in adversity, and there was a certain relation and resemblance in their stiffened walk, poor clothing, and dumb, imploring, empty hands." The spectacle, Garland continued, was "something tremendous, something far-reaching. The movement it represented had the majesty, if not the volcanic energy, of the rise of the peasants of the Vendee."[29]

The Colored Farmers' Alliance was the name of the group that organized black farmers alongside the whites-only southern Farmers' Alliance. Leaders from the Colored Alliance were essential in launching the People's Party; in some respects they were well ahead of their white brethren in calling for a third party.[30] But Black Populism, as it is now called, was ultimately a fruitless effort. Everywhere in the South, the Pops hit the wall of violence and vote fraud that blocked the progress of anyone who challenged white solidarity. When the new party made its debut in southern elections in 1892, black voters were attacked and a number of them were murdered, a direct reflection, according to a recent study of Black Populism, of "the political threat posed to the Democratic Party by the coalition of black and independent white voters." Violence of this kind continued here and there across the South until Populism was completely vanquished.[31]

Nor was the commitment to equality professed by many white Populists truly sincere. Some of them turned out to be just as committed to white supremacy as were the Southern Democrats they meant to defy. Many others thought racism and segregation were grounded in science.[32] And later on, once Populism had begun to weaken, the same Tom Watson who wrote such admirable words in 1892 reemerged as one of the nation's most notorious racists, producing (according to the historian Woodward) a stream of "tirades against his onetime allies of the Negro race that were matchless in their malevolence."[33]

The point here is not some precise accounting of the Populists' record on race—summary: they meant well but didn't deliver. The critical thing to understand, for present purposes, is that the Populists were not the great villains of the era's racist system. That dishonor went to the movement's archenemies in the southern Democratic Party, leaders who were absolutely clear about their commitment to white supremacy.[34]

THE MODERN-DAY ASSOCIATION of populism with "anti-pluralism" misses the historical target in several other crucial ways. For example, the Pops were the only party of their time to feature women in positions of leadership. In Kansas, the movement was singularly identified with the outrageous adventures of one Mary Elizabeth Lease, a dynamic orator who traveled around the state in 1890, damning Republican politicians and (according to legend) advising her audiences to "raise less corn and more hell." A quieter, more executive role was played in that same state by the journalist Annie L. Diggs, whom a Kansas City newspaper once called the "unqualified dictator of the

Kansas Populists . . . the first woman boss in American politics."[35] Again, not all Populists supported women's suffrage,
but enough of them did to secure women the right to vote in
several of the western states where the party was strong.

On the question of immigration, which was just as controversial then as it is today, the People's Party was of two minds.
Its 1892 Omaha Platform—like the platforms of the two major
parties—opposed "pauper" immigration on the grounds that
it "crowds out our wage-earners." The man the party chose as
its presidential candidate, however, was a forthright *supporter* of
open immigration, demanding in stormy Populist style:

> Are we still an asylum for the oppressed of all nations, or
> are we about to become a policeman for the monarchs and
> despots of the old world—a despicable, international slave-
> catcher, under a world-wide fugitive slave law—engaged in
> the business of arresting and returning to their cruel task-
> masters the poor slaves who are fleeing hither to become cit-
> izens and to escape from hopeless conditions?[36]

Toward immigrants themselves the People's Party was
remarkably open. A granular investigation of the attitudes of
Kansas Populists toward immigrants found precisely the opposite of what present-day theorists insist is always the case with
populism. Kansas in the 1890s was a state filled with just-
arrived people, and the Populists competed vigorously for their
votes; Populist officeholders, meanwhile, came from Ireland,
Germany, Sweden, and so on.[37]

As it happens, there *was* an anti-immigrant, anti-Catholic
hate group at work in the 1890s. But it wasn't called Populism. It was the American Protective Association (APA), and

the political organization through which it preferred to do its work was that norm-defending organization known as the Republican Party. Here is how the Populists of Kansas regarded the APA, as laid down in a resolution adopted ("nearly unanimously," according to the historian who discovered it) at the party's state convention in 1894:

> *Resolved*, That the People's party, as its name implies, is the party of the people, and hence the enemy of oppression and tyranny in every form, and we do most emphatically condemn such conduct as un-Christian, un-American, and as totally opposed to the spirit of the Constitution of our country and we pledge our best efforts to defeat such organizations and to protect as far as we are able every individual of every nationality, religious creed and political belief in his sacred right to worship God according to the dictates of his own conscience.[38]

This is curious, is it not? So many denunciations of populism for its "anti-pluralism," and yet here are the Populists themselves loudly attacking intolerance and anti-pluralism.

WHAT MAKES POPULISM truly dangerous, our modern-day anti-populist experts concur, is that it refuses to acknowledge the hierarchy of meritocratic achievement. In its deep regard for the wisdom of the common person, it rejects more qualified leaders . . . which is to say, it rejects them, the expert class.

The election of Trump, with its implicit rebuff of the Ivy League approach of the Obama years, inflated this particular fear into a kind of national nightmare. A man of remarkable ignorance about our system of government had been placed in charge of that system. A cartoon in the *New Yorker* captured the absurdity with a scene of airline passengers in a populist mutiny of their own: "These smug pilots have lost touch with regular passengers like us," bellows one of them. "Who thinks I should fly the plane?"

"If the elites go down, we're all in trouble," warned a 2017 headline in the *Boston Globe*. David Brooks informed readers of the *New York Times* that "populism" is the word we use to describe the hatred of "excellence" by the mediocre. Tom Nichols, a professor at the Naval War College, announced in *Foreign Affairs* that "America lost faith in expertise" due to a psychological syndrome in which stupid people are unaware of their own limitations while fine, scholarly people are peer-reviewed and know how to avoid confirmation bias. For good measure, he equated populism with "the celebration of ignorance."[39]

Understanding recent history as a showdown between peer-reviewed expertise and mass ignorance is at the core of the anti-populist tradition. "Voters are very ignorant, and always have been," write the political scientists Jonathan Rauch and Benjamin Wittes in a 2017 paper, "More Professionalism, Less Populism." Therefore, the two argue, the populist goal of increasing public participation is inherently wrongheaded; experts are the ones we should be empowering. "Like it or not," the two experts write, "most of what government does simply must be decided by specialists and professionals." Quoting one of their professional peers, they conclude that we must have a "new professional class to set the agenda."[40]

This is the recurring nightmare we will encounter throughout this book: the horror of populist anti-intellectualism. In its hyper-democratic folly, experts agree, populism believes that one person's ideas are just as good as another's, and hence it refuses to recognize learning or accomplishment. As a British politician put it just before the Brexit vote: "People in this country have had enough of experts."

Populism is the mob running wild in the streets of Washington, bellowing for beer and cheap gasoline. Meritocracy, meanwhile, is populism's diametric opposite: the mind that must rule the corpulent political body of America. Meritocracy is rule by well-graduated people who have dutifully climbed every ladder, rung every bell, and been rewarded for their excellence with their present high stations. Yes, meritocracy is an elitist system. But the only alternative to it is to place the fragile bureaucracy of, say, the State Department in the hands of a blundering dunce who can't find Pakistan on a map.

This harkens back to one of the essential philosophical problems of democracy: that the people will always be too ignorant to rule themselves. It's a question that vexed Jefferson and Madison, and now it vexes us, under the name of populism.

But does this archetypal dilemma really describe the Populist ideal? Was 1890s Populism a "celebration of ignorance" or a species of human stupidity?

No. The real problem with Populism—with all genuine populisms over the years—was the opposite: that ordinary people had come to understand their interests all too well and were now acting upon that knowledge.

Populism was a movement of books and newspapers, of reformers who believed in what the historian Postel calls "progress through education" with the earnest faith of the nineteenth-century uplifter. Think of the vast encampments of rural families listening to lecturers from the Farmers' Alliance, or of the lending libraries the Alliance set up all over the place, or of the universities that leading Populists helped to establish.[41] There were Populist newspapers, hundreds of them, started in order to contest the mainstream media of the day and to spread the gospel of reform. In their pages the reader would find cheap left-wing books for sale; the editor of the famous *Appeal to Reason* newspaper, for example, dispensed political tracts under the headline, "Books Laboring People Should Read: To Remain Ignorant Is to Remain a Slave."[42]

But neither did Populism call for rule by experts. Populism was about mass enlightenment, not the empowerment of a clique of foundation favorites or Ivy League grads. On the money question, Charles Postel tells us, the Pops thought it "could and must be understood by the people whose business interests and livelihoods were affected by it." Experts were regarded as helpful guides to the issue. But the Populists also understood that, in a democracy, ordinary working-class people were the ones who had to make the decisions, and so they educated themselves and prepared to "wrest the levers of monetary power from the corporate elite."[43]

In short, Populists both loved knowledge *and* rejected professional elites. The reason was because the economic establishment of that age of crisis was overwhelmingly concerned with serving business, not the people. The Populists mistrusted professional elites, in other words, because from their perspective those elites had failed.

A good illustration of what I am describing can be found in the 1895 pamphlet *What Is Populism?*, in which the author recounts all the different measures urged by "the financial doctors" upon "the plain people" as cures for their distress. Farmers and the government, we are told, followed the advice of these physicians, and "our illness continued and our suffering increased." In response, professional economists prescribed different, even sharper rounds of austerity, and still the economic disaster of the 1890s mounted.

"Let me tell you a secret," the Populist author confides. "The people have lost confidence in the professional skill of these physicians; they are reading up their own case; they reason that . . . a wrong financial policy must be the cause of financial distress; that a reversal of that wrong financial policy is the only rational and certain remedy."[44]

Does losing faith in professional economics mean that "the people" rejected learning across the board? Does it mean they celebrated ignorance? No: the author of *What Is Populism?* was in fact a professor of mathematics at Willamette University in Oregon. What he was criticizing was what we might call expert failure. The problem was not knowledge, it was orthodoxy: "financial doctors" who trusted blindly in the gold standard and in one another.

Proving that the experts had failed was a favorite set piece among reformers of the period. They loved to imagine leading financiers and academics—the stuffed-shirt, consensus crowd of their day—laid low by the steel-trap reasoning of some ordinary person. The outstanding example of this device is *Coin's Financial School*, William Harvey's best seller of 1894, in which bankers, economists, and newspapermen are humiliated by the overwhelming logic of a small boy who somehow happens to be an expert on free silver.

In the course of his story, Harvey mocks the mental processes of his exalted antagonists, depicting the minds of businessmen as tools of leading financiers. "On all such questions as a National finance policy their 'thinkers' run automatically," repeating whatever they have heard some banker say. And yet, as with other favorite Populist documents, *Coin's Financial School* was packed with tables and numbers: its point was not to discredit learning but to challenge conventional wisdom—to encourage people to figure out their predicament for themselves.

Mass enlightenment largely disappeared from the reform tradition in the decades after Populism was defeated. Instead of "self-education and self-mobilization," Postel reminds us, "the initiative passed to expert women and men, with professional training and administrative posts."[45]

And so it is today. Liberalism as we know it now is a movement led by prosperous, highly educated professionals who see government by prosperous, highly educated professionals as the highest goal of protest and political action. Where once it was democratic, liberalism is today a politics of an elite.

What makes this particularly poignant is that we are living through a period of elite failure every bit as spectacular as that of the 1890s. I refer not merely to the opioid crisis, the bank bailouts, and the failure to prosecute any bankers after their last fraud-frenzy; but also to disastrous trade agreements, stupid wars, and deindustrialization . . . basically, to the whole grand policy vision of the last few decades, as it has been imagined by a tiny clique of norm-worshipping D.C. professionals and think-tankers.

In this moment of maximum populist possibility, our commentariat proceeds as though the true populist alternative is simply invisible or impossible. You can either have meritocracy or you can have Trumpism. Those are the choices, the pundit-buro proclaims: You must either be ruled by gracious, enlightened experts or by racist, authoritarian dunces. Between them there is no middle ground and no possible alternative.

2

"Because Right Is Right
and God Is God"

One thing we know for sure about the Democracy Scare—the global revulsion against populism—is that it is a contemporary mode of thinking, as up-to-date as this morning's Twitter feed. How can it be otherwise? The horrors of populism only really registered in the pundit consciousness after the disastrous elections of 2016 delivered Brexit to the U.K. and Trump to the White House.

The argument of this book, however, is that anti-populism is in fact an old and surprisingly persistent habit of mind. No matter the guise or cast in which populism appears, each new generation of outraged critics thinks to describe it using the same stereotypes and the same images, as though they were reading from some long-lost script, lightly modified for current conditions.

We catch our first glimpse of the durable script to which the American elite persistently reverts when we look at the effort by elites of the 1890s to defeat the reform movement of the period.

Today we absorb our anti-populism from TV and social media, but the genre itself is a living fossil, a nineteenth-century smear campaign that is somehow still going.

LET US SET the stage. In the later decades of that century, the wealthy and the well-educated and the high-born—and they were all pretty much one group back then—saw their way of life come under threat by rising working-class movements: by strikes and boycotts; by anarchists and trade unionists. The fear of class war haunted the journalism and literature of the period; in the minds of the elite it was an ever-present peril.

The apocalypse seemed more imminent than ever as the U.S. economy sank into depression in the 1890s, as industrial conflict subsumed Chicago, and as the burgeoning Populist movement made its demands for currency reform and railroad nationalization. The country's respectables had laughed at Populism earlier in the decade, regarding it as a sideshow. Forced eventually to take it seriously, they came to see it instead as a sort of social earthquake, a peasant uprising right out of the French Revolution.

"The present assault on capital is but the beginning," moaned Supreme Court justice Stephen J. Field in 1895 as he struck down an early income-tax law, which had been pushed through Congress by Populists and reform-minded Democrats. "It will be but the stepping-stone to others, larger and more sweeping, till our political contests will become a war of the poor against the rich—a war constantly growing in intensity and bitterness."

Field had the aggressor and the victim mixed up, but the class war was most definitely on. At the Democratic convention in Chicago in 1896, working-class unrest appeared to triumph with the surprise nomination of a young former congressman from Nebraska, William Jennings Bryan, who had won the honor on the strength of his oratory against the gold standard.

To the establishment, there could be no doubt about what Bryan signified. One of the nation's main political parties had been captured by radicalism, and the shock was as great as that of a stock market crash. In the years before 1896, the differences between Democrats and Republicans on economic questions had been small; the two parties orbited each other in a tight system of limited government, gold-backed money, and friendliness toward big business. Bryan's nomination was the break that marked the system's collapse. The candidate himself was refreshingly direct about this. "We are fighting in the defense of our homes, our families, and posterity," he said in his sensational speech to the Chicago convention. "We have petitioned, and our petitions have been scorned; we have entreated, and our entreaties have been disregarded; we have begged, and they have mocked when our calamity came."

We beg no longer; we entreat no more; we petition no more.
We defy them.

The Nebraskan then proceeded to draw the distinction between the old philosophy and the new. "There are those who believe that, if you will only legislate to make the well-to-do prosperous, their prosperity will leak through on those below." But he proposed an alternative: "if you legislate to make the masses prosperous, their prosperity will find its way up through every class which rests upon them."

Bryan's chances appeared excellent in that summer of 1896, as he set off on a whistle-stop tour of America. The youngest major-party presidential candidate ever, Bryan seemed at first to be a man of destiny. His life story paralleled Lincoln's; his personal morality was without blemish; his oratorical ability was astonishing. To many ordinary people in the West and the South he was clearly the man of the hour, the answer to what ailed the depressed country. They became intoxicated with the pious Nebraska teetotaler.

But thanks to his attacks on gold and the wealthy, Bryan had virtually no funding and could afford none of the usual campaign accoutrements. For much of that year, the campaign consisted almost entirely of the Democratic presidential candidate riding around the country in a day coach, often carrying his own suitcases.[1]

Hard times was the inescapable campaign issue of 1896, but the way the candidates addressed it was via the proxy issue of the currency. Democrats and Populists blamed the country's deflationary gold standard for the unhappy fate of its farmers. William McKinley and the Republicans, meanwhile, saw gold as the rightful ingredient of "sound money" or "an honest dollar"; it was the metal of integrity.

Our concern in this chapter is with the latter group—the people who spoke for the economic consensus of the day. These men believed the gold standard to be the central pillar of civilization itself, and regarded the threat to dismantle it as a deadly peril. They may have been wrong on this issue and on many of the others as well, but nevertheless they prevailed. They contrived to crush Bryan's challenge and, in so doing, to build a lasting stereotype of reform-as-folly. The word with which they expressed that stereotype: Populism.

LET US OPEN a copy of *Judge* magazine for August 8, 1896, to get a glimpse of how respectable Americans the regarded the Populist threat. *Judge* was one of the premier humor magazines of the era, with several large, beautifully drawn political cartoons in each issue. The rest of its pages typically featured grotesque caricatures of blacks, Irish, Jews, immigrants, and farmers. Between the jokes at the expense of these subordinate people, you could also catch glimpses of the demographic for whose amusement the chuckles were collected: refined upper-class whites, people of manners and education and bank accounts, saying witty things about the burden of good taste. For them the magazine ran ads promoting Veuve Clicquot champagne and Golden Sceptre pipe tobacco; for them there was Prudential life insurance and high white collars.

With this particular 1896 issue of *Judge*, however, something has happened: the usual tone of genial amusement has given way to panic. At the magazine's center is a foldout illustration of stark American disaster, brought on by a gigantic figure labeled "Populism." This colossus is rustic and tattered but we are not meant to laugh at him: he glares with predatory eyes, he is armed with a brace of pistols and knives, he wears a French Revolution liberty cap marked "anarchy," he wields the torch of "ruin," and he towers terrifyingly over his fellow Americans. Before this monster flee the sort of tidy white people who made up *Judge* magazine's demographic: "Banker," "Capitalist," "Honest Citizen," "Respectable Democrat." One of them cowers on the ground beneath Populism's onslaught; another clutches his head in disbelief. "Has It Come to This!" blubbers the caption.

This was the Democracy Scare, 1896 version: our system was coming unraveled, with society's worst elements lining up against its best. Similarly frightful images appeared that year wherever people were dignified and accomplished together, always annotated with hysteria and hyperbole. Populism didn't merely threaten "norms"; it was bringing the country face-to-face with "anarchy" and "repudiation."*

On July 10, the New York *Sun* declared that the Democratic Party had been given over to "Jefferson's diametric opposite, the Socialist, or Communist, or, as he is now known here, the Populist." A few columns over from this pronouncement the reader was invited to savor this bit of doggerel, supposedly the chant of the radicalized Democratic Party:

> Pile the load on plutocrats' backs, sock it to 'em with the income tax. Of goldbug law we make a sport; when the time comes we'll pack the court. On with the programme without a hitch: skin the East and skin the rich. Lift the heart and lift the fist; swear to be an Anarchist. Our creed is ruin, our flag is red. On, brother Anarchists, and raise NED.[2]

This was the horror of democracy, live and in your face. A lead editorial that ran in the *Sun* a few days thereafter declared that there really was no Democratic candidate that year. Instead, "there are Populist-Anarchist candidates nominated on a Populistic-Anarchist platform." Similarly, in a pamphlet distributed by the Republican Party that fall, the novelist and statesman John Hay claimed that the Democrats no longer

---

* These were the two favorite scare words of 1896. "Anarchy" because the Democratic platform denounced the way the federal government crushed the Pullman strike and was thus supposedly in favor of lawlessness. "Repudiation" because, in seeking to take the country off the gold standard, Democrats were allegedly proposing that debts be repaid in dollars that were worth less than when the debts were incurred; thus they were supposedly "repudiating" those debts.

really existed: "The enemy which confronts us is the Populist party," which had swallowed the Democrats "as a python might swallow an ox."[3]

Thanks to William Jennings Bryan and "his new Red Circus," something miraculous had happened, the *Sun* proclaimed: "the business interests of the country are *all* arrayed on one side." The prospect of elite unanimity impressed many. E. L. Godkin, then the conscience of American journalism, clucked in the *Nation* that "no man has ever yet been elected President whom the business interests of the country . . . distrusted and opposed as unsafe; these interests in the controlling states are substantially unanimous against Bryan." Godkin was pleased even more by the harmony with which the nation's press came together against the Democratic challenger.[4]

It wasn't just business interests and respectable journalism that spoke as one: every species of orthodoxy joined hands that year. Eminent clergymen stood tall against the threat, joining the Methodist bishop who declared from the pulpit that "Populists were no better than Anarchists." A society preacher in New York denounced "Populist orators" as "the enemies of mankind." Another is said to have called Bryan "a mouthing, slobbering demagogue, whose patriotism was all in his jaw-bone."[5]

Scholarly elites hastened to join the consensus. Of fifteen university presidents polled by the *Nation*, not one supported Bryan. Yale sociologist William Graham Sumner, possibly the most famous intellectual in America, bitterly assailed the free-silver movement in a series of articles for *Leslie's Weekly*. Cornell historian Andrew Dickson White, a founder of that university, intervened with a pamphlet claiming that "for the first time in the history of the United States we have an Anarchist and Socialist platform" adopted by one of the two main parties.[6] Bryan himself was heckled by a crowd of Yale students as he spoke in New Haven—not because of his views on offensive Halloween costumes but because of his insolence toward the rich. As his speech was interrupted again and again, Bryan lashed out, saying, "I have been so used to talking to young men who earn their own living that I hardly know what language to use to address myself to those who desire to be known, not as creators of wealth, but as the distributers [sic] of wealth which somebody else created." It did not go over well.*

OF COURSE, THE Democratic Party was not really made up of anarchists, nor had it been captured by the Populists. Still, its shift to the Left was real enough, with huge potential consequences for the country's financiers and investors. Their fear was a tangible thing.

Republican leaders pulled out all the stops. Their candidate, the famed protectionist William McKinley, waged an avuncular "front porch campaign" from his home in Ohio. But behind the scenes, McKinley's friend Mark Hanna, the Cleveland tycoon, organized a bare-knuckle offensive in the great showdown

---

* Bryan reprinted his New Haven speech in his memoir of the 1896 campaign, *The First Battle* (W. B. Conkey, 1896), along with a resolution adopted by a joint meeting of the Cherokee, Creek, Choctaw, and Seminole tribes the next day. It read as follows:

Resolved, that we contemplate with deep regret the recent insulting treatment of William J. Bryan by students of a college in the land of the boasted white man's civilization, and we admonish all Indians who think of sending their sons to Yale that association with such students could but prove hurtful alike to their morals and their progress toward the higher standard of civilization (p. 487).

between the classes. If Bryan represented the producing masses of the country, as the Democrat claimed, Hanna would counter his appeal with Trump-like promises of prosperity-through-tariffs. He would enlist American business and the whole votes-for-hire political system of the nineteenth century to suppress the eloquent challenger.

In this war, Hanna was "a political generalissimo of genius," the historian Matthew Josephson has written, "risen suddenly from the councils of the leading capitalists, to meet and check-mate the drive of the masses by summoning up the berserk fighting power latent in his class."[7]

The dynamic Hanna set about raising and spending enormous sums for the GOP effort, even going door-to-door to the headquarters of the great American corporations soliciting funds to put down the Nebraska upstart. There were few campaign finance rules back then, and what Hanna levied was what Josephson calls a "political assessment"—which is to say, a private Republican tax—"upon corporate wealth."[8]

Armed with an unprecedented treasury, Hanna proceeded to crush Bryan under a mountain of money. He summoned up a blizzard of alarmist anti-Populist pamphlets—120 million of them, according to Josephson, distributed wherever Bryan's message seemed to have traction. A squad of paid Republican orators followed Bryan as he moved around the country. There were parades, mind-numbingly long and noisy and expensive. Every shady Election Day practice of the era was deployed; every last possible hireling was provided with generous outlays. Toward the end of the contest, business rolled out its ultimate weapon: coercion, allegedly threatening to shut down factories or cancel deals if Bryan won. Matthew Josephson's summary is chilly but exact: "Moral enthusiasm was to be beaten at every point in the line by a machinelike domination of the actual polling."[9] And so it was.

WHAT THE REPUBLICAN campaign defended was a culture of hierarchy and domination. "Some men must rule; the great mass of men must be ruled," Mark Hanna once said, and by and large America's elite agreed with him. People who thought like Hanna did taught at American colleges, preached from American pulpits, wrote for highbrow American magazines, and funded American politicians.

From the heights of this unanimity the men of quality denounced the rabble. Bryan's campaign aroused "the basest passions of the least worthy members of the community," announced an editorial in the *New-York Tribune* that ran on the day after the election. "It has been defeated and destroyed because right is right and God is God."[10]

Populism was the world turned upside down. It came from a dark place where society's guardrails were gone, where wealth and learning and status counted for nothing. "Populism" was a word used to express the horror of seeing hierarchies collapse and the lowly clamber to places where they do not belong.

Anti-populism's Magna Carta was *The Platform of Anarchy*, a pamphlet by the statesman John Hay that was distributed around the country as part of the Republican propaganda effort in the fall of 1896.[11] Hay's indignation was monumental. Populists, he wrote, valued nothing, throwing "their frantic challenge against every feature of our civilization." They longed to bind the hands of government "where it is inclined to protect order and property." They appealed "to the openly lawless." They waged a "shameful insurrection against law and national honesty." Their plans for funding the government were "the merest babble of the loafers around a rural livery stable." For the plumèd knights of the Republican Party, "it is as if a champion at a tourney, awaiting the onset of a chivalrous antagonist, should suddenly find himself attacked by a lunatic in rags."*

The future president Theodore Roosevelt echoed this view in *Review of Reviews*, where he descended into straightforward prole-bashing, performed in the key of aristocracy offended:

> That a man should change his clothes in the evening, that he should dine at any other hour than noon, impress [the Populists] as being symptoms of depravity instead of merely trivial. A taste for learning and cultivated friends, and a tendency to bathe frequently, cause them the deepest suspicion. A well-to-do man they regard with jealous distrust, and if they cannot be well-to-do themselves at least they hope to make matters uncomfortable for those that are.[12]

The respectable faced off against the contemptible. Quality and good taste were menaced by the riffraff for no reason greater than the supposed resentment of lower animals for higher ones.

I use the word "animals" deliberately. In 1894, Rudyard Kipling, then a resident of Vermont, published an allegorical story in which a group of horses on an East Coast farm trade

---

* In private, Hay's contempt was more ironic. Writing to his friend Henry Adams, Hay described Bryan's speeches as boring: "He simply reiterates the unquestioned truths that every man who has a clean shirt is a thief and ought to be hanged:—That there is no goodness or wisdom except among the illiterate and criminal classes—That gold is vile:—That silver is lovely and holy." *Letters of John Hay*, vol. 3 (Gordian Press, 1969), p. 74.

stories about the hard work they have done for their human masters. In a weird foreshadowing of Orwell's *Animal Farm*, a radical horse from Kansas shows up in their pasture and neighs about "degradin' servitood" and "inalienable rights" and the need to rise up against "Man the Oppressor." Readers at the time would have recognized his views as a parody of Populism; they are meant to sound ridiculous. The horse talks big, but in truth he is merely lazy. "I say we *are* the same flesh an' blood," the creature whinnies, insisting on equine equality regardless of how little work he does. The other horses are disgusted by his rebellion against their human masters and even more so by his democratic patter, which they correctly understand to be an excuse for shirking the life of labor that is every farm animal's lot in this world. The radical, Kipling teaches, is an animal who does not know his place in the hierarchy; the other horses gang up and give him a terrible kicking.[13]

The visual theme cartoonists favored as they went about illustrating Populism's upstart challenge was the eternal war of police and the poor. In an 1896 cartoon from *Puck*, another elegant humor magazine, William Jennings Bryan and his legion of disorder can be seen waving their red flag and marching down a city street behind three wild-eyed figures labeled "Riot," "Repudiation," and "Populism." The street is lined with stately banks and insurance companies, and—thank goodness—two lines of police representing the "sound money vote" are closing in to defend these honorable institutions from the "noisy mob."[14]

Cops vs. Pops was a recurring fantasy of those feverish days. Another *Puck* cartoon from the same period showed the Republican candidate, William McKinley, depicted as a prosperous gentleman with a noble lady on his arm, making his way through "The Slums of Popocracy." All around the glamorous couple lurk dark and shabby figures representing Democratic and Populist leaders. But fear not! Two beefy policemen are escorting the wealthy couple through this vale of proletarian menace.*

That cops exist in order to protect respectability from the dissolute was taken for granted by the editors of *Puck*. The humor, if you can call it that, was the way these cartoons fit political insurgency into this same template: a challenge to financial orthodoxy was equivalent to slum lawlessness; Populists were, essentially, lower-class criminals who obviously needed to be policed.

THE IDENTIFICATION OF Populism with demagoguery, a core doctrine of modern-day punditry, is descended directly from this original Democracy Scare. To prosperous Americans of the Gilded Age it was inconceivable that intelligent human beings would wish to crack down on banks or ditch the gold standard. Populist grievances were irrational by definition; indeed, as the renowned sociologist William Graham Sumner explained to readers of *Leslie's Weekly* in 1896, there really was no such thing as "hard times." Yes, people's lives were being ruined, but stuff like that happened all the time. Stuff like that was unremarkable. What deserved the reader's outrage and contempt, Sumner insisted, was when some "wily orator" showed up and

---

* Populism + Democracy = Popocracy. The allegory of the cartoon went like this: the lady represented the gold standard; the two policemen represented a breakaway faction of gold Democrats; and the caption ("Well Protected") was a nod to McKinley's protectionism.

told the losers "that this is somebody's fault." Somebody other than they themselves, that is.[15]

As we have seen, William Jennings Bryan won the Democratic nomination by virtue of his extraordinary skills as an orator; he campaigned by traveling the country and speaking to live audiences, which was something of an innovation in American politics. To his foes, what these things indicated was not that Bryan was a capable leader but that he was a demagogue, a man who made his way in the world by means of empty talk. By extension, the whole troublesome Populist insurgency was maybe just a matter of hypnotizing rhetoric.

It began on the very day of Bryan's surprise nomination. An editorial in the *New York Evening Post* declared the Nebraskan to be the Democrats' "chief demagogue," a man "who took the mob of repudiators off their feet by a speech of forty-blatherskite power." It wasn't so much Bryan's arguments that won the Democrats over, the editor continued, as it was "his wind power, which is immense."[16]

Another *Evening Post* editorial got all technical about the matter, attributing Bryan's victory to the enormous size of the building in which the Democratic convention was held, which permitted "a shouting, shrieking mob" to influence the proceedings. How has modern science overlooked this direct statistical relationship between architecture and mob psychology? It is the clear mathematical answer to the mystery of populism.[17]

A favorite image of the anti-Populists of the 1890s was the masquerade, the trick, the puppet show. Bryan and his followers were not real Democrats, everyone agreed; they were "masquerading in the Democratic garb," as Professor White of Cornell put it. *Life* magazine imagined Bryan as the leader of a pirate gang that had hijacked the Democratic vessel; as

Mephistopheles, luring the farmer astray.[18] In a more gothic vein, *Leslie's Weekly* depicted Bryan's face as a mask, behind which lurked a hideous howling "Anarchy" in a boar's hide and a bat's wings. This was, as the caption put it, "The New (Not the True) Democracy"; one of the monster's hands held its name tag; a second gripped the throat of a working man; a third used a knife to cut the dollar in half.*

Who was really in control of the uprising? Was Bryan some kind of mastermind, or was he merely the tool of others? According to the *New-York Tribune*, Bryan was "not the real leader of that league of hell," a verdict they handed down after the Democrat lost the election. "He was," the paper declared, "only a puppet in the blood-imbrued hands of Altgeld the Anarchist and Debs the revolutionist and other desperadoes of that stripe."[†]

And if he wasn't a puppet or a demagogue—if Bryan *wasn't* fooling when he denounced plutocracy—oh my God, don't even ask. "He is a dangerous man," editorialized the New York *Sun*: "if he is sincere, dangerous even as a fool is dangerous when he

---

* This was a page 1 image of what can only be described as an editorial sculpture, one in a series of efforts mocking Bryan. These were the work of the sculptor Max Bachmann and were somewhat famous in their day. Others in the series depicted Bryan as the serpent in the Garden of Eden, as a would-be slayer of the American eagle, and as a chick hatching from an egg marked "Anarchy." Several of them are collected here: https://john-adcock.blogspot.com/2013/01/max-bachmann-political-cartoonist-in.html?m=1.

† John P. Altgeld, the Democratic governor of Illinois in 1896, had pardoned the surviving Haymarket anarchists and opposed President Cleveland's military intervention in the Pullman strike, which was led by Eugene Debs. Altgeld was frequently depicted as the real force behind the Bryan campaign. The passage is from the *New-York Tribune* editorial, "Good Riddance" (November 4, 1896, p. 4).

raises a false alarm of fire in a crowded theatre; and if a demagogue, as he seems to be, doubly dangerous."[19]

The most extreme note was sounded by *Judge* magazine in a striking centerfold cartoon depicting Bryan as a bright-red Satan, complete with horns, bat wings, and a pointy tail. As in the Bible story, the demonic Nebraskan tempts the farmer with a vision of glittering cities, rivers, and hills, all made entirely of silver. The implication was not that free-silver's promise was false but that it was evil, a pact with the enemy of all that is rightful and holy. But the farmer, thank heaven, rejects the sinister offer.

None of this is to say that demagogues and evildoers and political puppets don't exist in American life; clearly they do. Nor is it to say that every politician who claims to love "the people" is sincere; many are not.

What that original Democracy Scare insisted upon is that *any* politician who uses the language of class-based grievance is probably either insincere or demonic; that *any* scheme for reforming capitalism by enlisting the votes of working people is most likely a fraud, a con game, a rebellion against God Himself.

THIS WAS NOT a hopeful way of thinking about democracy and its possibilities. On the contrary, to men of orthodox views, the people were the problem; they were the unpredictable oceanic force that had brought on the Populist threat. Dwelling on the people's mutability and menace, Gilded Age anti-Populists reached for the most frightening images available to understand how democracy had gone so very wrong.

The fight over the 1894 income tax law was an early example.

Before the Supreme Court, eminent Republican lawyer Joseph H. Choate described the tax as an instrument of mob rule, repeatedly mentioning its Populist origins as he made his case. "I have thought that one of the fundamental objects of all civilized government was the preservation of the rights of private property," he declared. "I have thought that it was the very keystone of the arch upon which all civilized government rests, and that this once abandoned, everything was at stake and in danger." Noting that the public supported the income tax and might be angry if it were deleted, Choate announced that this was even more reason for the Supreme Court to strike it down and remind the beast of its place, "no matter what the threatened consequences of popular or populistic wrath may be."[20]

John Hay, the author of *The Platform of Anarchy*, had served as Abraham Lincoln's private secretary during the Civil War, but in later years, as he contemplated what universal suffrage made possible, he began to doubt democracy itself. The people were suckers for demagogues; they were enlisting in strikes and riots; they were becoming the Mob.[21] "Most of my friends think Bryan will be elected and we shall all be hanged to the lampions of Euclid Avenue," he wrote to Henry Adams. In his pamphlet he compared the 1896 Democratic convention to the Reign of Terror, describing it as the sort of thing humans had not seen "since the half-demented clubs of Paris [which is to say, the Jacobins], when the old French civilization was rocking to its fall, delivered their daily defiances to all existing institutions."

Comparisons with the French Revolution were something of a cliché during those days of hate and trembling. Cartoonists loved to depict Populists as marching peasants wearing liberty caps, and on the morning after Bryan's nomination the New York *Sun* chose to dub the candidate "William Jacobin Bryan."[22]

The same publications were appalled at the notion that the people should have a greater say in running the place and settling questions that were the province of their betters. Then as now, faith in the people's wisdom was thought to be populism's original sin. Bryan was mocked in the *Nation* for supposedly starting his speeches with empty salutes to the genius of the common people: "Your wisdom is inexhaustible and infallible," he was parodied as saying. "I tell you that you are so great that you can ignore the rest of the world." A cartoon in *Puck* imagined Bryan on his whistle-stop tour, blowing the same sort of buncombe out of a bellows at a crowd of happy farmers, snaggletooth idiots wearing long agrarian whiskers. Bryan was driving them to ecstasy by saluting the wisdom of the hayseed:

Our people are capable of ruling! / They do not need the lessons of history! / They have nothing to learn! / They do not care for the experience of other nations! / They know it all! . . . Study and science are of no account, / the popular intuition is better than / reasoning and what the people say goes![23]

The imagined message—that the people had no need of experts—sent fear and outrage reverberating through the establishment. To the suggestion that the economic system be reorganized to benefit ordinary people, the financial elites replied: That's not how it works. We direct things the way we do not because we are greedy but because we know how they are to be directed. "A capitalistic system had been adopted, and if it were to be run at all, it must be run by capital and by capitalistic methods," recalled Henry Adams years later; "for nothing could surpass the nonsensity of trying to run so complex and so concentrated a machine by southern and western farmers in grotesque alliance with city day-laborers."[24]

That populism is at war with intellect, that it is an offense to meritocracy—this lasting axiom can also be traced to the original Democracy Scare, when Populism threatened to level both the hierarchy of money and that of established expertise. The institution where these two hierarchies came together was the gold standard, the bedrock of both classical economics and the banking system. For the Populists, as we have seen, the elites' faith in gold was a favorite target for mockery. But for establishment figures like John Hay, the only legitimate way to settle the currency question was "by the investigations of the leading economists of the world," gathered in solemn contemplation. The conclusion of such a gathering was certain: one couldn't adopt a silver standard in just one country and hope to succeed. America's economy was locked in an international system regulated by responsible expertise, Hay intoned, and upon this reasoning everyone who was anyone agreed. "All the intelligent bi-metallists of America . . . ; all those of England . . . ; all the German scholars . . . agree in this."[25]

A funny thing about that proud, scholarly consensus of the 1890s: it was wrong. As we now know, the gold standard was an archaic system that needlessly ruined millions of lives. Americans eventually replaced it with a fiat currency, just as the Populists advocated. In this most consequential Democracy Scare of them all, the cranks turned out to be right and the experts to be wrong.*

---

* One historian who has written about the ironic reversal of the antagonists of the 1890s is Richard Hofstadter, who in a 1963 essay mulled over the curious problem of "yesterday's crank" turning out to be right and

. . .

SUPPOSE YOU KNEW with utter certainty, however, that the reformers had it wrong and were pursuing an absurd and dangerous doctrine. How would you explain this mass enthusiasm for a false idea? Why, you would turn to what John Hay called the "mental constitution" of the person who believed in it: "You do not want to argue with him; you want to feel of his phrenological bumps."

Decades later, the historian Richard Hofstadter would famously assert that what Populism reflected was status anxiety and even a "paranoid style." His larger insight, which revolutionized social science in the 1950s and which persists in the anti-populism of our own day, was that mass protest movements in general could be understood as a reaction of maladjusted minds to the advance of modernity.

In truth, however, Hofstadter's discovery had already been made back in 1896, when Populism was repeatedly diagnosed as a form of mental aberration.[26] In September of that year, as the exciting presidential campaign unfolded, the *New York Times* announced the alarming discovery: William Jennings

---

"yesterday's accepted spokesman" turning out to be wrong. However, the historian derived no larger lesson from this, just noted it and moved on. It certainly didn't soften Hofstadter's views of Populism, a movement he persistently characterized as one of the main villains of American history.

But this reversal deserves to be taken more seriously. If the "crank" of the 1890s was right, he wasn't a crank after all; if consensus orthodoxy of that period was wrong, maybe we should reconsider our respect for consensus orthodoxy today.

Richard Hofstadter, "Coin's Financial School and the Mind of 'Coin' Harvey," his introductory essay to *Coin's Financial School* (Belknap Press, 1963), p. 45.

Bryan appeared to be clinically insane. It began with a letter to the paper from an anonymous "Alienist," or psychologist, who examined Bryan's heredity, his heretofore mediocre career, and his behavior on the campaign trail, and concluded "without any bias" that "Mr. Bryan presents in his speech and action striking and alarming evidence of a mind not entirely sound." Proof: the candidate was "an apostle of an economic theory without ever having a training in economics."

It was a scary situation, the alienist continued. After all, having "a madman in the White House" would not only be dangerous, but it would also damage democracy itself, since it "would forever weaken the trust in the soundness of republics and the sanity of the voting masses." The letter evidently caused a sensation, and the *Times* proceeded to mine the story for all it was worth, interviewing other professional psychologists and debating whether Bryan's obvious brainsickness was that of a "mattoid" or a paranoid.[27]

Economists concurred in this diagnosis. J. Laurence Laughlin of the University of Chicago analyzed the "Agricultural Unrest" for the *Atlantic Monthly* and quickly turned for his explanation to the minds of the Populists themselves. The reason they didn't understand their true economic situation was because of a peculiar malfunction of their "mental processes," Laughlin concluded. "Once the single-ideaed [*sic*] brain has been occupied by a theory, or craze," he announced, "the gate to all other ideas is thereby closed."

> In a brain incapable of economic and judicial reasoning, the one idea now in possession engenders prejudice, and even, in an emotional nature, frenzy. This class of minds may not always have the same craze, but, in its undereducated way, it

is sure to have one of some sort. The subject of the fanaticism may change in time, but with the fanaticism we must always reckon so long as the undereducated class exists and wields a large political power.[28]

Moreover, the problem of "the undereducated man, capable of holding but one idea at a time" was made worse, Laughlin charged, by the problem of the demonic manipulator, who sees in hard times an opportunity to mislead the gullible. "And the skill of the tempter is satanic," he continued. "I doubt if ever in our political history we have had more adroit manipulation and strategy than have been displayed by the managers of the silver party." The professional economist proceeded to blame the whole Populist uprising on "the great silver conspiracy, the equal of which has never been recorded."[29]

"A MOST LAMENTABLE Comedy" was the title that small-town newspaperman William Allen White gave to the anti-Populist novella he published in 1901. A thinly disguised account of insurgent politics in Kansas, White's novella is completely forgotten today. Once upon a time, however, it was highly regarded: it was quoted in history textbooks and recommended to curious foreigners by President Theodore Roosevelt.[30]

In White's telling, Populism was a form of mass hysteria, a "mental epidemic" that swept the region west of the Missouri River and that "held the people in a grip as vicious as a bodily distemper." His novella incorporates virtually the entire list of frightful characteristics that pundits of the day attributed to Populism: democracy gone haywire; the people transformed into a mob; churches and schools and other beloved institutions of small-town American life subverted by a demonic force.

It was a fanaticism like the crusades. Indeed the delusion that was working on the people took the form of religious frenzy. . . . At night, from 10,000 little white school-house windows, lights twinkled back vain hope to the stars. For the thousands who assembled under the school-house lamps believed that when their Legislature met and their Governor was elected, the millennium would come by proclamation. They sang their barbaric songs in unrhythmic jargon, with something of the same mad faith that inspired the martyrs going to the stake.

As for Populism's so-called issues, they all arose from what White called the "chief hallucination of the mania," which was "that the people owed more than they could pay; or in justice should be asked to pay." Times were hard; farmers were in debt—but so what? For the farmers' crisis White's sympathy was close to zero.

White describes the farmers holding their meetings, singing their stupid protest songs, and "cursing wealth for its iniquity." Their rebellion against the successful was so profoundly misguided that White calls it a rebellion against mind itself: "Reason slept and the passions—jealousy, covetousness, hatred—ran amuck, and who ever would check them was crucified in public contumely."

In this climate, the right order of things had been inverted. "Persons with reason were in disfavor." Losers prospered; the learned were ignored; the old leaders were cast out and professionals were replaced by cranks: "The doctor, lawyer, merchant and chief, were shoved aside for the horse-trader, the sewing-machine agent, the patent right pedler [*sic*], the itinerant preacher, the tenant farmer, the lawyer without clients, the school teacher without pupils."

White's novella tells the story of one of these cranks, a "town infidel" given to socialist politics and street-corner oratory who somehow becomes the leader of a local chapter of the Farmers' Alliance and is then swept by the lunacy of the moment into the governor's office. This character's one real talent is public speaking, which he has sharpened and perfected into a form of hypnosis, and in describing his performance at the state Populist convention White's horror transcends his prose:

> The speech could not be reported any more than the gyrations of a serpent charming a bird may be put in words. . . .
> As the wind makes billows in the prairie grass, Dan Gregg, who was not Dan Gregg, but a magician, swayed the great crowd at his whim. The delegates laughed, they cried, they shuddered; they clinched their fists; they cheered and knew it not, and orators and auditors, chained together by a common frenzy that each produced upon the other, went out of reason together.

This passage shows the obvious influence of the French social theorist Gustave Le Bon, whose book *The Crowd* William Allen White acknowledges having read and admired when it first appeared in English in 1896. Le Bon's most famous assertion, which White here applies to his fictional Populists, was that ordinary people, when gathered in crowds, became psychologically subhuman, akin to a person under hypnosis. Le Bon, who was no fan of democracy, also charged that crowds were irrational, impulsive, suspicious of progress, and fond of authoritarian leaders—precisely the bill of accusations that later generations of American social theorists would use to blast what they called "populism."[31]

Give the plain people a say, this kind of thinking holds, and by some deep, irrational instinct they will try to smash the social order and to topple the highly educated people who administer it, bowing down instead before what White elsewhere called "the lazy, greasy fizzle, who can't pay his debts." Now, as then, populism is the word we apply to this imagined war of madness against reason, of entropy against order, of the poor against the rich, of the unthinking rabble against society's brains.

EVERYTHING I HAVE mentioned so far in this chapter has shown the continuity between the anti-populism of the 1890s and that of the present day. On the important matter of populist intolerance, however, there is a surprising divergence. It is true that one of the words William Allen White and others favored when describing the mental failures of reformers was "bigotry,"* but what they meant by that word seems to have been something very different from what we mean by it today.

In his winding account of the madness of reform, White gives no examples of Populist racism or Populist hatred of Muslims or any other form of Populist intolerance. What tainted Populism with "bigotry" was its supposed antipathy to the successful: the movement, White writes, was "a wave of emotion

---

* "The world will not be made better," White wrote on the last page of his Populist novella, by "a movement too weak to conquer its own bigotry."

which has jealousy of the poor for the rich and envy of the strong for the weak for its impulse." The problem was the unthinking hatred of the lower orders for their betters.

Today, however, the bigotry of populism—its racism and its nativism—is by far its most prominent feature, with the word "populist" itself having become shorthand for "racist."

As we have seen, the Populists were not enlightened racial liberals by modern-day standards. Many of them were indeed racists and anti-Semites. Yet in all my reading of anti-Populist material of the 1890s, I came across no New York newspaper editorials or political cartoons that attacked the movement for its racial intolerance. This particular charge, so ubiquitous in our own day, seems largely to have gone missing back then.

How come? One reason, surely, is that the establishment publications of the time were themselves so frequently racist it would hardly have occurred to them to charge somebody else with the sin. For example, *Life* magazine, a relentless adversary of Populism, also gloried in publishing cruel stereotypes of blacks and Jews, often right alongside their cruel mockery of agrarian reformers. *Judge* magazine was pretty much the same, only in color. Flipping through its pages today is like walking through a beautifully appointed home where the dog has been permitted to defecate all over the floor, leaving you to step gingerly between the stinky cartoons, one after another, of grabby men with hooked noses.

Anti-populists did not hesitate to use racist images when they thought they might injure reformers by so doing. Caricatures of Populist senator William Peffer as the Jewish hypnotist Svengali were commonplace at one time, for example, and it's hard even to look at the anti-Semitic rendering of a pawnbroker that appeared on the cover of *Leslie's Weekly* one day in 1896 over the caption, "A Sure Winner If Bryan Is Elected."[32]

Speaking of Bryan, *Judge* magazine seemed to be on a sort of quest to publish the most poisonous imaginable image of the Nebraska idealist. The artist who depicted Bryan as Satan also thought to draw a centerfold cartoon labeling Bryan an "Assassin" who has just killed the creamy white maiden "U.S. Credit" with a long knife named "Repudiation." For this murderous occasion, the illustrator fitted Bryan out with a swarthy complexion and dressed him in the kerchief, earring, and leggings that the stereotypes of the day attributed to immigrants from southern Italy. (Four years later, when Bryan opposed American imperialism, the same cartoonist in the same magazine thought to call Bryan "The American 'Boxer,'" as in the Boxer Rebellion; now the Nebraskan is drawn in Chinese costume, his hair in a queue, a ferocious scowl on his face, and, of course, another gigantic knife in his hand.)[33]

Anti-Populist racism was not just a cartoon joke. In the South, where Populism once made a daring bid for transracial class solidarity, race hate was literally the third party's undoing. As we have seen, southern Populists initially bid for black votes by arguing that the class interests of black farmers were similar to those of white farmers, and that if the two came together politically they could improve their lot in life. Even more important was Populism's refusal of white solidarity, the keystone of the one-party rule of the Bourbon Democrats.

To put down the revolt, those Bourbon Democrats eventually turned to their one great weapon—insanely exaggerated racial anxiety. North Carolina furnishes the most outrageous example of how it worked. This was the state where Populism—in "fusion" with the local Republican Party—actually captured the government in 1894 and '96 and then made reforms that allowed blacks to sometimes gain political power in places where they were in the majority. It was also in North Carolina that the Democrats' racist campaign against the "Fusionists" grew so hot that it spilled over into murder, mob action, and the armed overthrow of a legitimate city government.

The name for that notorious episode is the "white supremacy campaign," an 1898 effort planned and mounted by the North Carolina Democratic Party to use antiblack hysteria to defeat forever their political rivals. The supremacist leaders played in particular upon the nightmarish threat black empowerment supposedly posed to white women. Amply funded by the state's business class, they issued an amazing assortment of racist cartoons, newspapers, and pamphlets. They brought in the South Carolina demagogue Ben Tillman to stoke the flames of racist hysteria even more. Then they used paramilitary gangs of so-called red shirts to intimidate Populist and Republican voters.[34]

North Carolina Populists claimed in response that white supremacy was a bogus issue and warned that any move to eliminate "the poor negro as a political factor" (which the Democrats promised to do) would ensnare "the poor white man" as well. The true aim of the white supremacy campaign, the Pops claimed, was to distract voters from the real issues—to elevate property over humans and to see to it that "the dollar is greater than the man."[35] It was to no avail.

At the conclusion of this campaign of vicious race hate and mob violence, North Carolina's ancestral Democratic rulers rode back to power over their Populist and Republican foes. In the city of Wilmington, they went even further. After the election was over, white Democrats armed themselves, formed ranks, and proceeded into the black parts of town, shooting, killing, and burning. The mob destroyed the offices of the city's black newspaper, dethroned the city's Republican mayor, removed its Populist police chief, threatened to lynch other politicians, and then saw their deeds effectively ratified by a federal government that declined to act.*

Is there is anything other than horror to be taken away from the story of this racist mob action of long ago? The civil rights historian Michael Honey tells us that "not 'Negro domination,' but too much democracy, through the fusion of Republicans and Populists, set off the white supremacy campaign."[36] The events that followed the white supremacy campaign certainly suggest that this interpretation is right—that the problem was democracy itself.

After winning their fanatical white-supremacy campaign, North Carolina Democrats set about reversing the reforms passed by the previous legislature. Then they moved to make their victory permanent by stripping the vote from blacks and poor whites. In the face of this final onslaught, the state's Populists vacillated and dithered and before long they were finished as a political force. A similar mania for disenfranchisement swept other southern states at about the same time—a movement that historians have attributed, in part, to elite fears

---

* A similar incident took place a short time later in a county in east Texas where Populists, with the support of black voters, had been able to prevail in elections until 1900. Populism was finally beaten there by a vigilante organization called the White Man's Union. Black Populists were murdered, black voters were intimidated, and then, at the climactic moment, the white supremacists took on the local biracial Populist constabulary in a gunfight. The Pops lost the shootout and Populism disappeared from that part of Texas forever. See the essay by Lawrence Goodwyn, "Populist Dreams and Negro Rights: East Texas as a Case Study," *American Historical Review*, December 1971.

aroused by the Populist threat to white solidarity. In North Carolina, at least, that was definitely the case, and disenfranchisement solved the problem . . . the problem of democracy itself.[37] And so the Populist revolt came to an end.

AFTER THE WHITE supremacists had worked their will in North Carolina, an anonymous black woman wrote to President McKinley, imploring him to do something about what the press had begun to call the Wilmington "race riot." "There was not any rioting," she wrote; "simply the strong slaying the weak."[38]

It is about as compact a summary of this chapter's themes as we will find anywhere. Anti-populism is always about the powerful lording it over the weak; the credentialed and the highborn reminding the world that the definitions of goodness and justice and truth are whatever they determine.

From 1896 to the present, anti-populists have polished an elegant archetype: The "undereducated class," as the economist Laughlin called them, are different from you and me. They are obsessive and suggestible and given to fanaticism. They fall for demagogues; they join the mob; they rise up against the experts who direct the system. Economics is beyond them, as are most forms of higher reasoning. And the weakness of democracy is that it is at the mercy of such people. This is the imagined threat that Populism presented and the threat that what is called "populism" will always present to the enlightened few who know how things should be run.

3

Peak Populism in
the Proletarian Decade

In 1929 and over the four years following, the global capitalist system slowly collapsed. It kicked off with the great crash on Wall Street, then descended slowly in a vicious spiral of contraction and despair. Banks failed; businesses went bust; farm prices plummeted. Every stock market rally ended in another capitulation; every coordinated corporate effort to hold the line on employment eventually failed.

By 1933, the Dow Jones Industrial Average had fallen some 90 percent from its high point. Unemployment had hit the almost unbelievable figure of 25 percent, or 12 million souls. There was no federal system of relief or unemployment insurance in place to deal with the crisis, and local charities had been tapped out after the first year. Middle-class savings had disappeared with the banks that had safeguarded them. The really unlucky lived in dumps, in boxes, and in doorways. The gold standard was still in effect, naturally, and dollars once again became scarce. In some cities Americans turned to barter in place of money.

Workers were still physically able to do their work, of course, and farmers were still producing food. But somehow that didn't suffice to make the great American machine go. Thus developed one of the decade's cruelest ironies: bumper crops in the countryside while people went hungry in the cities, and through it all both elements of society losing their livelihoods, their savings, their homes and farms. By the time the system hit rock bottom, workers with paychecks couldn't cash them, since the banks were almost all closed. "We are not in a mere business recession," announced New York senator Robert Wagner; "we are in a life and death struggle with the forces of social and economic dissolution."[1]

Civilization was unraveling before the nation's eyes, and the ultracompetent President Herbert Hoover—a Stanford-educated engineer who was renowned for organizing humanitarian relief efforts—seemed to have no idea what to do in the face of the disaster. The laissez-faire tradition had come to the end of its string.

"There have been financial depressions before but never one exactly like this—never one for which the defenders of the system could find so little justification," wrote Floyd Olson, the governor of Minnesota, a few years into the catastrophe.

The old shibboleths no longer have their catch and power. Rotary clubs and Lions clubs are at a loss to create "pep." It is hard to find something to cheer for. The average person laughs when the business man talks of restoration of confidence. Industrial leaders no longer speak of prosperity just

around the corner; an audience would howl a speaker down
if he made such a reference.[2]

The echoes of the 1890s were obvious. Farmers organized
themselves again and tried to take direct action. So did unemployed veterans, calling themselves the Bonus Army and stag-
ing a huge, multiracial march on Washington in 1932 after the
model of Coxey's Army. This time, on the orders of President
Hoover, the government met the ragged marchers with armed
force, with bayonets and tear gas and tanks.

The confrontation of rich and poor was on again. Mostly it
was a political war, a contest of words and votes, but sometimes
it was a matter of more forceful methods, of union organizing
and of business counterorganizing. Also of violence, on occasion. During the strike wave of 1934, an army of police depu-
ties fought an army of Teamsters on the streets of Minneapolis;
the strikers gave as good as they got. During the strike wave of
1937, police opened fire on supporters of a strike at a steel mill
in Chicago; ten people were killed. Throughout the decade and
across the country, employers hired thugs to restore order while
fascist groups sprang up to meet the demand for strikebreakers.[3]

There was an important difference from the experience of
the 1890s. Once Herbert Hoover departed the White House
in 1933, the federal government no longer automatically took
the side of the business class—and without Washington at their
back, employers found they could do little but rage against
strikers and then settle their demands for shorter hours and better pay. Ordinarily, hard times are particularly tough for unions,
since there is a vast sea of unemployed workers sloshing around
the economy, undercutting any demand that other workers might

make. But in the 1930s, with the capitalist faith in ruins, everything was different. People flocked to labor organizations as their
grandparents had flocked to the Farmers' Alliance during the hard
times of the 1890s. Organizing seemed like the only way out of
the crisis; unions won battle after battle; and as a result they tripled
in size in the eight years from 1933 to 1941.[4]

In truth the Great Depression discredited capitalism around
the world and made people into radicals in every land. This
did not happen because those people were especially enlightened, but because they were desperate. Communism suddenly
became appealing, to intellectuals as well as proletarians. France
and Sweden turned to socialism. Mexico nationalized the oil
industry. And Americans embraced our native radical tradition
of populism.

IN SAYING THIS, I do not mean that anyone called themselves
a "populist." In the 1930s, the p-word still referred strictly to
partisans of the long-dead third party of the 1890s; when it
made an appearance in the papers, it was nearly always in a
nostalgia story or an obituary for some colorful hero from the
radical days of yore. As a designation for a general political style
the word was extremely rare.

However, there were plenty of observers who made the connection between the politics of the Depression and those of
the 1890s. The adventures of Coxey's Army, for example, were
an obvious topic for reflection when the Bonus marchers were
in Washington. When two elderly Pops were retrieved from
obscurity and elected to the Kansas state legislature in 1932—
as Democrats, this time around—newspapers across the country
took the obvious lesson.[5] When indebted Iowa farmers rose in

revolt and blockaded cities in 1933, the comparison was made once more.[6]

William Allen White, the Kansas newspaperman who got his start describing Populism as a kind of collective madness, was still in the game during the Depression and in 1936 he wrote a retrospective on the matter for the *New York Times*. His views had mellowed with age and now when he looked back he saw Populism not as an episode of mass hysteria but as the respected granddaddy of all the reformers who had come since—Teddy Roosevelt, Woodrow Wilson, and now FDR.[7]

Franklin Roosevelt was, of course, a Democrat, and he did not call his New Deal "populist," but the lineage was clear to historians and popular writers of the day.[8] With the culture of the 1930s, the connection was even more obvious. Everywhere you turned in those days, optimism about ordinary people was the mood of the moment. There was populism in Hollywood movies, in plays, in popular poetry, in radio programs, in art photography, in strike manifestos, in folk music, in WPA murals, and in the patriotic propaganda the government issued as the nation prepared for World War II. There was populism in Congress, as it broke up banks, gave workers the right to organize, protected farmers from price fluctuations, investigated monopolies, and enacted landmark antitrust legislation.

But above all there was populism in the White House. This was the great difference between 1892 and 1932: in the latter contest, the man who brought farmers and workers together against Wall Street came out on top. And then he won again, even more triumphantly, four years later. Franklin Roosevelt and his successor proceeded to win three more times, serving five presidential terms in all. And this most consequential president of the twentieth century didn't merely talk in a populist way; he delivered. FDR bailed out farmers and homeowners, he protected unions, he pulled the teeth of the Wall Street wolves, he smashed oligopolies, he took America off the gold standard, and—although we don't remember it today—he was roundly condemned by the nation's respectables as the most dangerous demagogue of them all, a sort of one-man mob rule.

"WHAT WAS THE New Deal anyhow?" asked Frances Perkins in a speech in 1963. She had served as Franklin Roosevelt's labor secretary through his entire presidency, and she was in a position to furnish an answer. "Was it a political plot? Was it just a name for a period in history? Was it a revolution? To all of these questions I answer 'No.'"

> It was, I think, basically an attitude. An attitude toward government, toward the people, toward labor. It was an attitude that found voice in expressions like "the people are what matter to government," and "a government should aim to give all the people under its jurisdiction the best possible life."

Perkins understood that a concern for "the people" sounded trite to her audience in 1963, but she persisted: to Roosevelt it meant something very real. Before the New Deal, she said, "the people had been left out of the planning, except for the economic plans of their employers." Discovering the people and taking their well-being into account in economic policy—this was something new and radical in the thirties, something that our government still formally heeds even though the old, business-centric attitude is clearly dominant again.[9]

One chapter of Perkins's memoir of her days with Roosevelt is called, simply, "He Liked People." FDR, she reminds us, was a master of radio communication, speaking directly to ordinary Americans without journalistic intermediaries. After describing this famous talent of his, Perkins wrote that "the quality of his being one with the people, of having no artificial or natural barriers between him and them, made it possible for him to be a leader without ever being or thinking of being a dictator."[10]

Present-day observers sometimes find it difficult to think of the age of Roosevelt as a populist time. FDR was, after all, the consummate insider: the scion of an aristocratic New York family, a Harvard man, a devotee of no ideological system, and a master politician who did almost nothing else in his adult life except govern and campaign. In his spare time he loved martinis, yachting, and collecting postage stamps. In the first few years of his administration, he was open to the distinctly un-populist idea of a cartelized economy, in which business got to write its own rules (FDR turned strongly against that idea later). He was also the first president to methodically incorporate scholarly expertise into his administration, and for plenty of scholars, this is the most critical aspect of his twelve years in the White House. Here, they say, is the man who pushed the tycoons aside and placed experts like us atop the "commanding heights" of the economy.[11]

The best corrective to that understanding is the most direct one: listen to the words Roosevelt actually spoke. FDR talked constantly about the urgent need to take power away from economic elites and return it to the average American. The theme was there, for example, in his rousing 1932 acceptance speech to the Democratic convention in which he introduced the phrase "a New Deal" and in which he described that year's campaign as nothing less than a "crusade to restore America to its own people."

But before he got to that phrase, Roosevelt had echoed a famous passage from Bryan's 1896 convention speech, denouncing an administration that "sees to it that a favored few are helped and hopes that some of their prosperity will leak through, sift through, to labor, to the farmer, to the small business man." Roosevelt criticized orthodox economics, with its insistence that "economic laws—sacred, inviolable, unchangeable—cause panics which no one could prevent." And like an Old Testament prophet, Roosevelt even called on his audience of Democrats to repent, since "many amongst us have made obeisance to Mammon" and since "the profits of speculation, the easy road without toil, have lured us from the old verities."[12]

Roosevelt talked like this all the time: the virtue of toil versus the hollow allure of finance; the nobility of the many versus the perfidy of the economic elite. In September 1932, his campaign train took him to Topeka, Kansas—he would carry the home state of the old People's Party twice—to address the crisis of agriculture. Up until then, he pointed out to his audience, economic policy had been the province of bankers, not of the people. What this meant, he continued, was that our government had instructed farmers "to put their interests into the hands of their bitterest opponents—men who will go to any and all lengths to safeguard and strengthen a protected few, but who will coldly say to American farmers: 'One-third of you are not needed. Run a race with bankruptcy to see which will survive.'"

A "race with bankruptcy" turned out to be an apt phrase. FDR beat Hoover in an easy landslide that November, but by the time he was sworn in the following March, the numbers of unemployed had skyrocketed and the banks of the nation were closed. There was no economy to speak of. In the face of all that, Roosevelt delivered one of the all-time classics of populist oratory. "The unscrupulous money changers," which is to say, Wall Street bankers, had led the nation into disaster, Roosevelt declared in his inaugural address. And now:

> Stripped of the lure of profit by which to induce our people to follow their false leadership, they have resorted to exhortations, pleading tearfully for restored confidence. They only know the rules of a generation of self-seekers. They have no vision, and when there is no vision the people perish.
>
> The money changers have fled from their high seats in the temple of our civilization. We may now restore that temple to the ancient truths.

The virtuous people, brought to the brink of ruin by corrupt financial elites, had arrived at the seat of government to set things right.

Roosevelt played upon this theme constantly. His January 1936 State of the Union speech, delivered in the midst of an epic fight with the nation's business leaders, carried the idea to its most inflammatory expression. Everywhere you looked, Roosevelt said as he surveyed the nation and the world, "popular opinion is at war with a power-seeking minority." This minority, which he defined as the nation's "financial and industrial groups," was "numerically small" but had been "politically dominant" during the 1920s. The coming of the New Deal, however, had forged "a new relationship between Government and people." It had dislodged these tycoons from power and made government "the representative and the trustee of the public interest."

Now the war between the tycoons and the New Deal was on in earnest. Roosevelt had found it necessary, he said, "to drive some people from power and strictly to regulate others." In so doing, "we have earned the hatred of entrenched greed."

Simply put, our "resplendent autocracy" wanted their power back. They longed for an order in which the winnings again "went to the ruthless and the strong." But they faced a federal government—"a people's government," Roosevelt called it—whose power matched their own. And so, he charged, they aimed to conquer it and turn its powers to their own advantage. "Give them their way," the president warned, "and they will take the course of every autocracy of the past—power for themselves, enslavement for the public."

To repeat, these are lines that appeared in an American president's State of the Union speech, a speech of the greatest importance that was broadcast nationwide at prime time in an election year. The words shock the modern-day reader not because they weren't true, but because they are so starkly at odds with our modern-day conception of the office. The president, we think (or, rather, we thought until recently), is supposed to be a conciliator, a builder of confidence, a seeker of consensus. He or she is expected to avoid class conflict. So outrageous are Roosevelt's phrases that we can scarcely conceive he uttered them.

THE AGE OF Roosevelt was also the age of the mass movement. Huey Long, the senator from Louisiana, had his Share Our Wealth societies, and author Upton Sinclair had his End Poverty in California movement, which revived the old Populist idea of the "cooperative commonwealth." Farmers in the Midwest signed up for the Farmers Union; in Iowa for the Farmers'

Holiday Association; in Wisconsin for the state Progressive Party; and in Minnesota for the Farmer-Labor Party.

This last group, the "apostolic successor" of the old People's Party according to one historian, elected the aforementioned Floyd Olson governor of Minnesota in 1930.[13] Minnesota was the scene of spectacular agrarian protests and industrial strikes in those years, and as farmers and workers went through the tribulation of the Depression, Olson took extraordinary steps to alleviate their plight: spending on relief, proposing state-level versions of Social Security and health insurance, suggesting that government take over and run idle factories along with utilities and railroads, and, in 1934, declaring a moratorium on fore-closures. Olson had once been a member of the radical IWW union, and traces of its teachings persisted in his days as chief executive of the state. "We are in a fight," Olson said in a 1934 speech. "It is the people's fight."

> Let us not betray them. Let us answer predatory entrenched wealth as Maine answered, as California answered, and as the whole nation answered when it elected Roosevelt.[14]

The most dynamic mass movement of the era was organized labor. As in the depression of the 1890s, workers were growing militant again, and they were coming together in enormous numbers. Over the objections of the traditional craft unions and in the teeth of the country's biggest employers, an outfit called the Congress of Industrial Organizations (CIO) set about enlisting the country's millions of unskilled workers. It is not a coincidence that the nucleus of the CIO—the United Mine Workers—was one of the unions that had aligned with the People's Party back in the 1890s. This time around, though, their efforts succeeded, as the CIO's dramatic organizing drives swept the country's steel and automaking industries. Led in many departments by immigrants, the CIO organized African Americans as well as whites, and for about ten years it seemed unstoppable, the volcanic power that was rewriting America's social contract. The CIO was the emblematic social force of the period: populist-proletarian solidarity was its characteristic aspiration, and the sit-down strike was its great symbol.

Whatever else you may think of labor unions, their advance represented a gigantic step forward for popular self-determination. The growth of the CIO opened a vast new territory—the industrial workplace—to democratic participation. Suddenly, millions of workers got a say on the conditions of their employment, a development that would in turn bring about enormous changes in this country, making possible the middle-class society of the post–World War II years.

Thus began a flowering of populist culture that we would recall as spectacular were it not so familiar. "During the period from 1935 until the end of World War II," writes the cultural historian Warren Susman, "there was one phrase, one sentiment, one special call on the emotions that appeared everywhere in America's popular language: the people."[15] Entertainment as well as politics became saturated with reverence for "the common man," for the "average American," for the authentic democratic community.

In art and literature, thirties populism took the form of "social realism," a genre populated with heroic workers, salt-of-the-earth farmers, and ostentatious multiculturalism. Experimental or abstract techniques were suddenly out of vogue, replaced by the famous "documentary impulse," a determination to represent unflinchingly the actual lives of the stricken and the lowly. Always the new style incorporated attacks on elites and aristocracy and bankers and rich kids and highbrow dilettantes and pretense of every description.

The individual most responsible for the triumph of the documentary style was probably Roy Stryker of the government's Farm Security Administration (FSA), who sent a platoon of famous photographers out to record the lives of impoverished farmers and thus "introduce America to Americans." Stryker was the son of a Kansas Populist, and, according to a recent study of his work, "agrarian populism" was the "first basic assumption" of the distinctive FSA style. Other agencies pursued the same aesthetic goal from different directions. Federal workers transcribed folklore, interviewed surviving ex-slaves, and recorded the music of the common man. Federally employed artists painted murals illustrating local legends and the daily work of ordinary people on the walls of public buildings. Unknowns contributed to this work, and great artists did too—Thomas Hart Benton, for example, painted a mural that was actually titled *A Social History of the State of Missouri* in the capitol building in Jefferson City.[16]

There was a mania for documentary books, photos of ordinary people in their homes and workplaces that were collected and narrated by some renowned prose stylist. James Agee wrote the most enduring of these, *Let Us Now Praise Famous Men*, in cooperation with photographer Walker Evans, but there were many others. The novelist Erskine Caldwell and the photographer Margaret Bourke-White published *You Have Seen Their Faces* in 1937, while Richard Wright, fresh from the success of his novel *Native Son*, published *Twelve Million Black Voices* in 1941, with depictions of African American life chosen from the populist photographic output of the FSA. Wright described the awful conditions of sharecropping in the South and squalid rentals in the ghettos of the North, but nevertheless ended his essay on a hopeful note of solidarity and even of patriotism. "We black folk, our history and our present being, are a mirror of all the manifold experiences of America," he wrote. "What we want, what we represent, what we endure is what America *is*."

Leaders of organized labor, meanwhile, embraced what used to be called "Americanism," a flamboyant identification of their own quest for justice and equality with the national flag, with patriotic tradition, and with the country's political heroes: Washington, Jefferson, Lincoln, and Roosevelt. As the historian Gary Gerstle has shown, Americanism helped workers' organizations to reverse decades of propaganda casting their members as anarchists, aliens, foreigners, subversives, and so on. Now, and regardless of ethnic background, they were the people, demanding their rightful place under freedom's sun.[17] Here is what this variety of populist rhetoric looked like, drawn in this case from a CIO pamphlet dated 1944 and titled *This Is Your America*:

> If you are a worker, earning your living honestly—
> If you are a farmer, a small business man, or a housewife—
> If you are against people who think only of themselves and never of other people—
> If you have faith in America as a good place to live in for the common people—
> America belongs as much to you as to any other citizen.[18]

Through all of the proclamations of the era ran the ubiquitous, inevitable incantation, "the people." "Whatever was truly built the people built it," wrote Archibald MacLeish in his

somber 1939 poem, "America Was Promises." Similarly, in the
final seconds of the 1940 movie version of *The Grapes of Wrath*,
Ma Joad says (as her luckless family heads off in their old truck
for another low-wage agricultural job):

> We keep a'comin'. We're the people that live. They can't
> wipe us out, they can't lick us. We'll go on forever, Pa, 'cause
> we're the people.

And here are the words with which Franklin Roosevelt closed
his successful 1940 campaign for a third presidential term:

> Always the heart and the soul of our country will be the heart
> and soul of the common man—the men and women who
> never have ceased to believe in democracy, who never have
> ceased to love their families, their homes and their country.[19]

The Common Man. Americanism. The People. Even the
1939 New York World's Fair, a lavish corporate spectacle, was
officially supposed to be "The People's Fair." What did this glut
of rhetorical populism mean? The obvious goal of some who
used these phrases was to depict their left-wing views as exten-
sions of the country's traditions of democracy and patriotism,
rather than as subversive or alien, as they had always been in
the past. For others, populism was a way of calling for social
solidarity in the face of economic catastrophe and a world war
against fascism. It provided reassurance, a reminder of the old
Jeffersonian faith. It lent a sense of overwhelming righteousness
to the new ideas of the era.[20]

The literary critic Kenneth Burke, in a 1935 speech to a
left-wing writers' group, explained the decade's populist turn

in an unusually forthright way. Movements need myths and symbols in order to bring people together, Burke explained, and the highest symbol for those on the Left should be "the people" rather than the conventional one, "the worker." Burke's audience was largely made up of party-line Communists, and they did not appreciate his suggestion. But his reasoning rings true. "The people" was a "positive," aspirational symbol rather than a reminder of oppression and hard times, Burke figured, and besides it was better attuned to American traditions.

Here is Burke's key insight: "We convince a man by reason of the values which we and he hold *in common*." The alternative, Burke pointed out, is to scold your audience, to assume "antagonistic modes of thought and expression" and to "condemn" the unenlightened. What we ought to be doing is not scolding but persuading, trying to "plead with the unconvinced."[21]

Kenneth Burke may not have grasped the power of his observation, but he had touched the very core of a basic political dilemma. In politics, we can choose to apply purity tests to the public, or we can work to spread knowledge. We can embrace the people or we can scold them for not getting it. It is a subject to which we shall return later.

ANOTHER CHARACTERISTIC DILEMMA of the 1930s was the problem of the demagogue. Modern-day anti-populists would no doubt dismiss the kind of rhetoric I have been quoting here as the talk of unscrupulous scoundrels. After all, according to their theories, almost anyone who speaks of "the people" in opposition to "the elite" is some kind of anti-pluralist Trumpian extremist.

Curiously enough, however, many of the writers and politicians who generated that language were also concerned with the very same problem—with false leaders who stirred up the mob out of nothing but a desire for self-aggrandizement. One reason opportunists of this kind fascinated them was because they wanted to establish that not everyone who honored the "common man" was a racist or a mercenary; that there was a clear distinction between the genuine public servant and the smooth-talking con man.[22]

One could scarcely avoid the demagogue problem in thirties America. People who stirred up mobs were all over the place—the nightmare flip side of the era's populist hopes. There was Louisiana politician Huey Long, whose name became synonymous with demagoguery; Father Charles Coughlin, a radio priest from Detroit who eventually became a dealer in the vilest kind of anti-Semitic conspiracy theories; and newspaper baron William Randolph Hearst, who constantly used the symbols of patriotism to smear progressives.

Each of these men found ways to use the language of anti-elitism for gross personal advancement and for shocking anti-democratic ends. Coughlin started out protesting hard times and inequality but became a more or less open fascist by the beginning of World War II. Hearst admired the Nazis, and his papers actually ran columns by Hermann Goering, Hitler's right-hand man. Long's "Share Our Wealth" movement, which at first had admirable social-democratic aims, was taken over by a racist crank after Long was assassinated. The stories of all three men show how the vocabulary of protest can be imitated and swiped by the Right.*

----

* Many who write about the Depression today describe Coughlin and Long as "populists"; indeed, in some accounts these two spectacular demagogues were the *only* populists of the decade. It is important to remember, however, that neither of them ever applied that word to themselves or acknowledged any debts at all to the tradition of agrarian reform. In the case of Huey Long, at least, that debt was real enough, since his rhetoric often echoed that of the

The culture of the period was obsessed with demagogues like these men. The 1941 Frank Capra movie *Meet John Doe*, for example, tells the story of a quintessential average guy who somehow becomes the figurehead for a movement that celebrates average guys. The movement, however, turns out to be controlled by a fascist newspaper owner, an evil rich man with a private army who wants to use the cult of the average guy to cantilever himself into power.

But *Meet John Doe* does not denounce populism itself or conflate it with demagoguery or teach viewers that the people are too ignorant to rule themselves. It does the opposite. While it shows us the millionaire puppet master deceiving the public, it also introduces us to individual members of that public and urges us, in its corny Capra way, to admire these average Americans for their neighborliness and democratic goodness. The elites are grotesque, despicable, manipulative; they weave ugly plots as they conspire around their fancy dinner tables. But average Americans are honest and truehearted; one character even calls Jesus "the first John Doe." In the movie's final scene, the fascist tycoon is confronted by a delegation of average folks, one of whom delivers a classic Hollywood kiss-off: "there you are, [rich guy]: the people. Try and lick that."*

1890s. In other ways, though, Long was one of a kind, a man who played the American political game ruthlessly and with uncanny ability. (On this, see historian Alan Brinkley's account, *Voices of Protest* [Vintage Books, 1983], chapter 7.) A more accurate term for Coughlin and Hearst and the man who took over Long's movement would be "pseudo-populist."

* Elsewhere I have commented on the weird way this movie predicted the relationship between Fox News and the pseudo-populist Tea Party movement. What Frank Capra imagined in 1941 was reproduced for real by tycoon Rupert Murdoch and the everyman announcer Glenn Beck in

Or take *Citizen Kane*, the greatest Hollywood movie of the era, which is about exactly the sort of public narcissists and liars who are today indicted as "populists." The movie is a history of yellow journalism told through the biography of a man who seems a lot like William Randolph Hearst, and naturally "the people" is one of the movie's running themes: the newspaper owner's somewhat pathetic need to be loved by them and his belief that he can make people think "what I tell them to think." This master of fake news is eventually brought down, of course, but only after launching a campaign for governor of New York in which he makes vague promises to "the underprivileged, the underpaid, and the underfed"—and also to prosecute and lock up the other party's candidate. (There's a reason it's Donald Trump's favorite movie.)[23]

Does the movie's central story of a demagogue on the make mean that the grievances of "the underprivileged" were phony? No. Just as in *Meet John Doe*, the existence of fake populism doesn't discredit the real deal. "You talk about the people as though you own them, as though they belong to you," one of the characters rebukes Kane, the press lord:

As long as I can remember, you've talked about giving the people their rights, as if you can make them a present of liberty, as a reward for services rendered. Remember the working man? . . . You used to write an awful lot about the working man. He's turning into something called organized labor. You're not going to like that one little bit when you find out it means that your working man expects something

---

2009–10, with the ultimate result being the election of TV tycoon Donald Trump to the presidency.

as his right, not as your gift! . . . When your precious under-privileged really get together, oh boy.

Orson Welles, the star, director, and co-writer of *Citizen Kane*, was no anti-populist. On the contrary, he was a prominent advocate of what was called People's Theatre; his obsessive concern (according to historian Michael Denning) was anti-fascism. He was given to denouncing the powerful in the same thirties manner as everyone else I have described in this chapter.[24]

How is this possible? How was Orson Welles able to embrace the people and simultaneously attack demagogues? How was Frank Capra able to do it? Or, for that matter, Franklin Roosevelt, or Henry Wallace, or Floyd Olson? How could they see something so clearly that has entirely escaped our present generation of political experts?

It was because the word these people used to describe demagogues like Coughlin or Hearst was not "populist." It was "fascist." Or, to be precise, "pre-fascist."

The distinction was easy enough to make: leftists and liberals who spoke the language of "the people" in such a fiery way aimed to use democratic instruments to make the country's economic system more democratic. They did not try to shut democracy down in order to stave off changes that were displeasing to the elite. In the 1930s that kind of thing was the preserve of fascists.*

---

* This is, roughly speaking, the definition proposed in a study of demagoguery by the veteran journalist Raymond Gram Swing called *Forerunners of American Fascism* (J. Messner, 1935). In chapters about Coughlin, Long, Hearst, and a handful of others, Swing described them not as fascists proper but as the kind of leader that comes just before fascism, a bridge to the brown-shirted future.

. . .

ANOTHER DISTINCTION IT'S important to recall: for all its populism, the Depression was not really a period of mob rule, or of wisdom trampled by public ignorance, or even of plebiscitary democracy. The Roosevelt administration did not put every detail of its program up for a public referendum, despite its many invocations of the "common man" and despite the overwhelming landslides it won. The Age of Roosevelt was also the age of regulation, the period when the administrative state came into its own, launching the Securities and Exchange Commission, the National Labor Relations Board, the Social Security Administration, the Tennessee Valley Authority, and the Federal Communications Commission. I am aware that in recalling all this I am breezing by decades of controversy and thousands of pages of carefully considered history, but that's because the point I want to make is a relatively simple one: the populist tradition just isn't as stubbornly hostile to representative bodies as anti-populist theory makes it out to be.

Nor did the populism of the Roosevelt era translate into a renewed suspicion of international trade and globalism. For all the isolationist agitation of the period—and, yes, lots of good progressives were leery of foreign entanglements—FDR and his State Department were America's all-time champion believers in international organizations and free trade, constantly attacking the high-tariff policies of their Republican predecessors and, later on, working to build the United Nations.

What surprises the modern observer is that even globalism was cast in populist terms back then. For example, when the publisher of *Time* and *Life* magazines announced the "American century" in 1941, Vice President Henry Wallace gave a radio speech pushing back against him: it was not our century at all, Wallace declared, but the "Century of the Common Man," a "people's century" in which cartels and monopolies must come under "international control for the common man."[25] A short while later, with World War II having engulfed the United States, Undersecretary of State Sumner Welles delivered a famous address in which he anointed the conflict "a people's war" and then explained why the postwar world had to reject protectionism, a policy in which, he said, "small vociferous privileged minorities" had once tried to choke off trade and thus "brought ruin to their fellow citizens."[26]

And I must confess it astonished me to discover that, in his closing speech to the 1944 Bretton Woods Conference—the very font and source of globalization—Treasury Secretary Henry Morgenthau described the launch of the World Bank itself as though he were addressing a meeting of the Farmers' Alliance. The new organization, he predicted, would destroy the power "certain private bankers have in the past exercised over international finance." Under the World Bank's program of handing out cheap loans, Morgenthau continued, "The effect would be . . . to drive only the usurious money lenders from the temple of international finance."[27]

POPULISM'S SUPPOSED HOSTILITY to intellect, so widely condemned today, becomes something very different when seen through the lens of the 1930s. It is true that the Depression discredited economic scholars and captains of industry and that, in the depths of the economic crisis, Americans laughed bitterly at the country's former wise men. One of the most popular books of the decade was made up of bum predictions by economists, politicians, and bankers, reprinted verbatim with no commentary except headlines giving the true facts. Its title was literally a sneer: *Oh Yeah?*

That was pretty crude, I suppose, and Lord only knows the thousands of ways the populist culture of the Depression years has been criticized since then for its vulgarity and philistinism. A whole generation of artists and thinkers, it is said, abandoned the experimental styles of the 1920s in favor of corny folksiness. They stopped exploring the vacuous stupidity of American life in order to paint pictures of farmers and workers and compose sentimental odes to the sons of toil and write books with titles such as *I Like America* and *American Stuff*. Suddenly even the most highbrow culture workers were writing and painting for an audience of ordinary people.

But regardless of what we think of the art of the Depression, there is no denying that it was produced by people who took ideas seriously, figures like Kenneth Burke, Orson Welles, Diego Rivera, Carl Sandburg, John Dos Passos, Ben Shahn, and James Agee. We might not appreciate the low-rent direction in which they chose to take modernism, but it remained modernism nonetheless. This isn't the place to get into it, but perhaps the real philistines in this picture are the ones who dismiss artists and writers because they started to care about the experiences of ordinary people.[28]

In the case of the economics profession, its mass shaming by the Depression proved to be a supremely fortunate development. In 1932, "respectable opinion was all on Mr. Hoover's side," the economist John Kenneth Galbraith wrote years later. The ones who thought America should detach itself from the gold standard, bail out agriculture, and spend lots of money on public works were "cranks, crackpots, eccentrics, and the vaguely irresponsible. . . . These were not the ideas of men of established reputation," Galbraith concludes. "If Roosevelt had mastered and accepted the ideas of the men of established reputation, his views would not have been different from those of Mr. Hoover."[29]

Thank goodness Roosevelt didn't care about "established reputation." Thank goodness he was willing to put the well-being of ordinary people above economic orthodoxy. Yes, professionals eventually learned to honor FDR as the patron saint of academia-in-government, since he was advised by a so-called Brain Trust of college professors. However, FDR took their advice not because he was a meritocrat who automatically deferred to orthodoxy, but because he was a pragmatist who wanted to try new approaches to things. In fact, FDR was decidedly unimpressed by academic prestige. At a press conference in 1935, the president recounted reading articles by fifteen different economists. From these, he concluded, "two things stand out: The first is that no two of them agree, and the other thing is that they are so foggy in what they say that it is almost impossible to figure out what they mean. It is jargon; absolute jargon."

Indeed, one of the idiosyncratic ideas Roosevelt aired a number of times during his presidency was that highly educated people were a "class" enjoying "privilege" every bit as much as those of great wealth. He saw these two groups—the rich and the well-educated—as distinct elites, albeit on the same side of most questions. If you legislated as degree-holders demanded, he once said, you would be helping not the "whole community" but their particular social cohort. FDR liked to repeat the following homily, which he attributed to Harvard president

Charles William Eliot: "If the ballot of the United States were limited to the holders of college degrees"—not a far-fetched proposal in our current springtime of seething anti-populism—"the country would probably last about two years."[30]

Putting the well-being of the "whole community" above norms, prestige, and academic orthodoxy doesn't sound scary to me; it sounds like good government. It's an attitude that had a salutary effect on the ivory tower as well. In 1938 a group of young academic economists published a book repudiating their conservative elders and endorsing FDR's New Deal in its broad populist outlines. "The conception of government as the organized expression of the collective strength and aspirations of the great mass of the people," they wrote, "has come to stay."[31] Not a ringing declaration really, but still quite remarkable in the context of the economics profession, which had previously insisted—and which would someday insist again—that the hopes of the "great mass of the people" didn't matter; that the only ruler that government needed to heed was economic law.

ON THE OTHER hand, we have been instructed in recent years to understand that when we hear someone dedicating themselves to the "great mass of the people" or to the "whole community" or to the "common man," they are always, perversely, leaving somebody out. Specifically, we know that they are secretly confessing themselves to be guided by racism, or xenophobia, or nativism, or anti-pluralism.

And sure enough, there were plenty of high-profile racists and anti-Semites in the 1930s, and a few of them liked to talk about "the people"—for example, Father Coughlin, the

Jew-hating radio priest, or Democratic senator Theodore Bilbo of Mississippi, the country's champion bigot.

But by 1936, Bilbo's Democratic Party—the traditional enforcer of the racist system in the South—had begun to change. In that year, the party commenced its historic outreach to black voters in the North. This effort was assigned to a Democratic group called the Good Neighbor League, set up for the purpose of persuading African Americans and other traditionally Republican groups to join Roosevelt's liberal coalition. The high point of the effort was a spectacular rally in Madison Square Garden featuring Cab Calloway and his orchestra; it was broadcast across the country—except in the South, that is. The League's political message was simple: look at what the New Deal agencies had done for African Americans. Let's allow one of the scholars who has studied the episode to recite the list. The federal government, he recalls,

> had employed 25,000 young black men and women in the National Youth Administration, and 200,000 blacks had been enlisted in the Civilian Conservation Corps. The Works Progress Administration provided earnings for 1,000,000 black families. . . . In addition to these accomplishments, nineteen housing projects for black residents were undertaken by the Public Works Administration, and $7,500,000.00 was appropriated for black schools and colleges in fifteen southern states.[32]

As countless writers have pointed out over the years, the New Deal failed African Americans in all sorts of ways. The great reforms of the 1930s coexisted with Jim Crow and were sometimes crafted specifically to exclude black workers from benefits, thus tiptoeing around the ever-so-delicate sensibilities of the white South. New Deal housing agencies refused to subsidize black homeownership, a costly mistake with consequences that are still felt today. It was not until 1948 that the Democratic Party truly committed itself to civil rights; it was not until the 1950s that Social Security was finally expanded to cover almost everyone. Still, what FDR achieved was impressive when compared to the pittance Hoover had done during his rounds with the Depression. Accordingly, the Democrats' outreach in 1936 was a massive success, with black neighborhoods in northern cities going overwhelmingly for FDR that year.

Viewed from a wider perspective, the populist culture of the thirties—always deliberately inclusive and glaringly anti-racist—permanently changed how Americans think of themselves. The historian Michael Denning calls it "pan-ethnic Americanism," a "pride in ethnic heritage and identity combined with an assertive Americanism." It was, he continues, "perhaps the most powerful working-class ideology of the age of the CIO, and it significantly reshaped the contours of official U.S. nationalism."[33]

Examples: Louis Adamic, a writer on class conflict in America who moved on to eulogizing the immigrant experience in books such as *From Many Lands* and *A Nation of Nations*. And: All the social-realist murals of the era, with their obligatory scenes of proletarian heroism and their representations of humanity in all its multihued righteousness. Even: the multicultural American propaganda during World War II, which was supposedly about smashing the Nazi idea of a "master race" in the name of "all free peoples" everywhere, and which has been remembered ever since for the flagrant way we disregarded it, interning people of Japanese descent, rescuing the British and French empires, and so on.*

Or think of *Ballad for Americans*, the 1939 cantata made into a gigantic popular hit by the African American singer Paul Robeson. It's OK, nobody else remembers it, either. Still, it was a sensation when it was first broadcast, the granddaddy of all the schmaltzy July 4 patriotic entertainment from that time to this. The song is a ten-minute rendering of the country's history with Robeson singing the part of the people. In political-science terms, his populism is clinically exact: "I represent the whole," he announces at one point, quoting Lincoln, hailing the Founding Fathers, singing the first lines of the Declaration of Independence. The elites are, of course, the bad guys: the "everybody who's anybody" who have persistently doubted democracy. Robeson, conversely, declares himself the "everybody who's nobody," the "nobody who's everybody." And then Robeson recites a series of lists—occupations, religions, and nationalities. *Ballad for Americans* is basically pluralism set to music:

> I'm just an Irish, Negro, Jewish, Italian, / French and English, Spanish, Russian, / Chinese, Polish, Scotch, Hungarian, / Litvak, Swedish, Finnish, Canadian, / Greek and Turk and Czech / and double-check American.

---

* The quotation comes from onetime undersecretary of state Sumner Welles in his wartime book *The Time for Decision* (Harper & Brothers, 1944), p. 298. Fighting a world war against Nazi racism in which we bailed out the racist empires of our allies and ignored the official racism of our own southern states was obviously a grievous contradiction in this philosophy, a contradiction that Welles never resolved except with evasive banalities about postwar organizations that would fix everything and give everyone national determination, etc.

Just as in *Citizen Kane* and *Meet John Doe*, the deep baritone voice of "the whole" then takes a slap at demagoguery and racism—"out of the cheating, out of the shouting / out of the murders and lynching / out of the windbags, the patriotic spouting."

One reason Robeson's multiculturalism made as much sense as it did in 1939 was because immigrants and children of immigrants were everywhere in Depression-era populist culture. Frank Capra, the great votary of the small-town myth, was born in Italy. Floyd Olson, the radical Minnesota governor, was the son of Scandinavian immigrants; so was the poet Carl Sandburg. Sidney Hillman, one of the most creative labor leaders of the period, was born in Lithuania. The proletarian parable that all these people embraced was, to a surprising degree, a polyglot populism of the recent arrival. The CIO, the voice of mass working-class mobilization, was particularly fond of it; you might even say populist multiculturalism was their house style.[34]

I have in mind here a pamphlet produced by the CIO's political action committee called *The People's Program for 1944*. It is filled with typical pop-talk of the World War II variety, making shout-outs to farmers and small business owners and dreaming of a plan for universal prosperity after the war. ("Ultimate victory, of which we are certain," the pamphlet trumpeted, "must bring with it the assurance of lasting peace . . . and the development of an abundant life for the Common Man of this earth.") Then the pamphlet comes to civil rights. "The hateful practice of discrimination because of race, religion or national origin against which we are fighting abroad must be stamped out at home," it declared.

> Anti-Semitic and anti-Negro practices undermine the very foundation of our democracy. Full economic, political, and

civil equality must be guaranteed to every American, regardless of his race, creed or national origin.[35]

Again, this was not unusual; it was what populist unionism was all about. We were all part of "the people"; we were all together in the war against fascism and reactionary elites. This was the message of another CIO pamphlet, *The Negro in 1944*, which trumpeted advances made under the Roosevelt presidency.

> In this year of decision, 1944, Negro Americans find themselves at a crossroad.
>
> They are not there alone.
>
> The small farmer, the small businessman, the white collar worker, the professional, the housewife, both white and colored, are there.
>
> The foreign-born are there.
>
> So are all the people who live by the sweat of their brows.
>
> All the "little people" are at the crossroad this year.[36]

Let us conclude this section by recalling an amazing War Bonds advertisement denouncing bigotry that ran in labor newsletters in 1944 and was uncovered by the historian Gary Gerstle. The ad accused a woman who worked hard to support the troops of undermining the war effort. How so? She had failed America, as Gerstle describes it,

> by making "thoughtless remarks" about neighbors "who go to a different church," and "about folks whose skin is a different color, or whose names are hard to pronounce." "As surely as though you landed on these shores in the dark of night

from a submarine, bent on blowing up factories and burning bridges," the advertisement charged this witless mother, "in spite of your charming manner and your 'all-out' war record, lady, *you* are a saboteur."[37]

THE GRANDEST, MOST eloquent evocation of Depression-era populism came from the Lincoln biographer Carl Sandburg, whose 1936 offering was a book-length poem called *The People, Yes*. Aside from its iconic title, the work is almost completely forgotten today, a strange outlier amidst the last century's highbrow taste in poetry. Sandburg's verse is not abstract; it is not avant-garde. But let us put our cynicism aside for a moment. As the title suggests, *The People, Yes* was a full-throated celebration of ordinariness: the manners of the people, their dreams, their folly, their aspirations, and above all their speech, the "plain and irregular sounds and echoes from / the roar and whirl of street crowds, work gangs, sidewalk clamor," as he wrote in the introduction.

As with *Ballad for Americans* and so many other works of the time, there is a compulsive listing of identities, repeated efforts to name-check everyone. Sandburg gives us cantos that are lists of occupations, cantos made up of slang expressions and lines from folktales and popular jokes. There are strikers, angry farmers, tricksters, soldiers, armies, and, of course, a big fat rich guy, ordering others off his property.

Naturally Sandburg attacks the elite, mocking the pretenses of aristocracy and reminding his Depression-era audience of something they knew all too well—that justice treats rich and poor differently. He reminds us that bank robbers go to prison but, if you're a bank officer who loots the company, "all you have to do is start another bank."

Sandburg may have been the perfect embodiment of the populist sensibility of the Depression years. He was known as the "People's Poet," the heir of Walt Whitman, the bard of the ordinary, "writing his raw, muscular verse for his peers out of a spontaneous native wisdom," as his biographer put it.[38] Over the course of his remarkable career he organized for the Socialist Party, wrote groundbreaking newspaper stories about the black experience in Chicago, and collected folk songs.

The virtuosity of the ordinary was Sandburg's lifelong fascination. This ultra-democratic theme was unpopular with highbrow critics at the time, as it is again today: what we expect from our poets is abstruseness, exclusivity, peer-reviewed professional excellence. Sandburg's modernism carried him to a different place, where the vernacular of the everyday was made to describe the nobility of the average.

WHAT I HAVE offered in this chapter is, again, not an ambitious new theory about the past. Everything I've recounted here has been a deliberately noncontroversial summary of famous quotes and events. My purpose in bringing it all together in one place is to point out in the bluntest way possible that populism is not at all what modern anti-populist theory holds it to be . . . and to suggest, furthermore, that populism may well be the key to turning our nation around.

I make no claim that the New Deal ushered in utopia or even that it practiced what it preached. It didn't, as everyone knows. Regardless of how Paul Robeson stirred his listeners' souls, there were hotels and restaurants all across the country that could lawfully have refused him service. And while the CIO represented democratic aspiration of the best kind, it came a cropper in the South just as Populism did, a shortcoming for which middle-class Americans everywhere eventually paid the price.

Even so, it is vitally important to remember the words and the deeds of those days. The years when American liberals laughed at "economic laws," sent the "money changers" packing, and declared "the people are what matter" were also the years of peak liberal greatness. Populism's days of cultural ascendancy in this country coincided with the gradual conquest of economic depression and with America's victory in World War II. Populism is what strengthened the unions and built a middle-class democracy. Populism, rightly understood, is what allowed Roosevelt to win four presidential elections (and Harry Truman a fifth); it is what gave Democrats such a solid majority in the House of Representatives that they didn't lose it, except for two brief interregnums, until 1994.

American liberals need to remember how their tradition thought and how it talked when it was strong and vital—in order to figure out how it might do so again.

4

"The Upheaval of the Unfit"

Not everyone loved the common man in the Age of Roosevelt. For all the tears that liberals shed over Dust Bowl migrants, the Depression also saw a powerful backlash against democracy in general and against economic democracy in particular. The decade that produced "The People, Yes" also gave us *The Revolt of the Masses,* in which Jose Ortega y Gasset deplored the empowerment of the vulgar herd, and also *The Hour of Decision,* in which Oswald Spengler defined democracy as mob rule and bad taste, a system so weak that it could never last.

Looking back on the decade of the thirties, it is easy to forget how many people around the world decided in those years that democracy was finished—that the global economic depression had revealed government by the people to be a failure. Democratic governments everywhere dithered and crumbled, their glad-handing politicians useless in the face of the crisis.

Americans lost faith as well. At the end of his landmark three-volume history of this period, the historian Arthur Schlesinger Jr. assembled a series of shocking quotes from prominent Americans in the early thirties, all of whom were convinced that democracy was either doomed or that it deserved to die. A sampling:

"The moral and intellectual bankruptcy of liberalism in our time needs no demonstration. It is as obvious as rain and as taken for granted."

"Political democracy is moribund. . . . Civil liberties like democracy are useful only as tools for social change. Political democracy as such a tool is obviously bankrupt throughout the world."

"Modern Western civilization is a failure. That theory is now generally accepted."[1]

These were fairly extreme statements. But pessimism about the future of democracy was common during the Depression, talking at you from the radio or the pulpit, scolding you from the editorial page. The form it ultimately took was what I have been calling anti-populism.

The problem, the anti-populists maintained, was excessive democracy. Just as in 1896, the right order of things was menaced by mob action, by a rising up of the ignorant. Government by the people had become a threat to property, to the Constitution, and hence to democracy itself.

DEPRESSION-ERA ANTI-POPULISM TOOK a while to find its voice. In 1932 the ideological opposition to Roosevelt was weak. The Hoover administration had failed by any standard of judgment and no one really knew how much would change when the gloomy Republican was replaced by the sunny aristocrat from upstate New York. What FDR meant by "a New Deal" was still vague and his party's platform in '32 was perfectly conventional, recommending balanced budgets and an end to Prohibition. Perhaps it would merely be another instance of the outs replacing the ins, lots of noise signifying nothing.

Very quickly, however, it became clear that Roosevelt was working an enormous change in the economic role of the federal government—or, as he himself put it in his State of the Union address in 1936, "a new relationship between Government and people."

Under his direction, the United States finally left the gold standard. It handed out relief to the unemployed. It hired armies of people to build bridges and buildings, to paint murals and shovel snow. It set up a national old-age pension scheme. It bailed out homeowners. It bailed out farmers. It regulated banks and countless other industries. It protected unions and encouraged workers to join them. There were strikes in every city, new walkouts were happening all the time, and in an alarming number of them business owners were being forced to settle.

Each of these developments, by itself, would have been a momentous change; now they were happening together, all at once. The big-business community reeled in shock. Its leaders looked for a way to fight back.

The showdown came in the election of 1936. As the political parties maneuvered and the nation's elites chose sides, it became plain that this campaign would be a battle royal, an all-or-nothing war over the future direction of the nation. A crusade, from one perspective, for freedom and the Constitution. Or, viewed slightly differently, an attempt by the once-privileged to regain their former position. Either way, it was to be a referendum on big government and the welfare state.

There were three main components of the anti-Roosevelt forces. The Republican Party furnished the presidential candidate: Kansas governor Alf Landon, who had been something of a progressive in earlier days but was now willing to commit himself to the defeat of the New Deal. He would attack all of it, from Social Security to the WPA, as an imposition on freedom itself.

Even more important than the Republican Party in 1936 was the independent political effort mounted by big business. The organizations through which business leaders distributed their propaganda were many, but the one that mattered most was called the American Liberty League. The first of the nation's great right-wing front groups, the Liberty League was set up by a handful of wealthy people, chiefly from the DuPont family, who had special reason to hate and fear the triumph of progressives.* With the lavish budget its wealthy backers furnished, the League followed the strategy pioneered by Mark Hanna forty years previously, producing speeches, radio broadcasts, pamphlets, and a blizzard of panic-screaming headlines. The Liberty League was better funded and far better organized than a traditional political party, which made it the de facto "leading opposition to Roosevelt," as one scholarly study recalls.[2]

---

* Because DuPont was preeminent in the explosives business, the company had been targeted in congressional hearings on war profiteering and criticized in detail in a popular 1934 book by H. C. Englebrecht called *Merchants of Death: A Study of the International Armament Industry* (Dodd, Mead, 1934).

The third part of the '36 crusade was the newspaper industry, which came together against the would-be dictator Roosevelt the same way it had united against Bryan in 1896. The
reason for journalism's overwhelming hostility to the president
seems obvious in retrospect: the owners of the nation's papers
were wealthy figures who regarded themselves as spokesmen
for their local business communities; they also felt their immediate interests to be threatened by the unionization that the
New Deal encouraged. Whatever the reason, their cohesion was
remarkable. FDR himself believed that the press was 85 percent against him; the historian Arthur Schlesinger Jr. put it at
75 percent of the country's big-city newspapers; Frank Luther
Mott, in *American Journalism*, suggests that 63 percent of all the
nation's papers were opposed to the president.[3]

The year 1936 was to be a great mustering of society's elites,
assembling for war against populism once again. The Roosevelt
administration, they would charge, was a dangerous departure
from established and bipartisan economic consensus. It was the
work of cranks, radicals, and demagogues. It was the product
of one man's mental illness. It was the tragic outcome of a system that permitted ordinary people to hand down judgments
on matters that were far above their station. And so another
Democracy Scare gripped the country.

ONE NODE WHERE the fear began was the National Association of Manufacturers, the great ideological union of American industry, which had been waging a propaganda war against
organized labor for decades before the New Deal arrived on the
scene. The Depression and its political consequences, however,

would prove to be the greatest challenge in the NAM's life, requiring its most advanced efforts.

The central idea in the NAM's vast output in the thirties, according to historian Richard Tedlow, was the "harmony of all classes." There need be no conflict between business owner and business employee, the NAM maintained; nor was there any need for friction between business and government. Consensus was the natural and normal condition of economic life: "Prosperity dwells where harmony reigns," as the NAM slogan had it.[4]

The reality of the Depression was anything but harmonious. In 1934, the NAM made a series of proposals to President Roosevelt to get the economy going again, asking him to reverse himself on nearly every front—put the country back on the gold standard, balance the federal budget, crack down on labor, and generally to do whatever would make business owners happy.[5]

Roosevelt did not comply. His aides scoffed at the NAM's suggestions, and the New Deal chugged onward. Workers organized, regulators regulated, and the WPA continued to hire unemployed people.

An ugly mood began to sweep the business community. In a controversial 1935 article, the financier E. F. Hutton said he felt the pain of the stockholder who got to "watch the value of his securities gradually destroyed by unwarranted attacks of demagogues in high places," meaning by New Deal regulation. Then Hutton urged his corporate colleagues to join forces and enlist in the class war. "I say:—'Let's gang up!'"

Gang up on the elected government in Washington, that is. Business leaders, Hutton said, needed to build an "unbroken front" of upper-class solidarity. "The business men of the country," he urged, the owners of stocks and bonds or any other property, the holders of insurance policies, and the depositors in banks, must realize that the only way to prevent regimentation, collectivism, or any other ism . . . is for all groups to join together in one great group which will come to the help of any individual group when it is attacked.[6]

When E. F. Hutton talked, people listened.* Many of them were outraged by what they heard him saying, but a few saw the wisdom of his remarks.

Gang up is precisely what business leaders did. A few months later, at their next annual meeting, the members of the NAM enlisted for the duration. "Industry . . . has been forced to enter the political arena," proclaimed the association's president, "or be destroyed as a private enterprise." The scene at the gathering was electric. The assembled businessmen approved a passionate manifesto denouncing the New Deal's "dictatorship" and espousing the "American System" of private enterprise. One eminent man after another declared his selfless concern for his country and the working masses.[7]

A Detroit steelmaker counseled the NAM's members to talk politics with their employees and take control of the Republican Party. A business school professor advised them to "submit to regulation but to resist control," in the description of the *New York Times*. A ferocious anti-populist note was struck by shipbuilder Clinton Bardo, who berated the "economic crack-pots, social reformers, labor demagogues and political

---

* Another achievement for which E. F. Hutton gained renown in his lifetime was the construction of a fabulous mansion in Palm Beach, Florida, named Mar-a-Lago.

racketeers" who, he claimed, had made the Depression so much worse. The New Deal, he continued, was "the most savage and concerted political attempt ever made toward the destruction of our industrial system."[8]

THE SAME SORT of gripe could be heard in every corner of upper America. One fine day in 1934, a vice president at DuPont wrote a letter to a former chairman of General Motors to complain about the New Deal. Here is how it had ruined his life:

> Five Negroes on my place in South Carolina refused work this Spring, after I had taken care of them and given them house [sic] rent free and work for three years during bad times, saying they had easy jobs with the government. . . .
>
> A cook on my houseboat at Fort Myers quit because the government was paying him a dollar an hour as a painter when he never knew a thing about painting before.

The former GM bigwig felt his colleague's pain. Something was indeed going very wrong in this country. In his reply, he suggested that the DuPont exec set up "some very definite organization" to instruct Americans on "the value of encouraging people to work; encouraging people to get rich; [and] showing the fallacy of communism."[9]

So was born the American Liberty League, the central organization of the business resistance to Roosevelt. Spawned by an executive's frustration at uppity working people, the Liberty League was anti-populist by birth but also by nature. As it began its "educational" work, it quickly became clear that the organization's grand purpose was to demonstrate elite consensus, to show that the nation's respectables stood shoulder to shoulder in solid agreement against the Rooseveltian experiment. Bipartisanship was an essential ingredient in this display—the Liberty League enlisted many prominent Democrats in its war on the Democrat in the White House, including two of the party's former presidential candidates. Credentialed prestige was another component: the League's spokesmen were drawn conspicuously from the most authoritative circles of economic and legal thought.

The overarching message of the Liberty League's resistance to Roosevelt was simple and monotonous. The New Deal, went the complaint, was a form of dictatorship akin to those in Italy, Germany, and Russia. It was trampling upon the American Constitution. It was crushing American liberty. Who knew or cared if FDR was on the Left or the Right: he was clearly a would-be authoritarian and the country needed to be saved from him and his monster government. Cue hysteria. Crank it all the way up.

A 1935 Liberty League pamphlet, authored by an economics professor from Vanderbilt University, labeled Henry Wallace, then the secretary of agriculture, a "Little Dictator" who might yet become "a real Stalin." Another pamphlet, published later that year, compared the New Deal both to the "autocratic power" of King George and also to the fascist systems of Mussolini and Hitler. The subtitle of a third, a description of FDR's farm program, ran as follows: *An Analysis of a Vicious Combination of Fascism, Socialism and Communism Which Cannot Be Harmonized with the Basic Principles of Constitutional Government in the United States.*[10]

"If there are any items in the march of European collectivism that the New Deal has not imitated it must have been an oversight," roared former president Herbert Hoover at the

Republican convention in the summer of 1936. The administration was a hodgepodge of usurpations, declared a Liberty League pamphlet a short while later—a would-be "totalitarian state" along the lines of European dictatorships.[11]

At a white-tie dinner sponsored by the League, Al Smith, the failed Democratic presidential candidate of 1928, stepped before the microphones and let loose a torrent of red-baiting. The New Deal, Smith charged, had enacted Socialist rather than Democratic Party principles and was at war with basic American freedoms. It was OK with him, Smith clarified, if the administration's "young brain trusters" wanted to "disguise themselves as Norman Thomas or Karl Marx, or Lenin, or any of the rest of that bunch, but what I won't stand for is allowing them to march under the banner of Jefferson, Jackson, or Cleveland." Nor would the country, with its proud democratic tradition. "You can't mix socialism or communism with that. They are like oil and water. . . . They refuse to mix."[12]

Smith had once been a close friend of Roosevelt's, and his speech made the sort of splash that grand personal betrayals of this kind always do. But the image that stuck in the public mind was the glittering audience that had dressed up in evening clothes to applaud this son of the New York streets as he denounced his former pal. Among them was a Vanderbilt, a Guggenheim, an Aldrich, a Russian princess, and Jay Cooke IV; assorted bankers and industrialists and lawyers; the owner of the *Washington Post*. One couldn't ask for a better illustration of the true nature of the Right's hand-wringing over freedom and the Constitution.[13]

Ah, the poor, forsaken Constitution. Conservatives talked as though it were a covenant that had been handed down by God, but from which we had strayed thanks to the infernal temptations of FDR. Now the blight of economic depression was our punishment. "Whatever caused our past prosperity," declared prominent attorney William H. Stayton in a 1935 Liberty League radio broadcast, "we know that there was a time when we obeyed our Constitution and were blessed above the rest of the world; and we know too that today our prosperity and happiness have given place to unemployment and distress which accompany our neglect of the Constitution."[14]

The nation's press joined in the chorus of rebuke, issuing invitations to the most extreme sort of political dread. The *Los Angeles Times,* to choose one paper, routinely made the darkest kind of accusations against the liberal president. Aghast at some long-forgotten episode of New Deal meddling in 1936, the paper announced that whether it was done with "deliberate intention of wrecking the social structure to let 'collectivism' inherit the earth, or whether it was merely inept blundering, makes little difference." A few days after that, the *Times* suggested that Rooseveltian bad-mouthing of business constituted the same sort of "leadership" responsible for "Russia and Spain and Italy and Nazi Germany."[15]

The way the *Chicago Tribune* urged panic upon its readers that year has become the stuff of legend. Here is how journalism critic George Seldes told the story in his 1938 book *Lords of the Press*:

> Every day the *Tribune* editorial page was a biased attack on Roosevelt with the heading "Turn the Rascals Out"; every day the *Tribune* telephone operators said "Good morning. *Chicago Tribune.* There're only forty-three (or less) days left in which to save the American way of life." Every day truthfulness, accuracy, impartiality, fair play and decency were flouted in the most vicious campaign against the President.

In the *Tribune*'s editorial cartoons, FDR could be seen marrying off "Miss Democracy" to a bristly-headed Communist; exploiting thuggish "Class Hatred" along with his Communist pals; denying everything though his hands were covered with "The Red Jam of Moscow." On October 20, the *Tribune*'s lead editorial was titled, "The Dictatorship Emerges"; the inevitable comparisons to Stalin and Hitler were duly made. A few days later, a *Tribune* editorial announced "It Will Happen Here, Unless—"; a column of full-throated red-baiting unfolded beneath. ("Some squeamish citizens resent calling such a program a program of communism, though that is obviously what it is.")

A front-page *Tribune* editorial just before Election Day declared, "You should realize that Nov. 3 is the most fateful day in the history of the American people. Do not consider that statement an exaggeration. If Landon is not elected you may have seen the last of free government as you have known it." A nearby cartoon showed FDR happily urging a blindfolded Uncle Sam over a cliff marked "Dictatorship."[16]

And then a shot right out of 1896. In the first of a long series of editorials titled "Turn the Rascals Out," the *Tribune* declared that Election Day 1936 was "the chance to get rid of repudiators, devaluators, and inflationists, of the men responsible for the tampering with the national currency, the national credit, and the national honesty." It was an almost exact repeat of the bill of grievances with which the nation's newspapers had charged William Jennings Bryan.

OF COURSE, THE Liberty League and its spokesmen also tried to present themselves as the voice of ordinary people. They loved to quote Jefferson, rail against tyranny, and cry out in the name of "that great big middle class we refer to as the backbone and rank and file," as Al Smith put it at that ultra-fancy League dinner.

The League's elitism was obvious in its face, however. Its pamphlets proudly listed the names of the extremely wealthy individuals who sat on its National Executive Committee. And whatever cultural authority the organization had was derived not from its intimacy with the rank and file but from its relationship with the dignified and the credentialed, by which I mean distinguished scholars and high-ranking corporation lawyers.

A consensus of the respectable was, as always, the form that the opposition to populism took, and in the publications of the Liberty League men of eminence and standing demonized the challenge to social hierarchy. Roosevelt represented mob rule, they said. Roosevelt violated norms and flouted the accepted boundaries of politics and economics. Roosevelt prioritized the shiftless and the lazy over the capable and the talented. Roosevelt coddled the weak and enslaved the strong. Roosevelt was mentally ill.* Roosevelt's New Deal represented an uprising of

---

* In an election-eve radio address, a former secretary of state named Bainbridge Colby described FDR as "swept headlong by hysterical resentment; shaken by the intensity of his hatreds." Colby proceeded to quote the famous psychologist Carl Jung:

> I have just come [from] America where I saw Roosevelt. Make no mistake, he has the most amazing power complex, the Mussolini substance, the stuff of a dictator absolutely.

Colby was quoting from an interview with Jung that ran in the London *Observer*. The Swiss psychologist, it seems, was a full-blown anti-populist, perceiving commonalities between (as he put it) "Hitler, Mussolini, Stalin, yes, and Roosevelt." Jung was also a hard-money man, complaining about the "fake money" that governments were producing under the guise

the lower orders, who wanted merely to pillage their betters. Like Bryan before him, Roosevelt was the emblem of a world gone mad.

At the pleasant resort of Sea Island, Georgia, at a 1935 meeting of the state's bar association, nightmares of a world turned upside down—of the end of American civilization!—stalked through the heads of the ruling class. Liberty League official Ralph M. Shaw, a name partner at the Chicago mega-firm known today as Winston & Strawn, summed it up thus:

> The New Deal is . . . an effort sponsored by inexperienced sentimentalists and demagogues to take away from the thrifty what the thrifty or their ancestors have accumulated, or may accumulate, and to give it to others who have not earned it, or whose ancestors haven't earned it for them, and who never would have earned it and never will earn it, and thus indirectly to destroy the incentive for all future accumulation.

The eminent lawyer thundered on: "Such a purpose is in defiance of everything that history teaches and of the tenets upon which our civilization has been founded."[17]

Civilization's downfall was even more alarmingly illustrated by the New Deal's revival of the old system of slavery, under

---

of "devaluation." After declaring that "nature is aristocratic," Jung continued as follows: "Communistic or socialistic democracy is an upheaval of the unfit against attempts at order." Furthermore: "A decent oligarchy—call it aristocracy if you like—is the most ideal form of government." I draw these quotations from a reprint of the Jung interview that appeared in the *Washington Post* on December 11, 1936. Bainbridge Colby's remarks appeared in the *Chicago Daily Tribune*, November 3, 1936, p. 10.

which some people "had the right, by law, to expropriate the
time and labor of other groups." Now, Shaw accused, it was
back, in different form:

> Under this new status, it is proposed by taxation to confis-
> cate the property of some citizens; expropriate the time and
> labor of those who work and are still willing to work and to
> give the proceeds thereof to those who don't work, many of
> whom are unwilling to work. The latter have a legal right
> to enjoy the property, the time and the service of the former.

The welfare state was bondage all over again. "The only difference between this present status and the slavery that obtained
prior to 1860 is this," Shaw continued: "That in the present status the inefficient become the masters and the efficient and the
thrifty are the slaves. That is the logic of the New Deal."[18] The
natural order of human society was being tragically reversed
before these respectable gentlemen's very eyes.

For the Liberty League and its allied forces, what the New
Deal represented was not merely a political reversal but a
scrambling of the entire hierarchy of existence. It had worked
this evil by obeying the preferences of people who, while they
might constitute an electoral majority, really had no business
making such decisions . . . which is ultimately to say that the
real problem was democracy itself.

The point was made in a League pamphlet by the attorney
William R. Perkins, the man for whom Duke University's main
library was later named. After musing upon the various outrages
the Roosevelt administration was then supposedly inflicting
on the Constitution in the name of "the people," Perkins declared
that "this is but the old, old rule of numbers, a form of government

which proved the scourge of national existence and became thoroughly discredited long, long ago for an unanswerable reason." That reason: "It vests complete, direct power in those who are least endowed, least informed, have least, and thereby reduces government to the lowest common denominator."[19]

Popular sovereignty, Perkins continued, was "utterly un-American," the sort of thing advocated by Karl Marx, who "to the unending turmoil and suffering of Europe, likewise taught the proletariat to use their numerical superiority." And now Franklin Roosevelt had brought this pernicious doctrine to America. The "democratic mass" was in control, Perkins warned, and disaster was around the corner.[20]

Another problem with the people was that there were just too damn many of them. For Thomas Nixon Carver, a renowned Harvard economist, the vast numbers of undistinguished folks was not a godly virtue; it was another nightmare. Let the poor "multiply out of all proportion to the need for them," he wrote in *Nation's Business* in 1935, and they would undoubtedly destroy the capitalist system—either by "voting heavier and heavier taxes on property for the benefit of the propertyless" or else "by violence," should it come to that. He dubbed this "the population problem," an explosive variable in a difficult economics equation. These people had to be carefully controlled by enlightened planners lest they swamp us all with their unbridled breeding.[21]

Even the idea of equality was attacked. Speaking to an audience of lawyers in 1936, Frederick Stinchfield, a Liberty League personage who was soon to become the president of the American Bar Association, griped that "we used to be a virile, self-reliant people." But something had gone wrong, and with the Depression Americans began looking to Washington to solve their problems. To help explain this degeneration, Stinchfield quoted from a then-popular book, *Man, the Unknown*, by the French biologist and Nobel laureate Alexis Carrel:

> "Another error, due to the confusion of the concepts of human being and individual, is democratic equality. . . . Indeed, human beings are equal. But individuals are not. The equality of their rights is an illusion. The feeble-minded and the man of genius should not be equal before the law."*

Unfortunately, however, they were equals before the law, and the sad result of this democratic "error" was that, thanks to politics, losers were permitted to evade the losing that was their rightful lot in life. In truth it was even more perverse than that: democracy gave the weak a way to lord it over the strong. Stinchfield quoted Carrel some more:

> "The standardization of men by the democratic ideal has already determined the predominance of the weak. Everywhere, the weak are preferred to the strong. They are aided

---

* If we turn to Alexis Carrel's then-celebrated, now-forgotten book, we find that the passage Stinchfield quoted continues as follows: "The stupid, the unintelligent, those who are dispersed, incapable of attention, of effort, have no right to a higher education. It is absurd to give them the same electoral power as the fully developed individuals. Sexes are not equal. To disregard all these inequalities is very dangerous. The democratic principle has contributed to the collapse of civilization in opposing the development of an élite."

Of course races were not equal, either. Elsewhere in *Man, the Unknown*, Carrel speculates that "the most highly civilized races" had the fairest complexions while "the lower races" lived in places that were hot and sunny. *Man, the Unknown* (Harper & Brothers, 1935), pp. 271, 214.

and protected, often admired. Like the invalid, the criminal, and the insane, they attract the sympathy of the public."

Science taught a lesson different from the populist folly of democracy, however. Humans succeeded or failed, science supposedly told us, largely because they were born to succeed or fail. If they were successful, it was often because they had better genes, or better blood, or were descended from better stock—that sort of thing. If they failed, heredity was again the reason. Once more the eminent lawyer cited the words of the Nobel laureate:

"In democratic countries, such as the United States and France, for example, any man had the possibility during the [nineteenth] century of rising to the position his capacities enabled him to hold. Today, most of the members of the proletarian class owe their situation to the hereditary weakness of their organs and their mind. . . . Today, the weak should not be artificially maintained in wealth and power."

Oddly enough, the ideal for which Stinchfield marshaled all this genetic fatalism was self-reliance. What was missing from the political debates of the thirties, the lawyer charged, was some understanding by ordinary Americans that the responsibility for the Depression lay with each and every one of them— some recognition that the way you dealt with hard times was by toughening up and looking within, not by pointing at big external forces. Ah, "what a difference it might have made, could we have heard from someone in official authority in the last six years that a man's misfortune is brought about by himself in part or in whole."[22]

But why should anyone feel personal responsibility for his

or her situation when it was really determined by centuries of breeding? To ask the question is to answer it. Given the political requirements of the American Liberty League in 1936, both the sunny credo of individualism and the ugly science of eugenics led to the same imperative: You must not challenge or overthrow society's elites. The weak must learn their place and be satisfied with their lot.

The pamphlet with which the Liberty League spread Frederick Stinchfield's ideas across the land does not tell us how his audience of accomplished professionals reacted to his talk; whether they grasped the contradiction of celebrating hereditary elites and the American way at the same time; whether they understood the paradox of aligning FDR with fascism while using quasi-fascist arguments against him. But we do know that the business community stood united against Roosevelt. As one CEO put it in 1936, the president was opposed "almost unanimously by the business and professional men of the country."[23]

It is to those "professional men" that we turn now. Today we think of the New Deal as the historic dawn of professional power, the moment when expertise finally came together with government. After all, Roosevelt was famously advised by a "brain trust" of college professors, and the New Deal was staffed with hundreds of idealistic young college grads. As the sociologist Edward Shils put it years later, much of the backlash against FDR was no more than "friction" caused by "the entry of the intellectuals into politics and administration."[24]

What we find difficult to recall is how very far outside the professional and academic orthodoxies of the time the New Deal intellectuals actually stood. From monetary theory to wage-and-hour regulation, the policies FDR pursued were massive violations of the reigning faiths of classical economics, and just as in 1896, academics let the public know it. In 1933, ninety eminent economists got together to decry FDR's departure from the gold standard, and in 1934 the New Deal got the full Harvard treatment, with seven notable economists from that institution publishing a book-length rebuke of FDR's program.[25]

"Money-tinkerers" and "demagogues" were the terms favored by Professor Walter E. Spahr, chairman of New York University's economics department, when describing Roosevelt and his advisers in 1935. The Great Depression was unlike all others, Spahr fumed, not only because it was more severe, but also because the nation had—foolishly, incredibly—turned over control of its government to the worst sort of "rabble rousers": money cranks who had, in their madness, taken the nation off gold. "It should be an arresting fact that not one of these demagogic leaders is ever a well trained person in monetary affairs," he vituperated. Oh, the president had been given the opportunity to listen to real experts. "Instead of profiting by such expert advice," however,

> this Administration has chosen to surround itself with monetary advisers of an exceedingly unorthodox sort—in most instances men of no standing or reputation or experience whatever in the field of monetary affairs. The consequence has been an orgy of wild and fantastic monetary legislation which has been the laughing stock of the leading monetary authorities of the world.[26]

The economic heresies of the New Deal were enumerated in a roll call of respected American economists published by the Liberty League in 1936. Professors "of the highest standing" from Chicago, Brookings, and every Ivy League university cautioned against Roosevelt's zany ideas. After heaping up all this evidence of professional consensus, the League pamphlet proceeded to its inevitable, contemptuous conclusion: The doctrines of the New Deal "do not find acceptance with the overwhelming majority of the academic profession."[27]

The point reverberated across the media landscape of the day. "The so-called 'brain trust' which has been advising the administration," a 1936 editorial in the *Los Angeles Times* announced, "was selected not because the views of its members were considered sound by the consensus of eminent scholarship, but because they chimed in with what the administration wanted to do." Or, as the Liberty League put it in one of its rare moments of brevity, "there are professors and professors." There were accepted communicants in the church of orthodoxy and then there were heretics and outsiders—and FDR's bunch were most definitely the latter.[28]

One of the professors customarily name-checked in essays and pamphlets of this kind was the Harvard economist Thomas Nixon Carver, whom we met a few pages ago; he was an elder statesman of the discipline who had become a particularly determined opponent of the New Deal. In April 1936 he was appointed to head a division of a Republican brain trust that was supposed to study and explain the New Deal; no doubt he got the job because the year before he had authored a booklet called *What Must We Do to Save Our Economic System?* that had become a cult favorite among conservatives.[29]

Carver's views seem unremarkable when you first encounter them. In an article he wrote for the *Los Angeles Times* in 1935, for example, he could be found lamenting the way government

regulation and unemployment relief were undermining traditional American values and turning respectable people into
"chiselers."[30]

But when Carver turned to the subject of working people—
the nonrespectable ones whose lives had actually been ruined by
the Depression—something in his manner seemed to change.
As we have seen, he regarded these people not as strivers whose
values needed to be respected, nor as the plain people honored
by Carl Sandburg and Abraham Lincoln.

They were a menace. Carver deplored immigration from
Mexico and the Philippines and then sighed over the "fact"
that "people of low mentality cannot have a standard of living
like that of people of high mentality and will therefore multiply according to their animal impulses and not according to
any standard of family building." He longed for a "population
planner" to sort out this mushrooming mess. He expressed
admiration for "Hitlerism" because Nazis dared to sterilize
"defectives." He urged us to "lend every possible encouragement" to entrepreneurs. He looked forward to a day when "the
highly capable" had more children and "the less capable and
less prosperous" had fewer. And then he suggested, by way of
concrete policy proposals, that couples be forbidden to marry
until they were able to buy a car.[31]

This was stupid stuff, but the man pushing it was no crank.
Thomas Nixon Carver was one of the country's most celebrated
economists and a confirmed believer in laissez-faire in most
aspects of economic life.[32] But the private lives of ordinary people: oh, that was different. That was an area where intrusive
supervision by super-planners was fully warranted and urgently
required. After all, the system needed workers—that was just

math—but not so many workers that they might pull off some kind of uprising against the system.

Up until this point in our story, anti-populism had real potential as a political approach. Finding some Harvard man to deplore the unorthodox ideas of the vulgar and the lowly had been a sound strategy in 1896.

But in 1936, appointing a man like Carver to lead a division of the Republican brain trust discredited not only Republicans but brains as well. About a month after his role in the GOP commission was announced, newspapers got wind of his booklet on population control and began mocking his prescriptions. Calling for the exclusion of certain races, requiring people to buy a car in order to marry, praising Hitler, and doing it all in the name of freedom—this was too much.

Americans don't like to be told that their love lives are economically problematic to their betters. To chase such a noxious assertion with a shot of *Sieg Heil* is to make it even more toxic still—to place a cyanide cherry atop a creosote sundae, if you will.[33]

HOW WAS THE great business offensive against the New Deal received in the cities and towns of America? We get a street-level view of the 1936 campaign in the memoirs of Thomas Hart Benton, the regionalist painter, who was struck by the angry expression of upper-class righteousness that he began to notice here and there. "In many polite houses" that summer, the painter remembers, "the voice of suspicious hate was directed toward the riffraff."

Benton spent much of the '36 election season touring his home state of Missouri, and in his recollections he tells of how he visited the tastefully decorated home of a retired banker, a

man with a "highly developed sense" of "standing and prerog-
ative." During their conversation, Benton made the grave faux
pas of saying something nice about the regulatory state. The
banker erupted.

"The class of people who run the business of this country
are the ones who know how to run it," this grandee insisted.
"It has come to an awful place when a lot of incompetents who
won't work when they have a chance can get up the nerve to
insist that those who do work should divide with them." Then
his vehemence took a gory turn. Addressing the painter, the
banker declared, "You have no respect for the traditions of your
country but when the time comes you are going to learn, you
and all your dissatisfied friends, that there are machine guns in
the hands of the right people here to bring you back to your
senses."[34]

Benton chalked the man's outburst up to the newspapers,
whose propaganda campaign "against Rooseveltian radicals"
was "in full blast" that year. Something larger was going on as
well: a certain kind of class bitterness was awakening in 1936—
but "at the wrong end of society," as Benton puts it. It was
the exact mirror image of the decade's proletarian plays and
its social-realist murals—the well-to-do were discovering the
peculiar grievances of the strong and the privileged.

IN 1936, THOSE grievances were not nearly enough. When
November came, Franklin Roosevelt beat Alf Landon in one of the
greatest landslides of all time, with Landon losing even his home
state of Kansas. Even though prestigious polls declared a Republican victory to be inevitable, and even though newspapers like the
Chicago Tribune and the Hearst chain spread alarm with every drop

of ink they could muster, Roosevelt won all but two states. The Liberty League's crusade for the Constitution had failed utterly.

African American voters abandoned the Republican Party for the New Deal. Unions backed the president overwhelmingly. Working-class districts everywhere ran up a gigantic score for Roosevelt. The American people had been asked to negate a political turn that, they were told, would lead to the destruction of freedom, to the rise of dictatorship, to mob rule and the end of civilization—and by and large the American people didn't listen. The election of 1936 was to be a plebiscite on the regulatory welfare state, and through its actions the public, as New Deal historian William Leuchtenburg puts it, legitimated "the Leviathan state."[35]

The results were especially painful for the so-called Lords of the Press. They had come together as one, they had impugned the New Deal with the most emphatic words in the English language, and none of it had worked. Not only did the public ignore their warnings; the public did the opposite of what the media had instructed. As George Seldes pointed out at the time, Roosevelt seemed to run especially well in cities where he "had not one newspaper on his side." The only possible conclusion was that people were casting votes for Roosevelt and also "against the newspapers in general."[36]

The Depression had proven too overwhelming an experience for ordinary people to dismiss the New Deal out of abstract, upper-class fears. Arthur Schlesinger put it well: "The spectacle of the rich men of the nation declaring that America was in the grip of revolution because their servants were no longer content with their wages was not one which deeply moved many of their fellow countrymen."[37]

This was the winning hand in 1936: not that reform threat-ened liberty, but that tycoons and bankers and newspaper publishers—the people who ran the country into the Great Depression—were using "liberty" as a fig leaf for their priv-ilege . . . and it was their privilege that constituted the real issue.[38] As Roosevelt himself put it in his State of the Union address in 1936, "they steal the livery of great national consti-tutional ideals to serve discredited special interests."

The language the president used to describe his adversar-ies at the Democratic convention that summer was even more explosive. "These economic royalists complain that we seek to overthrow the institutions of America," he thundered. "What they really complain of is that we seek to take away their power. Our allegiance to American institutions requires the overthrow of this kind of power. In vain they seek to hide behind the Flag and the Constitution. In their blindness they forget what the Flag and the Constitution stand for."

A few days before Election Day 1936, continuing his "cru-sade to restore America to its own people" in a speech at Madi-son Square Garden, Roosevelt attached the most damning label of all to "business and financial monopoly"—they were "the old enemies of peace." What Americans learned during the years when such forces dominated the government, he continued, was that "Government by organized money is just as dangerous as Government by organized mob." And now organized money wanted its Government back.

Never before in all our history have these forces been so united against one candidate as they stand today. They are unanimous in their hate for me—and I welcome their hatred.

. . .

EXPLAINING THE POLITICAL results of 1936 feels like an exercise in obviousness. Anyone could see that regulation of banks wasn't mob rule—given what had happened during the 1920s, it was common sense. Calling FDR a mentally unhinged, would-be dictator was flatly preposterous: he had been in the White House for several years by that time and ordinary people could see the president was no Hitler and that their prospects had improved considerably during his tenure.

Still, it is important to note the broad outlines of what happened that year: the elites of this country came together in an extraordinary united front against the New Deal; they embraced all the traditional elements of the anti-populist ideology—one that is again in vogue in our own time—and they fell flat on their faces.

The distinguished professors, the captains of industry, the lords of the press, the grandees of Wall Street—Americans no longer respected them. "The election of 1936 brought out the fact," wrote the New Dealer Thurman Arnold, "that a very large number of people, roughly representing the more illiterate and inarticulate masses of people, had lost their faith in the more prominent and respected economic preachers and writers of the time, who for the most part were aligned against the New Deal."[39]

Writing on the same subject a few years later, President Roosevelt himself declared that, throughout American history, two "schools of political belief," liberals and conservatives, had fought endlessly for primacy. Regardless of what it was called at any particular moment, he wrote, "the liberal party . . . believed in the wisdom and efficacy of the will of the great majority of the people, as distinguished from the judgment of a small minority of either education or wealth."[40]

What Roosevelt could not have foreseen was a party system in which the divide fell not between the few and the many, but rather between the small minority of wealth and the small minority of education, in which the captains of industry were at odds with the distinguished professors and the lords of the press, and in which each group had captured control of one of the political parties. In other words: the system that has prevailed for the last few decades, in which the public is invited to choose between the candidate of resentful oil billionaires on the one side and the candidate of enlightened private-equity billionaires on the other.

IN 1896, ANTI-POPULIST contempt helped carry the day for William McKinley.

In 1936, anti-populism went down with a resounding crash. In the aftermath, Republicans moderated their defense of the pre–New Deal order; they accepted regulation and the welfare state. In succeeding decades, their presidential candidates— from Wendell Willkie to Dwight Eisenhower to Richard Nixon—would campaign as economic moderates, swearing to protect the signature achievements of the New Deal and even out-liberalizing the Democrats from time to time. They would not again attack the existence of the regulatory state until many administrations had passed—until they had perfected their own form of pseudo-populism, a story we shall read in chapter 7.

For corporate America, snarling anti-populism was an obvious dead end. There were friendlier ways to make the sale. In the mid-thirties, as the business historian Roland Marchand has put it, ad agencies and PR firms began "translating corporate imagery into the vernacular," explicitly aiming their sales pitches at working-class people. The DuPont company, whose principals had underwritten the American Liberty League, tackled its dreadful public image by taking to heart the cultural populism of the day. Beginning in 1935, the company began broadcasting a radio program called *The Cavalcade of America*, in which incidents from history were excitingly dramatized, often with individuals chosen from what the company magazine called "the common mass," ordinary Americans who were supposed to illustrate "heroism, virtue, ingenuity and public service."[41]

Not all conservatives would choose to mimic populist language. The famous libertarian Albert Jay Nock would advise his readers to forget "the masses" and focus on the "remnant" of worthwhile people; neoclassical economists would learn to speak in math and would set up exclusive societies where they perpetuated their ideas; and, of course, there was that novelist who would fantasize about a hidden valley in the Rocky Mountains where righteous billionaires might retreat from the world, set up a gold standard of their own, and await the inevitable collapse of the liberal order.

The only important anti-populist survival on the right that I'm going to describe here was Herbert Hoover, who was not chastened by the back-to-back (-to-back-to-back) Democratic landslides and who spent the rest of his life carping bitterly about Franklin Roosevelt and the New Deal. In 1948, nine days after yet another shocking, populist-flavored Democratic victory, Hoover phoned in to a gathering at Wilmington College in Ohio to deplore what he called the "cult of the common man" and to strike a blow for the forgotten men of quality and talent.

"Let us remember," Hoover intoned, "that the great human advances have not been brought about by mediocre men and women. They were brought about by distinctly uncommon men and women with vital sparks of leadership." He saluted higher education for producing such excellent people and saluted students for "striving to become uncommon men and women."[42]

What makes these banal sentiments interesting is how universal they have become in the years since—universal among liberals, I mean. These days Democrats are the ones who give commencement speeches saluting the graduates of fancy schools for the innovations they will one day contribute and the enlightenment they will bring to the land. These days it is liberals who arise, like Herbert Hoover, from the ranks of the white-collar meritocracy, who deplore the reverence shown to the common man, and who take the views of highly educated professionals to be revealed wisdom itself.

ONE FINAL LESSON I wish to take from the politics of the 1930s is this: The *Los Angeles Times* was not wrong when they described the New Deal as an attack on "the consensus of eminent scholarship." Those hundreds of economists I described above were not mistaken when they depicted the New Deal as a risky experiment. But they *were* wrong to think that its embrace of new ideas meant the New Deal would fail. Orthodox economics had led the world into the Great Depression. Orthodox economics would never have permitted the measures that got us out of it. But Roosevelt knew somehow that orthodoxy was wrong. The thinkers who stood outside the professional consensus were the ones who turned out to have the correct answers. Just as in 1896, the cranks turned out to be right.

The New Deal succeeded precisely because it, too, was outside the consensus. Franklin Roosevelt was able to do what he did because he was willing to close his ears to "men of established reputations." Had he handed over the task of recovery to the best and the brightest, this country might never have recovered. Discontent would have mounted, the forces of "entrenched greed" would have drilled their private armies and stockpiled their machine guns, and their moment would eventually have come.

At the Democratic convention in 1936, President Roosevelt described himself as a worker for a "great cause"—the cause of "the people." He allowed that in other lands, leaders had given up on that cause and on democracy itself. But "here in America we are waging a great and successful war. It is not alone a war against want and destitution and economic demoralization. It is more than that; it is a war for the survival of democracy. We are fighting to save a great and precious form of government for ourselves and for the world." Painful though it may be for liberals to acknowledge nowadays, it was Roosevelt's willingness to disregard elites that won that war. These were the reasons the New Deal succeeded and democracy lived. If the heroes of those days were cranks, then thank God for cranks. Thank God for populism.

5

Consensus Redensus

Once World War II was over—once the energy behind the New Deal had dissipated and agrarian radicalism had disappeared, a peculiar thing happened: populism went into the academic interpretation machine and came out as something different, something sinister.

What I have been calling "anti-populism" changed as well. Up until this point, its prime constituency had been comfortable and conservative business interests lashing back at radical troublemakers. But now anti-populism was taken up by a new elite, a liberal elite that was led by a handful of thinkers at prestigious universities.

This group translated anti-populism into the language of theory and built it into a full-blown system of big, intimidating ideas. It continued to serve the same function as always, rationalizing the power of the powerful. But now anti-populism did its work by means of psychology and social theory.

In short, the highly educated learned to deplore working-class movements for their bigotry, their refusal of modernity, and their borderline madness. The single word with which they expressed that finding: "populism."

THIS PART OF our story begins in the mid-1950s, a time of confidence and unprecedented middle-class prosperity. The economic collapse of the Depression was behind us, and the abiding faith among American intellectuals was that economic collapses in general were behind us, having been permanently solved by the managerial state and the managerial corporation. Even more obsolete were the vast political struggles of the preceding decades. Huge public fights over ideology need never happen again, American intellectuals agreed; thankfully, the era of mass mobilization had given way to a political system of interest groups and experts, of plenty and of contentment.

A famous book described this new era of pluralism and consensus and managed affluence as the "end of ideology."* Other scholars argued that ideology couldn't have ended because it had never really existed in America in the first place. A much-read work of history implied that, whatever their purported differences, all American politicians had pretty much believed the same things. From its very beginnings, another prominent historian maintained, America had always been a land of Lockean liberalism, permanently given to pragmatic experimentation

---

* "In the Western world," pronounced Daniel Bell in *The End of Ideology: On the Exhaustion of Political Ideas in the Fifties* (Free Press, 1962), "there is today a rough consensus among intellectuals on political issues: the acceptance of a Welfare State; the desirability of decentralized power; a system of mixed economy and of political pluralism. In that sense, too, the ideological age has ended" (pp. 402–3).

within constitutional limits. Americans were said to be untroubled by the peculiar ideas and wild politics that roiled the rest of the world. We did not go for abstract systems of political theory, and we never had.

The "liberal consensus" is the name that is sometimes applied to this smug worldview, and until it went up in flames in the late 1960s, it was the orthodoxy of the age. Whatever problems the country had, it was thought, were on their way to being solved. Civility was the rule in political speech; pragmatic dealmaking was the political method; and pluralism was the unalterable political fact of the day. "The problems of modern America were no longer ideological but technical and administrative," American thinkers agreed, according to a history of the period, and the way to address these was "by knowledgeable experts rather than by mass movements."[1]

"Knowledgeable experts" enjoyed something of a boom in the 1950s. Universities expanded dramatically. All the smart young men had good paying jobs at some center for advanced something, or were introducing modern management techniques to a federal department, or were working as "systems analysts" in some giant corporate bureaucracy.

Consensus thinkers were obsessed with the social position of the expert. After all, you couldn't have stability and prosperity without them. So intellectuals cheered when white-collar professionals rose through the ranks and booed when they were criticized. In a once-famous 1962 essay, sociologist Daniel Bell, the author of *The End of Ideology*, hailed the "technical and professional intelligentsia" who had ascended to the top echelons and the "new system of recruitment for power" that had wisely plucked them out of the mass. Even the military, Bell marveled, was now in the hands of this deserving cohort. As he put it, "the problems of national security, like those of the national economy, have become so staggeringly complex that they can no longer be settled simply by common sense or past experience." Bell went on to narrate the rise of a new generation of "technicians and political theorists" who had come to rule the Pentagon under the visionary leadership of Defense Secretary Robert McNamara.[2]

There was a wonderful coincidence behind the intellectuals' newfound faith in consensus: those who now organized and administered the great administrative organization were people exactly like them—highly educated professionals. The consensus thinkers saw American society as stable and harmonious because they were now part of its elite, members of the insiders' club just as surely as the press lords and steel magnates of the past.

THERE WAS A second coincidence behind consensus theory—this one kind of frightening. The early 1950s saw the rise of Wisconsin senator Joe McCarthy, whose name became synonymous with a particularly abusive form of red-hunting; he was cheered on by millions of average Americans as he accused innocent people willy-nilly of being Communists. Under the influence of this bullying Republican demagogue, America became hysterical with fear. It indulged in a carnival of persecution that was largely aimed at intellectuals—authors and college professors, for example. In response, intellectuals began to believe that paranoid hatred of the educated elite was a permanent threat lurking always just beneath democracy's surface. Open societies like ours, they concluded, were in constant danger of convulsions of intolerance brought on by the uneducated rank and file.

So: intellectuals in the fifties were more respected and prosperous than ever. At the same time, they were the targets of a spasm of manufactured hate that (as they saw it) had clouded the minds of the country's lower orders.

The effect of McCarthyism was to turn the country's intellectuals against ideology even more forcefully. Acting out of both complacency and alarm, they pushed toward a theory of democracy in which the passions of the millions were muted in favor of stability or "equilibrium"—a form of democracy in which everyone accepted that the real power lay with professionals like themselves.

"Pluralism" was the name the intellectuals gave this model, but the name was misleading. The key to the pluralist system, as the consensus thinkers imagined it, was not people from different walks of life having their say; it was the *leaders* of different groups coming to agreement quietly around a big mahogany table somewhere. Forget angry crowds marching in the streets by the millions: what you needed to make democracy work was a bunch of professional interest-group leaders, representatives who were highly civilized and who got along well with one another. These leaders and representatives were the key. They would reach across the aisle. They would compromise and make deals. They would find and inhabit the warm and "vital" center.[3]

"Representative government," wrote Daniel Bell in 1956, was the only way to put "a check on the tyrannical 'popular' majority." It was the only way to "achieve consensus—and conciliation."[4]

You could trust representatives. They were professionals. What you could not trust were ordinary citizens coming together in mass movements. The men of the fifties knew that nothing good could ever result from such a thing. Mass movements were unstable and given to extremism. Mass movements did not listen to intellectuals. Their grievances were irrational—expressions of declining status or psychological maladjustment or bigotry or something even worse. Mass movements were swept along by moral passion to do terrible things. Herd average people into mass political groups, expose them to demagogues, and they became . . . a mob. Awful developments followed inevitably: McCarthyism today, perhaps fascism tomorrow.

Then came a peculiar turn. The specific mass movement that the gentlemen of the consensus fixed upon as an example of everything that was foolish and destructive about democracy was the farmer-worker rebellion of sixty years previous known as Populism. Of its name the consensus thinkers forged a generic noun for the unreasoning folly of mass democracy. "Populism" became their pet term for the opposite of themselves—the "ism" that we use to describe demagoguery and intolerance and the crazy passions of the crowd.

THIS UNDERSTANDING OF Populism was not entirely new. In its essential points it was the same bill of hysterical accusations that had been leveled at reformers in 1896 by men of eminence and social standing. It also owed more than a little to the anti–New Deal propaganda generated by outfits like the Liberty League. Neither of these obvious forebears, however, was ever acknowledged by the thinkers of the 1950s. Instead they retrieved pieces of a long-forgotten conservative stereotype, tricked them out with the fashionable academic jargon of their era, and launched the result as a shiny new diagnosis handed down by the well-adjusted administrative mind. From there it grew to become the vast academic-journalistic enterprise that today holds "populism" to be the source of all that is wrong with modern politics.

It began, as I noted before, with McCarthyism, which was a phenomenon of the extreme Right. Each of the consensus thinkers agreed, however, that the paranoid, red-hunting suspiciousness of the 1950s was in fact a descendant of the democratic agrarian Left of the 1890s. In this view, all discontent that is expressed via mass movements of ordinary people is equally vulgar and fraudulent and irrational and scary. The original Populist movement, wrote the famous historian Richard Hofstadter in 1955, "seems very strongly to foreshadow some aspects of the cranky pseudo-conservatism of our time." In 1958, the sociologist Seymour Martin Lipset described McCarthyism as a "recent expression of populist extremism," reasoning that the two were the same since McCarthy vilified "the traditional enemy of populism, the Eastern upper class." The historian Peter Viereck went further: "McCarthyism is actually a leftist instinct behind a *self-deceptive* rightist veneer."[5]

"Populism" was thought to incorporate many sins in the eyes of the liberal consensus, but most of them were attributed to the same perceived error that conservatives had identified in decades before: a refusal of deference. Populism was egalitarianism taken to such an extreme that it rejected legitimate hierarchies along with wrongful ones—legitimate hierarchies being, of course, the ones that the intellectuals themselves had climbed, the hierarchies of scholarly achievement. Populism represented the denial of their expertise. As Daniel Bell put it in *The End of Ideology*, "populism goes further" than merely rejecting economic status: "that some are more qualified than others to assert opinions is vehemently denied."[6]

We have heard several versions of this view already. That democracy means the overthrow of all standards of excellence is the baseline fear of the anti-populist tradition going back at least to the 1890s if not to the French Revolution. But Bell didn't acknowledge that he was part of any such tradition. Nor did he name any actual Populists when he made the above statement; he just asserted it and moved on. As we shall see again and again with the consensus intellectuals, they seemed to believe they could say whatever they wanted about populism without any obligation to prove it—a suspension of the rules of academic engagement that would lead to tremendous confusion in years to come.

ONLY ONE OF the leading consensus thinkers seemed actually to know who the Populists were. Richard Hofstadter, the most famous American historian of his day, retold the story of the 1890s People's Party in his enormously influential 1955 book, *The Age of Reform*. Hofstadter had, of course, read much of the Populist literature and he clearly understood the nineteenth-century context in which they rose up. For all the romance of the third-party effort, however, Professor Hofstadter ultimately flunked the Pops for what he saw as a tendency toward the paranoid and the irrational.

Specifically, he accused the Populists of losing faith in progress, instead looking "backward with longing to the lost agrarian Eden" from which the country had fallen. He argued that the Populists despised immigrants—indeed, that "everyone remote and alien was distrusted and hated" by them. Also, that they were "profoundly nationalistic and bellicose," even though they often said they weren't. Furthermore, the Populists understood history by referring to crackpot conspiracy theories having to do with bankers and gold, he charged, and they were "chiefly" responsible for anti-Semitism in America, blaming Jewish bankers for the farmer's problems.[7]

The Populists believed all this nonsense, Hofstadter explained, because they were not people of the city, "the home of intellectual complexity." What's more, farmers of the 1890s were a group that was on the way down, "losing in status and respect" in comparison to successful, upwardly mobile city folk. Losing status made them anxious, and anxiety, in turn, made them reach for irrational explanations and embrace the politics of resentment.[8]

Hofstadter returned to the subject of Populism again and again in the course of his career, always singling out this particular reform movement for its sins against academic and cultural respectability. In a 1953 speech on anti-intellectualism, for example, Hofstadter declared the Populists to have been enemies of higher learning, since they supposedly "raised hob with the University of Kansas" when they were in the majority in that state.* In his famous 1964 essay, "The Paranoid Style in

---

* Hofstadter gives no source for this assertion. "Although many writers cite Populist interferences with academic freedom," writes political theorist Michael P. Rogin,

> "in point of fact there is only one example. In Kansas, the Populists ignored academic tenure in reorganizing the Kansas State Agricultural College. This was not, it should be pointed out, because they were suspicious of 'overeducation'; they rather had a somewhat naïve faith in what education could accomplish. In Kansas, they desired to introduce a liberal arts curriculum into an exclusively agricultural college. In this case the interference with academic freedom resulted not from anti-intellectualism but from enthusiasm for education."
> Rogin, *The Intellectuals and McCarthy*, pp. 180–81.

It is important to note that the University of Kansas and Kansas State are

American Politics," he again highlighted the Pops' fondness for the language of conspiracy. A few years later, Hofstadter had the honor of being the sole representative from North America at the very first academic conference on what we now call global populism studies; he took that occasion to emphasize, one more time, Populist naivete in the face of sophisticated international markets.[9]

Hofstadter's psychoanalysis of the People's Party was hugely influential in its day, powerfully reinforcing elite fears of grass-roots movements and relaunching "populism" as the generic name for the familiar political specter that always haunts the respectable. Few of the details in the historian's dark portrait stood the test of academic scrutiny, however. Many of the items I mentioned above turned out, upon investigation, to have been based on either a tendentious reading, or a whopping exaggeration, or else an outright error.

Looking back from sixty years on, the motives behind Hofstadter's war on the reformers of the 1890s appear to have been both petty and distinctly of-their-time. What I mean by this is that Hofstadter seems to have chosen Populism as a proxy in his lifelong personal war against a previous generation of scholars, the so-called progressive historians, who cherished memories of Populism but whose symbols and theories had degenerated into patriotic clichés by the 1950s.[10] What better way to spite them than to revive the old anti-populist stereotypes of the 1890s?

The central idea of the progressive historians' vision of the

---

not the same institution. Also: once Republicans had beaten Populism down in Kansas, they orchestrated a retaliatory mass firing at the same college. See Clanton, *Kansas Populism: Ideas and Men* (University Press of Kansas, 1969), pp. 205–6.

past had been social conflict, Hofstadter later wrote, meaning a struggle that always featured the same two sides, changing form but recurring throughout our history: radical versus conservative, farmer versus capitalist, the heirs of Jefferson versus the heirs of Hamilton. Thus when we find Hofstadter accusing the Populists of oversimplifying the political struggle in which they were engaged, imagining it as a war between "the people" and the "money power," we understand that he is also criticizing his scholarly predecessors, who said similar things all the time.[11]

But by 1955 that older generation of historians was gone. In putting Populism behind us, *The Age of Reform* was meant as a sort of manifesto for the new breed, with their faith in pluralism,* professionalism, and benevolent, administrative capitalism. Hofstadter sifted through the nation's reform tradition, dismissing things that were no longer useful—mass movements, for example—and celebrating what he felt had paved the way for the post-ideological present. So while crusading mass movements like Populism were said to have achieved little for the farmer, the historian strongly hinted that modern-style corporate lobbying outfits like the Farm Bureau got the goods.[12]

When reform came from the bottom up, in other words, it was moralistic, demagogic, irrational, bigoted, and futile. When reform was made by practical, business-minded professionals— meaning lobbyists and experts who were comfortable in

---

* Hofstadter later described his generation's contribution to scholarship as "the rediscovery of complexity in American history. . . . The Progressive scheme of polarized conflict has been replaced by a pluralistic vision in which more factors are seriously taken into account." *The Progressive Historians*, p. 442.

the company of lobbyists and experts from other groups—
prosperity was the result.

Another consequence of *The Age of Reform*, important for our
purposes, was the mutation of the word "Populism" from a reference to a specific political party to a general term that could
apply to anyone—what Hofstadter called "a kind of popular
impulse that is endemic in American political culture." The
People's Party may have been its most prominent example, but
"Populist thinking," the historian continued, "has survived in
our own time, partly as an undercurrent of provincial resentments, popular and 'democratic' rebelliousness and suspiciousness, and nativism."[13]

Reviving the 1890s depiction of social protest as a species of
resentment and unreason turned out to be exactly the thing to
do in 1955. *The Age of Reform* perfectly captured the rationality-
worshipping tenor of its times. It won the Pulitzer Prize. It has
been described as "the most influential book ever published on
the history of twentieth-century America."[14] And it transformed
"populism" back into a term of top-down abuse . . . a move that
raises hob with us still.

ANTI-POPULISM BEGAN TO change sides as well. Now it was
prominent academic liberals who regarded mass movements as
dangerous dens of demagoguery, and who began to use "populism" as a generic term for an ugly, down-market political sensibility. Using the tools Hofstadter provided them, American
intellectuals quickly built anti-populism into a towering structure of liberal social theory.

Before the consensus generation started on its work, the
political theorist Michael P. Rogin tells us in a 1967 study

of this period, "McCarthyism meant something like character assassination, and Populism was the name of a particular
historical movement for social reform at the end of the nineteenth century. Through their influence Populism has become
an example of and a general term for anomic movements of
mass protest against existing institutions—the type of movement typified by McCarthyism."

The most memorable effort along these lines was *The Torment of Secrecy*, a 1956 study of McCarthyism by the sociologist
Edward Shils. Over the course of his career, Shils would pile up
an awesome record of scholarly attainment—prizes and profes-
sorships and prestigious appointments—but when he turned
to populism, the sociologist did not proceed empirically as
Richard Hofstadter had done, combing through Populist books
and manifestos. Instead, he advanced on his target by means of
assertion and stereotype; indeed, it is not clear from his writing
on the subject that he knew what the People's Party had been.*

"Populism proclaims that the will of the people as such is
supreme over every other standard," Shils announced at the
opening of his chapter on populism, defining populism as a
form of nihilism that respected no institutions except public
opinion. This was, of course, the same old fear of democracy-as-
anarchy that we saw during the Democracy Scares of 1896 and

---

* For example, at the beginning of the chapter of *The Torment of Secrecy*
(Free Press, 1956) on the subject of populism, Shils provides the names of
two supposedly admirable representatives of the species—George Norris of
Nebraska and Robert La Follette of Wisconsin. It is true that both of these
men were prominent progressives from the Midwest, but neither of them
was actually an affiliate of the People's Party. The closest Shils gets to the
movement itself is when he name-checks William Jennings Bryan several
pages later.

1936, and Shils proceeded to establish that populists held these views in the same way that his predecessors had: simply by saying so. When Shils asserted it, however, it was not the same as when a conservative Republican asserted it in a pamphlet with a hysterical title like *The Platform of Anarchy*. What Edward Shils wrote was social science. It was scholarship.[15]

Shils advanced then to the next logical step in his program: asserting that populism was the shared ingredient in each of history's worst moments. "Nazi dictatorship had markedly populistic features in its practice, in its constant invocation of the will of the people," he wrote. "Bolshevism has a strand of populism in it too. . . . In the United States, populism lives on in persecutory legislative investigations," by which he meant McCarthyism.[16] It was as if the nightmares of the Liberty League in the 1930s had actually come to pass. All the villains were united by a common thread: Nazis and Communists; reds and red-hunters, all cherishing the same Satanic faith in the common man.

Before long we come to Shils's real concern: the threat populism posed to intellectuals like him and his colleagues. Obviously the danger was substantial: "When populism goes on the warpath, among those they wish to strike are the 'overeducated,' those who are 'too clever,' 'the highbrows,' the 'longhairs,' the 'eggheads,' whose education has led them away from the simple wisdom and virtue of the people." Shils knew that populists did things like this because those are things that Joe McCarthy did, and in the example of that renowned demagogue, the eminent sociologist assured us we could clearly see the Populist of the past, "the 'grass roots' prophet assailing the aristocratic battlements of pure learning which have despised the wisdom of the people."[17]

As a description of the actual Populist tradition this was

nonsense, but Shils sailed right on, enlarging the populists' supposed hatred of learning into a hatred of quality and refinement in general. "Populists, whether they are radical reformers or congressional investigators," he wrote, "are all extremely suspicious and hostile towards the more sophisticated person." In Shils's system, populism is the name one gives to any situation in which "there is an ideology of popular resentment against the order imposed on society by a long-established, differentiated ruling class."[18] In other words, any objection that ordinary people might have to any system of domination is in fact little more than nihilistic demagoguery and the rejection of all standards.

The populist, Shils went on in his bombastic way, "denies autonomy" to any institution of government. Populists hate bureaucracy. They despise the justice system and politicians in general. They hate learning. They deny the right of privacy. But oh, they love bullshit: this is the definition of the species. "Populism acclaims the demagogue who, breaking through the formalistic barriers erected by lawyers, pedants and bureaucrats, renews the righteousness of government and society."[19]

It's kind of a peculiar experience to see someone defending intellectualism so ferociously while engaging in intellectual practice of the kind that would score him a flat "F" were *The Torment of Secrecy* turned in as a sociology term paper. Virtually nothing in Shils's denunciation of populism is tied to supporting evidence. Individuals and even institutions are sometimes accused of being tainted with populism simply because they come from "the Middle West." The book was basically a Democracy Scare unto itself, with accusations of world-historic fiendishness thrown down one after another, unsubstantiated by anything besides the imaginary target's imagined views on some abstract subject—the highbrow equivalent of a Bircher conspiracy theory, you could say.

Still, *The Torment of Secrecy* was another influential work. This was where the word "populist" left the historical rails and began its long career wandering hither and yon, haunting the scholarly mind. This was the missing link where the anti-populist stereotype built up for six decades by American conservatives was adopted by the theorists of liberalism and then spread into every corner of the international world of scholarship.

The reason for the book's influence is clear enough: it flattered the powerful. What Shils meant to do with his attack on populism was build support for a liberal democratic system where political actors wisely limit their ambitions to what he calls "gradual increments of change." To achieve such a system, what was required from working-class people was acceptance of hierarchy, meaning "deference" toward "those who govern," like in Britain.[20]

What was required from those who ruled, meanwhile, was a certain chumminess toward one another—"a sense of affinity among the elites," as Shils put it. People on top, he pleaded, must respect others on top.[21]

From this nifty hierarchy "only extremism is excluded." Only populists are to be ostracized.

Perhaps you recognize what Shils is describing: It is the current liberal ideal of Washington, D.C. It is the philosophy of mainstream American journalism. It is the strategic model for the cautious, scholarly, consensus-minded Clinton and Obama administrations, extending their hands in friendship to fellow elites in Wall Street and Silicon Valley. This is where it all begins.

• • •

TO DECLARE THAT the people were the problem with democracy was to make a spectacular break with the Jeffersonian tradition, but the strictures of social science required more. One had to be precise. Which group of people, specifically, was the problem?

The answer was provided by the sociologist Seymour Martin Lipset. In 1959 he discovered that the great danger to self-government was what he called "working-class authoritarianism."

Lipset was perfectly candid about this. What he called the "lower-class individual" was not really suited to democratic self-government. The "norms of democracy," he wrote, could only be appreciated by someone with "a high level of sophistication and ego security." Working-class people weren't "sophisticated" by definition, and this led to all sorts of problems: they fell for demagogues, they hated minorities, they were suspicious of intellectuals, and so on.[22]

The reality that working-class organizations often promote complex ideas that are the opposite of nativism or anti-intellectualism was something Lipset considered and dismissed. That meant nothing, since "the fact that the movement's ideology" might be "democratic does not mean that its supporters actually understand the implications."[23] The way to judge those supporters was with the metrics of social science, not their own words. The scientific facts were straightforward: low-status people held low-status views—authoritarian views. That's simply the way things were. The authoritarianism of working-class people was baked in, psychologically determined by their social position.

"Populism" was one of the terms Lipset used to describe this unfortunate psychosocial situation. Indeed, the word was a kind of shorthand for a whole understanding of the latent authoritarianism of all working-class movements. In Populism's original incarnation, Lipset continued (following Hofstadter), its partisans could be seen to despise immigrants and Jews; and "latter-day" vehicles like the Ku Klux Klan also represented the populist impulse. Its most recent "expression" was, of course, McCarthyism.[24]

Tellingly, Lipset introduced his findings about "working-class authoritarianism" not as useful information in its own right but as "a tragic dilemma for those intellectuals" who had once believed in ordinary people. In the world of the consensus it was intellectuals who mattered, and Lipset merely wanted to draw their attention, in a collegial and scholarly way, to the fact that when they said noble things about "the proletariat," they were making an unfortunate mistake.[25]

This, too, was a viewpoint that would reverberate down through the decades. "Authoritarianism," scholars would come to agree, was a property associated with working-class voters, with populism, and the answer to it was rule by elites. White-collar authorities had to be strengthened in order to fend off working-class authoritarianism.

Now, we have seen lots of authoritarian deeds in this book—strike-breaking private armies and so on—but precious few of them can be laid at the feet of the working class. On the contrary: it has consistently been elite fears of working-class votes that gives rise to Democracy Scares. This historical contradiction of the "working-class authoritarian" thesis seems to have been obvious to no one, however. Elites must have greater authority, the argument went, or else authoritarianism will win out. This can only mean that some group's authority is nonauthoritarian by definition—and it is of course the enlightened authority of the highly educated who are always the heroes of consensus literature.

They are the ones who know how to meet the grievances of the working class with stone-faced discipline. The populists may crave authority, but we the authorities will break them of that.

THANKS TO THE work of Hofstadter, Bell, Shils, and Lipset, anti-populism became one of the great themes of the consensus years. Everyone wanted it to be true. Everyone agreed on it. Mass movements of working people were dangerous.

And then: the whole scholarly edifice came crashing down. The redefinition of populism as proto-fascism, you will recall, was based on the psychohistorical portrait of 1890s Populism by Richard Hofstadter. Soon it became clear that Hofstadter had done little archival research on Populism. He had not read deeply in the movement's literature or studied its record in government. His grasp of the movement was based on just a handful of primary sources, some of them only loosely connected to the People's Party itself—cherry-picking taken to a kind of extreme.

Historians who did do research in Populist archives set to work enthusiastically demolishing the Hofstadter thesis. They proved that Populism wasn't any more backward-looking than any other movement that protested capitalism. That the Pops weren't against industrialization, although they didn't like the particular way the robber barons were directing it. That they weren't hostile to education. That they weren't nativists; in fact, they competed for immigrant votes. [26]

Hofstadter's most sensational accusation against Populism— that it was the fountainhead of American anti-Semitism—turned out to be a wild exaggeration. It drew a ferocious, fact-filled rebuke from the historian Norman Pollack, who showed that, while there were indeed anti-Semitic Populists here and there, radical farmers on the Great Plains were probably *less* anti-Semitic than were other elements of 1890s society. His conclusion, after conducting research in a number of midwestern state archives: "the incidence of Populist anti-Semitism was infinitesimal."[27]

To identify "status anxiety" as the source of mass pro- test movements—and also as the reason to dismiss them as irrational—sounded ever so scientific, but it turned out to be completely arbitrary, a label the critic (or historian) could affix to almost any group he chose in order to disparage it. To apply the term to the Populists, Hofstadter basically had to ignore the movement's voluminous and extremely rational concern with practical economic matters. Remember, the Pops came up during a time of terrible farm prices and a severe busi- ness depression. They faced these developments squarely and with comparatively little scapegoating, kind of an impressive achievement for the nineteenth century when you think about it. Dismissing their discontent as "status anxiety" comes close to denying the reality of economic hardship altogether.[28]

Under this hailstorm of rebuke, Richard Hofstadter even- tually gave up trying to defend the Populism chapters of *The Age of Reform*.[29] His status-anxiety theory was tossed into the dumpster of discredited hypotheses, joining the Frontier thesis in the pile of scholarly discards. Charles Postel, the historian whose authoritative 2007 book on Populism buried what was left of *The Age of Reform*, has described the Hofstadter view as "largely intuitive." This is being polite. Christopher Lasch, who was Hofstadter's protégé at Columbia, believed Hofstadter's contempt for Populism in fact betrayed his cohort's "cultural prejudices" against the lower middle class.[30]

• • •

HERE'S THE CRAZY thing, though. Academic anti-populism lives on. Indeed, it thrives. The almost complete discrediting of its founding text seems to count for nothing. Today, seemingly every well-educated person in America and Europe knows that populism is the name we give to mass movements that are bigoted and irrational; that threaten democracy's norms with their anti-intellectual demagoguery. Upon Hofstadter's famous mistake the burgeoning pedagogy of "populism studies" builds its theories and convenes its panels. Out of this scholarly blunder of the 1950s has grown the common sense of ruling elites everywhere.

But of course it's not just Hofstadter's mistake. Consensus-era anti-populism built upon prejudices that were inherited from conservatives in the 1930s, which they had inherited from conservatives in the 1890s. All that was really new in the post-war years was the advanced sociology and the slightly more sophisticated psychological put-downs. Otherwise, the elements of the anti-populist stereotype remained stubbornly the same, and so did the social position of those who embraced it. Indeed, it seems that whenever we find someone attacking populism, their underlying purpose is to shore up the legitimacy of whatever system it is that has made them an elite.

What motivated adherents of this anti-populist creed, in each historical iteration, was raw self-interest. The core of the consensus school's viewpoint, as Michael Rogin described it, was "the hope that if only responsible elites could be left alone, if only political issues could be kept from the people, the elites would make wise decisions."[31] This is the essence of anti-populism always.

Today the "hope" for wise decisions by elites rolls irresistibly on, while the war on populism continues in almost exactly the same terms used by Hofstadter and Shils in the consensus days of 1955, the same terms used by America's eminent lawyers in 1936 and by America's leading economists and aristocrats in 1896. It doesn't seem to matter that the theory is based on a debunked historical hypothesis. On it goes, repeating the same eternal archetype: the bigotry of ordinary people, the folly of protest movements, and the wisdom of elites.

The context of the Eisenhower years is long gone, of course: self-assured liberalism evaporated decades ago, the Cold War is over, the academy is in love with forms of conflict that the fifties mind could never have imagined. But somehow the consensus faith plays right on through it all, tootling its one-note song of anti-populist indignation even as the liberal sun sets and the right-wing night falls.

It lives on because the archetype is the thing, the system of symbols and characters that has been incorporated into our modern-day canon of political myths. When someone moans about populism, we know instantly that they are summoning up a vision of a society directed by responsible professionals, always including themselves, always concurring prudently with one another, always doing their best to steer the world through complex problems. These professionals are all highly educated; in fact, they probably all went to a tiny handful of schools. If it's pundits we're talking about, they work for one of a tiny handful of media outlets; if it's policy advisers, they work for one of a tiny handful of think tanks. They might not all agree with one another down to the letter, but agreement itself—consensus— remains for them the noblest of goals.

6

Lift Every Voice

At the conclusion of the 1965 march from Selma to Montgomery, Alabama—in some ways the last great, unambiguous triumph of the civil rights movement—Martin Luther King Jr. stood before the Alabama state capitol building, its Confederate flag flapping in the breeze, and recited the words of the "Battle Hymn of the Republic." Before he came to that famous peroration, however, he gave his fellow marchers a short lesson in a different chapter of American history—the origins of racial segregation. Where did this awful system come from, anyway? King's answer: it began, in part, as a stratagem to defeat Populism, which had made a shocking bid in the 1890s to bring together poor blacks and poor whites into overwhelming majorities across the South.

> The leaders of this movement began awakening the poor white masses and the former Negro slaves to the fact that they were being fleeced by the emerging Bourbon interests.

Not only that, but they began uniting the Negro and white masses into a voting bloc that threatened to drive the Bourbon interests from the command posts of political power in the South.

The powerful, however, didn't fancy being unseated from their position of dominance in the South. To protect themselves, they tried to divide their working-class enemies, falling back on the old ruse of white supremacy. "They saturated the thinking of the poor white masses with it," King continued, "thus clouding their minds to the real issue involved in the Populist movement."

They then directed the placement on the books of the South of laws that made it a crime for Negroes and whites to come together as equals at any level. And that did it. That crippled and eventually destroyed the Populist movement of the nineteenth century.

What followed was one of King's all-time great images. The Bourbons, he recounted, "took the world and gave the poor white man Jim Crow."

And when his wrinkled stomach cried out for the food that his empty pockets could not provide, he ate Jim Crow, a psychological bird that told him that no matter how bad off he was, at least he was a white man, better than the black man. And he ate Jim Crow.

That, King concluded, was the tragic story of how the original Populist revolt was squashed. The masters of the South trashed their own society, set human against human in a racist death struggle, all to keep themselves secure in their exalted place. They segregated their world to death:

> They segregated southern money from the poor whites; they segregated southern mores from the rich whites; they segregated southern churches from Christianity; they segregated southern minds from honest thinking; and they segregated the Negro from everything. That's what happened when the Negro and white masses of the South threatened to unite and build a great society: a society of justice where none would prey upon the weakness of others; a society of plenty where greed and poverty would be done away; a society of brotherhood where every man would respect the dignity and worth of human personality.[1]

It was a remarkable speech in many ways, not least because in this passage King got the broad sweep of the Populist story right. By 1965 that word and that story had grown cloudy with demonization of the sort we saw in the last chapter. Indeed, before the decade of the 1960s was out, the media would crown as America's premier populist none other than King's nemesis George Wallace, the snarling segregationist who sat in the Alabama governor's chair at the moment King spoke.

But for now that poisonous irony was still in the future. In 1965 idealism was still capable of carrying the day, and King looked back through the fog of confusion to recall how America's original movement of working-class unity was defeated. It wasn't just a historical point of interest for him. By describing Populism's goal as a "great society"—President Lyndon Johnson's name for his civil rights and anti-poverty measures—King was suggesting that the movement of the 1890s had an obvious modern counterpart. Working people of both races could come together once more to build a nation of justice and plenty.

What King hinted at, others stated directly. Michael Harrington, the democratic socialist author, was in the audience in Montgomery that day and set down the message for readers of the *New York Herald Tribune* on March 28, 1965: this movement was not going to stop with civil rights. "King and the others made it clear that they look, not simply to the vote, but to a new coalition of the black and white poor and unemployed and working people," Harrington wrote. "They seek a new Populism."

Harrington knew whereof he spoke. By "populism" he meant a transracial movement of the working class that aimed to reform capitalism from the bottom up and distribute its wealth more evenly. Harrington was right to attribute such aspirations to King and his fellow leaders in the civil rights movement. He was also right to understand that a populist sensibility, stirred up by the successful struggle for civil rights, was sweeping over the country, building enthusiasm for "participatory democracy" and popularizing catchphrases such as "Power to the People."

Consensus intellectuals had proclaimed "the end of ideology" just a few years previously, telling the nation that the big political problems had pretty much been solved. Mass movements were things of the benighted past. Today, the leaders of every group were seated comfortably around the boardroom table, and they got along famously with one another. Rationality and pluralism reigned, with stability and equilibrium for all.

But now the men of consensus were rubbing their eyes behind those heavy horn-rimmed spectacles and gaping at what was transpiring outside the faux gothic windows: there were millions of people in the streets, demanding an end to segregation and then to poverty, war, and sexism. There were students sitting in at lunch counters, cops unleashing dogs on protesters, Klansmen blowing up churches, and racists going mad on TV, dumping acid into the swimming pool rather than see it integrated. There were protesters surrounding the Pentagon, fighting the cops in Chicago, ransacking the dean's office; there were bomb threats and sometimes real bombs; there were consumer advocates and wildcat strikes and even farmer protests, all over again. Never has so cocksure a worldview seemed to crumble so completely so quickly.

TODAY, MARTIN LUTHER King is far better remembered for his heroic battles against segregation than for his determination to humanize the capitalist system. But by the time of the Selma march, King was deeply immersed in workers' issues. He had spoken at many union gatherings, labor leaders had attended his marches, union lobbyists had helped get the civil rights acts through Congress, and union members had donated heavily to King's organization over the years. The civil rights movement's various tactics—boycotts, sit-ins, mass demonstrations—were consciously borrowed from the labor actions of the 1930s.* Before King became the country's preeminent civil rights figure, that role was arguably filled by A. Philip Randolph,

---

* "Emulating the labor movement, we in the South have embraced mass actions," King said to the National Maritime Union in 1962, "boycotts, sit-ins and, more recently, a widespread utilization of the ballot." Martin Luther King Jr., "*All Labor Has Dignity*," ed. Michael K. Honey (Beacon Press, 2011), p. 70.

president of a union of railroad workers. It was Randolph who first proposed a civil rights march on Washington (in 1941) and who helped organize the 1963 March for Jobs and Freedom at which King delivered his famous speech from the steps of the Lincoln Memorial.

The explanation for this relationship is simple: the labor movement and the civil rights movement were natural allies that shared similar goals and similar techniques. King returned to the point again and again in his speeches. "Negroes are almost entirely a working people," he observed in his remarks to an AFL-CIO convention in 1961. "There are pitifully few Negro millionaires and few Negro employers."

> Our needs are identical with labor's needs: decent wages, fair working conditions, livable housing, old-age security, health and welfare measures, conditions in which families can grow, have education for their children, and respect in the community. That is why Negroes support labor's demands and fight laws which curb labor. That is why the labor-hater and labor-baiter is virtually always a twin-headed creature spewing anti-Negro epithets from one mouth and anti-labor propaganda from the other mouth.[2]

The South had always been hostile to labor unions, but with the success of the civil rights movement, King ventured, that would change. Help blacks secure their right to vote, he promised a gathering of the United Auto Workers, and "a new day will dawn which will see militant, steadfast and reliable congressmen from the South joining those from the northern industrial states to design and enact legislation for the people rather than for the privileged."[3]

Those last few words deserve our attention because they are a classic variation on the traditional populist formula. In truth, King used a lot of populist phrases. He spoke, for example, of the "forgotten men" imprisoned in the ghettos of the big cities. He charged that America "takes necessities from the masses to give luxuries to the classes."[4]

King's great goal—to move beyond legal equality and secure democratic economic reforms as well—became especially clear in the later 1960s, when he advanced to what he called a "new phase" of the struggle. If the first phase was devoted to recovering citizenship rights, the next one was aimed at securing the economic equality that this country has never granted anyone without a fight. As the movement advanced to this next objective, King pointed out, many of its white allies would probably drop away. It had been easy for a certain sort of prosperous white American to support civil rights, he told an audience of Teamsters in 1967, "when there was a simple objective of curbing brutality," of taming "the coarse sheriffs" of Birmingham and Selma. There was a dualistic clarity to those early struggles, with their brave stands against racist laws and pigheaded enforcers.*

But the next phase, King told his audience, would be different. It would carry a "real cost" for people outside the South; a cost that would be measurable in dollars. Demanding economic equality would mean massive federal "appropriations to create

---

* Although King didn't mention it on this occasion, another factor bringing clarity was the international context in which those coarse sheriffs did their brutal thing. In the competition with the Soviet Union for the nonaligned nations of Africa and Asia, TV footage of police dogs attacking children in the streets of Birmingham made good propaganda for those denouncing the American way.

jobs and job training; it means the outlay of billions for decent housing and equal education." Still, this war against poverty had to happen:

> Today Negroes want above all else to abolish poverty in their lives, and in the lives of the white poor. This is the heart of their program. To end humiliation was a start, but to end poverty is a bigger task. It is natural for Negroes to turn to the labor movement because it was the first and pioneer anti-poverty program.[5]

Later that year, King began working on what would prove to be his final campaign: a poor people's march on Washington in which the marchers would remain in the capital city, living in tents and presenting their demand for what he called an "economic bill of rights." The phrase itself was borrowed from Franklin Roosevelt, and King's logic was similar to the former president's: ordinary political rights only took Americans so far; now it was time for this prosperous country to guarantee its citizens a job, a minimum income, housing, and a decent education. His strategy was to re-create the protest of the Bonus Army, which had camped in Washington in 1932 while demanding payments for World War I veterans (and which, in turn, had been inspired by Coxey's Army, the 1894 march on Washington that had meant so much to the original Populists).[6]

King interrupted his work on the Poor People's Campaign in early 1968 to make a fateful intervention in a strike of black sanitation workers in Memphis, Tennessee. In that particular city, the civil rights cause had morphed into a movement for workers' rights, and the going was as tough as it had been in Selma and Birmingham, with huge rallies met by martial law and plenty of police violence. The mayor of Memphis turned out to be as much of a hard-liner against public-sector unions as other southern officials had been against integrated schools and black voter registration.

In a powerful speech to the strikers there, King looked back over his career as a leader in the struggle for freedom and explained the move from civil rights to economic rights. "With Selma and the voting rights bill one era of our struggle came to a close and a new era came into being," he recalled.

> Now our struggle is for genuine equality, which means economic equality. For we know now that it isn't enough to integrate lunch counters. What does it profit a man to be able to eat at an integrated lunch counter if he doesn't earn enough money to buy a hamburger and a cup of coffee? . . . What does it profit one to have access to the hotels of our city and the motels of our highway when we don't earn enough money to take our family on a vacation?[7]

KING'S STATEMENTS ON economic issues often reflected the thinking of his close associate Bayard Rustin, the political strategist who had helped put together the 1963 March for Jobs and Freedom. Rustin was the supreme pragmatist of the civil rights movement, by which I do not mean he was a lukewarm consensus-seeker who believed that interest-group lobbyists in D.C. could sort everything out. Like King, Rustin imagined big, bold things for the movement, for African Americans, and for the country, and he meant to achieve those things by means of clear-eyed left-wing realpolitik. A master of class analysis, Rustin believed in working through (as one profile of him put it) "the ballot, the union card, and coalition politics."[8]

Like King, Rustin understood that the movement had to advance to the next challenge after the landmark civil rights acts of 1964 and '65 had been signed into law. And so, in a much-discussed 1965 article in *Commentary* magazine, Rustin announced the transition of the civil rights movement from "a protest movement," as he put it, "into a full-fledged *social movement*," by which he meant a shift from "removing the barriers to full *opportunity*" to "achieving the fact of *equality*."[9]

Economic equality, that is. Rustin hoped to eliminate poverty in America with a massive federal employment and housing proposal called the "Freedom Budget." The cost would be enormous; to achieve the goal, he wrote, would require nothing less than "a refashioning of our political economy." Rustin well understood the political difficulties ahead. "It is one thing to organize sentiment behind laws that do not disturb consensus politics," Rustin wrote the next year, "and quite another to win battles for the redistribution of wealth."[10] How could he hope to bring such a gigantic change about?

"The answer is simple, deceptively so," Rustin continued: "*through political power*." How to take that power? Again, the answer was straightforward: by building a "coalition of progressive forces which becomes the effective political majority in the United States," a coalition made up of "Negroes, trade unionists, liberals, and religious groups."[11]

Especially trade unionists. In the years to come, as Rustin drew closer to the AFL-CIO, he often wrote about the role of organized labor in building his grand coalition of economic reformers. As it happens, these were also the years when the stereotype of white union members as right-wing "hardhats" was coming together, which makes their central position in Rustin's plans even more remarkable.

In 1970, union construction workers in New York City attacked and scattered a protest against the Vietnam War; a few weeks later they held a massive pro-war rally in the streets of Manhattan. In 1971, the archetypal blue-collar bigot Archie Bunker made his debut on television—yet, in the face of all that, Rustin published "The Blacks and the Unions," in which he insisted that the unions of the day were in fact more integrated than nearly any other American institution, even with the reactionary construction unions taken into account. What's more, Rustin went on, unions naturally gravitated toward integration because they understood (after many hard lessons) that dividing the working class by race meant certain defeat. Most important, for Rustin's purposes, was that the unions' political program was identical to the demands of African American leadership. "The problems of the most aggrieved sector of the black ghetto cannot and will never be solved without full employment," Rustin wrote, "and full employment, with the government as employer of last resort, is the keystone of labor's program."[12]

In this way Rustin surveyed the same ground as other figures I have described in these pages, and ran into the same problem: Lifting up people crushed by centuries of racist exploitation meant not only winning the rights of citizenship but also reforming the capitalist system. Any structural reform along these lines was going to be costly, however, and this would make such change difficult. Moral suasion would not suffice here: the only way to get it done would be with a grand coalition of working-class people—a mass movement from the bottom up. Racism was (in addition to everything else) a deadly poison to that coalition, since it fatally undermined solidarity.

Rustin also faced something new: the problem of liberal anti-populism, by which I mean the growing contempt of enlightened professionals for the lower orders, meaning the white working class. For well-educated liberals in the early 1970s, such people, along with their organizations, appeared to be the nation's single most reactionary element—supporting the war in Vietnam, resisting busing, putting Richard Nixon in the White House, and so on.

Rustin would have none of it. After quoting a handful of condescending liberal remarks about union members, he came right to the point: this was not "political opposition" but "a certain class hatred." More specifically, it represented a "hatred of the elite for the 'mass.'" The upper-class liberals of 1971, he continued, understood alienation rather than solidarity as the heart of radicalism, ignoring organizations of ordinary people that aimed by their very nature for "greater social equality and distributive justice."[13]

What surprises the disenchanted modern reader about all this is Rustin's optimistic assumptions about ordinary citizens. It's a theme that recurred throughout his career. Describing a voter-registration drive in a 1958 letter to Martin Luther King, for example, Rustin wrote, "We urge people to vote. We do not want to influence them to vote for any particular party. We believe in the people. When they are aroused to vote, they will vote intelligently."[14]

This optimistic thread ran all through the civil rights movement. "I Am A Man" read the placards carried by strikers in the Memphis sanitation workers' strike—an assertion of rights and equality as fundamental as anything we've seen in these pages.

When King spoke to those men—trash collectors, remember, who came from society's lowliest ranks—he said, "So often we overlook the work and the significance of those who are not in professional jobs, of those who are not in the so-called big jobs. But let me say to you tonight, that whenever you are engaged in work that serves humanity . . . it has dignity, and it has worth."[15]

"All labor has dignity," King continued that night in March 1968—an expression that could have come straight out of a Populist manifesto circa 1891.

THE MOST DYNAMIC populist innovations of the 1960s came not from adults but from radical youth groups like the Student Nonviolent Coordinating Committee, which was formed after sit-in protests at segregated lunch counters in North Carolina in 1960. SNCC's leaders stood up to spectacular racist violence during the Freedom Ride campaign and then during efforts to register black voters in the Deep South, and their bravery quickly captured the imagination of liberals nationwide. But what made SNCC remarkable wasn't really its leaders—it was the group's determination to enlist ordinary African American citizens for direct actions against the racist system of the South. By "ordinary citizens" I am referring, in many cases, to tenant farmers and sharecroppers, the same group that was the focus of so much Populist activity in the 1890s and of populist culture in the 1930s.

Traditional civil rights groups would typically build support for their agenda with a charismatic leader, but SNCC took a different approach. Its idea was to move into some area in the Deep South—which was still, one hundred years after the Civil War, more of a giant carceral work farm for African Americans than it was a modern capitalist economy—build a movement among the people who lived there, then continue to organize somewhere else. It was the organized, not the organizer, that mattered in this model. In its early years SNCC was boldly and thoroughly antihierarchical, practicing democracy in its meetings as well as demanding democracy from the white masters of the South. The group insisted, for example, that ordinary people's knowledge of civil rights law was in some ways superior to that of law professors and law makers; it understood that, as one history of the movement puts it, "experts and leaders did not know how to break down Jim Crow." Only the people themselves could do that, and so SNCC's object came to be "to create leadership in each community so that formal leaders would no longer be necessary."[16]

SNCC's language was often straightforwardly populist. "We all recognize the fact that if any radical social, political and economic changes are to take place in our society, the people, the masses, must bring them about" was one of the famous lines deleted from SNCC leader John Lewis's speech at the 1963 March on Washington. "It's not radical if SNCC people get political offices, or if M. L. King becomes President, if decisions are still made from the top down," said SNCC leader Stokely Carmichael in 1965. "If decisions get made from the bottom up, then that's radical."[17]

"Participatory democracy" was the name the decade gave to the idea that motivated SNCC. The actual phrase was introduced by another student-led group, Students for a Democratic Society—SDS, the main organization of what was then called the New Left. To hear the group's leaders explain what they meant by "P.D." you might think you were listening to some latter-day adherent of the old People's Party, their red-hot Great Plains calamity-talk having somehow been translated into the subdued language of the mid-century multiversity. As SDS's 1962 *Port Huron Statement* explained, "participatory democracy" meant

> that decision-making of basic social consequence be carried on by public groupings;
>
> that politics be seen positively, as the art of collectively creating an acceptable pattern of social relations;

and furthermore that big economic decisions "should be open to democratic participation and subject to democratic social regulation."

There was more to it, of course. Probably too much more—as political platforms go, *The Port Huron Statement* was a wordy one, with the early printed versions running to some sixty-three densely argued pages. Suffice it to say here that "participatory democracy" eventually became one of the glowing desiderata of the era—like "authenticity," like "revolution"—a fad concept that students were all on fire to actualize.[18]

A fad, yes, but also something genuinely hopeful. Participatory democracy arose from SDS's wildly optimistic first principle: that all humans were "infinitely precious and possessed of unfulfilled capacities for reason, freedom, and love." It was succinctly stated in a later SDS slogan: "Let the people decide." The echoes of Populism in this kind of talk were obvious, if not always acknowledged by New Leftists themselves: the reverence for the ordinary citizen, the longing for collective democratic action. And, of course, all of it flew straight in the face of the cardinal doctrine of modern anti-populism—that the people are far too ignorant to manage their own affairs.

The other important way in which the sixties student Left

fit the populist profile was its transracial quality. Organizing across color lines was, obviously, close to the heart of what the New Left thought it was. In the early sixties, SDSers enlisted in SNCC's campaigns for desegregation and black voting rights in the South, learning from them the power of direct action. In the late sixties they came to regard groups like the Black Panthers as the "vanguard" of the socialist revolution they meant to make. In both cases it was the militant black Left that they looked to for leadership.

This marks a change in the populist tradition, and its significance deserves to be underscored. "For the first time," writes Michael Kazin, a historian of populism who was also an SDS leader at Harvard University, "significant numbers of white activists proclaimed a desire to take their cues from a primarily black movement."[19] Generally speaking, populist movements of the past had involved white organizers including blacks in their movements; this time the equation was reversed. African Americans were the leaders; the white Left was a sort of auxiliary to their insurgency in the South.

Like its predecessors, the New Left was also a mass movement—or, rather, it eventually became one. After 1965, as the Vietnam War became issue number one, the New Left exploded in size. At its zenith, SDS had around one hundred thousand members—small by historical standards, but with a cultural reach that far exceeded those numbers. Its ideas spread from the elite campuses to the vast world of college students, giving us "the Sixties" as everyone remembers it: constant protests, occupations of campus buildings, battles with police outside the Pentagon or the Chicago Hilton, Vietcong flags, gigantic rallies on the Mall in Washington, D.C.

• • •

BY THE END of 1968, however, nothing was working out the way it was supposed to. Martin Luther King was murdered less than a month after he declared that "all labor has dignity," his assassination touching off riots in cities across the country. The Memphis sanitation workers eventually won their strike—today they are AFSCME Local 1733—but the Poor People's Campaign floundered without King's leadership. The tent city on the National Mall was constructed as planned, but only after endless organizational difficulties and without ever achieving the spectacular impact of the 1963 March on Washington.

The shift of emphasis toward economic equality planned by King and Bayard Rustin fared even worse. The Vietnam War absorbed all the resources that the Johnson administration—the last one led by a real New Deal liberal—might have put toward achieving full employment. Rustin's hopes for the Freedom Budget and a powerful left-wing political coalition were smashed in the process. Although it was hard to see it coming at the time, liberalism was smashed, too, its different factions pulling the Democratic Party to pieces.

Organized labor never did recover the boldness of the CIO era, as Martin Luther King often urged it to do; instead most unions settled into bureaucratic torpor. King's plan for reforming the Democratic Party fared no better. As black voters made their numbers felt in the South, the racist political machinery of the region simply changed sides, defecting to the Republicans.

The Democratic Party itself did the opposite of what the reformers hoped. Instead of embracing a bold agenda of redistribution, the party descended into a civil war in the wake of the

Vietnam debacle. The winners of that tussle were ultimately the party's anti-populists—technocrats who believed that reforms, if any were warranted, had to come from the highly educated leadership class.

As for the New Left, it failed to become the next step in the grand march of progress, always remaining a movement of college students, not "the people". Its members never transcended their essential identity: these were proto-professionals, young people in training for positions in the upper reaches of America's middle-class society. They were a charming elite and even an alienated elite, but an elite nevertheless.[20]

And they acted like one. In the early days of SDS, the group's understanding of capitalism didn't have a whole lot to do with traditional working-class concerns—with hard work for lousy pay, for example, or with monopoly, or with the power of banks.[21] Indeed, what made them a "new" Left was the singular belief that educated people like them, rather than the working class, were now the agents of political progress. In this they bore a strong resemblance to the consensus intellectuals who taught them, scholars who believed progress would come from the enlightened people in society's higher-educated ranks, not from mass movements or blue-collar workers. "The key was not the proletariat, as socialists for more than a century had believed," as historian James Miller summarizes one SDS leader's thinking in the early days; "the key was students." As Tom Hayden, the principal author of *The Port Huron Statement*, recalled years later, he had believed that humanity had entered "a whole new period of history in which the Left had to go from a belief in labor as the agency of change to students as an agency of change."[22]

Social class was a persistent stumbling block for the New

Left. One anecdote Miller relates in his history of SDS is how the group's organizers, trying to bring together the unemployed in several northern cities, eventually lost interest in the poor folks they were trying to help—because those poor folks often turned out to think America needed to fight communism in Vietnam.[23] Let the people decide . . . and they will disappoint you every single time.

Eventually the romantic populism of the early 1960s drained away completely. It happened in movement politics and it happened in the larger culture. "The Sixties," as middle-class Americans remember it, began with a folk-music revival; with a thousand super-authentic performances of blue-collar despair; with "The Ballad of Hollis Brown" and all those different versions of the sad, sad story of "The House of the Rising Sun." The way it ended was with anger, with the Jefferson Airplane yelling, "Up against the wall, motherfucker."

By the time the clock ran out on the New Left, its activists had come to believe that the American people were not the protesters getting fire-hosed by the police in Birmingham, Alabama; the American people were now seen as the ones turning the fire hoses on those protesters. The people were not the would-be beneficiaries of progressive reform; they were *the enemy*, facilitators of the evil Amerikan empire.

"Working people" here in the USA were not anything special, a 1969 SDS manifesto declared; just another "particular privileged interest" bought off with imperialist plunder. The only "people" who mattered by then were the "oppressed peoples of the world," the peasants of Vietnam and the Third World, and with them the white New Left boldly declared its solidarity. SDS was a "Revolutionary Youth Movement" now, an armed ally of the global people's uprising in whose eyes *all* Americans (with the exception of African Americans) were suspect.[24]

This, at any rate, was one of the movement's great, lasting legacies. The New Left succeeded in stripping the aura of nobility away from what the Pops called the "producing classes," and in inventing an understanding of radicalism in which politics was no longer really about accomplishing public things for the common good. Instead, politics was becoming, at least in part, a path to personal fulfillment or healing. Protest degenerated into "street theater"; "radical style" came to trump "radical substance," as the historian Christopher Lasch put it; a satisfying sense of personal righteousness became the ultimate end of political action.[25]

It was the opposite of what King and Rustin were after, what populism is always after: a grand coalition of social forces that would reform capitalism in the interests of the great majority. That was lost in the late sixties—drowned in the muddy Mekong or clubbed to the pavement on Michigan Avenue.

I DO NOT want to judge the New Left too harshly. I wasn't there. To those who were, the horror of the Vietnam bloodbath was overwhelming and in bringing it to a stop, extreme measures must have seemed justified. Also, SDS was right about the exhaustion of liberalism, and they were right, in part, about the traditional institutions of the Left. Liberals were indeed too cozy with corporations and with imperialism. Many unions were indeed bureaucratic and un-progressive back then—after all, there were no more solid supporters of the Vietnam War than the top brass of the labor movement.

Not all working-class leaders were so hidebound, however. Walter Reuther, the president of the powerful United Auto Workers and a veteran of the CIO campaigns of the thirties, spent the sixties marching in civil rights demonstrations and looking for ways to join forces with the New Left. He was slow to turn against the war, out of loyalty to President Lyndon Johnson. But in 1970 he was able to look back over the history of his union and claim, with justification, that no organization in the world had done more "to place human rights above property rights."[26] This was an insight the protesters of that era missed: organizations of ordinary working people are often a force for democratic progress by their very nature, regardless of the ignorance or bigotry of individual members of those organizations.

The radicals missed the point then, and everyone misses the point today. The social stereotypes established in those last awful years of the sixties have stuck with us. Like the geriatric Rolling Stones, they chug along imperturbably though they are now decades past their rightful retirement. We cannot shake them. When we recall that King and Rustin and Walter Reuther hoped for a grand alliance of ordinary people, we have trouble imagining what they might have had in mind. But white working-class people as enemies of progress—oh, *that* we understand.

The big counterculture think-book of 1970, *The Greening of America*, described "blue-collar workers" as "those arch opponents of the new consciousness." This was stated matter-of-factly; the author assumed that everyone knew what he meant by then. The book's twist was that it exhorted us to have pity on these monstrous proles. "Look again at a 'fascist'—tight-lipped, tense, crew cut, correctly dressed, church-going, an American flag on his car window, a hostile eye for communists, youth, and blacks." You might hate this stock blue-collar character, but his life is really quite sad:

> He has had very little of love, or poetry, or music, or nature, or joy. He has been dominated by fear. He has been condemned to narrow-minded prejudice, to a self-defeating materialism, to a lonely suspicion of his fellow men. He is angry, envious, bitter, self-hating. He ravages his own environment. He has fled all his life from consciousness and responsibility. He is turned against his own nature.

And so on. Maybe all "he" really needs is to be slipped a dose of youth culture.[27]

The Greening of America is dedicated to "the students at Yale," where its author taught in the Law School. That the stereotype the book did so much to bolster might have been a straightforward expression of his cohort's structural antagonism to working-class people appears not to have occurred to its author. In hindsight, however, it is obvious: in 1896 the young gentlemen of Yale heckled working-class champion William Jennings Bryan; in 1970 their votary trolled the white working class generally for its lousy consciousness. And somewhere in between this myth was blithely cemented: The Ivy League elite were not only society's rulers, but also society's rebels and revolutionaries, its designated conscience. The successful were not only more capable than those who toil; they were morally superior as well. The reasoning had been flipped but the conclusion remained the same: the ruling class ruled because it deserved to rule.

Think of the enlightenment that clouded the mind of the celebrated author Terry Southern, who wrote parts of the 1969 movie *Easy Rider*—another accolade for the counterculture—and who described its horrifying final scene as "an indictment of blue-collar America, the people I thought were responsible for the Vietnam War."[28] Which is to say, Southern thought the people serving in the Vietnam War were the people who got us into the Vietnam War. Hollis Brown and the Masters of War had turned out to be one and the same.

And now think of that scene itself, the ultimate expression of the decade's anti-populist sensibility. *Easy Rider*, a motorcycle adventure movie starring and produced by Peter Fonda, has often been described as a generational answer to *The Grapes of Wrath*, which starred Fonda's dad, Henry. And in that final scene, the glamorous young bikers with the awesome rock 'n' roll soundtrack are brutally and pointlessly shot to death by a pair of heavily accented, obviously impoverished rednecks riding in the cab of an old pickup truck. Who are these villains? As the sharp-eyed historian Jefferson Cowie points out, "It is almost impossible to not see these characters as a quote from *The Grapes of Wrath*."[29]

In other words: they were the Joads, the very symbols of resilient thirties populism, reimagined for the sixties and for the decades to come as murderers . . . as pigheaded killers of everything that is fun and joyful and enlightened and tolerant and cool in American life. As fascists.

IN THIS WAY the consensus school's anti-populism was elevated by its enemy the counterculture into wisdom for the ages. The consensus view on nearly everything else—mass movements, post-ideology, the sanctity of the university, and so on—was shattered by the sixties, but this essential bit of class profiling was set in stone. Working-class whites were reactionary and authoritarian. The university president in his three-piece suit believed it, in his quiet, scholarly way—and so did the long-haired student who had just trashed his office and chugged his sherry: democracy is a system meant for enlightened people like them.

The 1968 third-party run for the presidency by the Alabama segregationist George Wallace represented either the final confirmation of this thesis or a backlash against it, depending on your perspective. Touring northern cities as well as his familiar southern haunts, Wallace denounced hippies and journalists and Hollywood celebrities and liberal college professors, always from a position of long-suffering averageness. White working people from every corner of the nation briefly rallied to Wallace's message of hardscrabble anguish, his savage resentment of the high-minded and the well-educated. And so a man straight out of the southern-demagogue tradition came to be seen as an honest expression of the average American's new sense of bitterness.

"Populism" was the noun journalists started using to categorize that southern-demagogue tradition. Thanks to the labors of Richard Hofstadter and the others described in the last chapter, writers everywhere knew that this was the exact word for Wallace's venomous combination of racism and his appeal to the "great silent American Folk," as one account put it. Besides, Wallace was said to be vaguely liberal on economic questions, and he was running as a third-party candidate. So the p-word seemed to make sense. Although Wallace apparently never used it to describe himself—indeed, he objected to it—journalists depicted him as the ne plus ultra of populism as he went about his mission of political disruption.[30]

In retrospect it was clearly a misnomer. Alabama was capable of producing left-wing, man-of-the-people politicians in the 1960s, but George Wallace wasn't one of them. Where populism had once been defined by its transracial aspirations, Wallace was the nation's champion segregationist, a mouthpiece for the very sort of people who terrorized actual Populists in the 1890s. Wallace was no rebel: he was the authority under whom Alabama officers beat and hounded civil rights protesters so many times in the 1960s, perhaps the ultimate anti-populist act.[31]

Nor was Wallace's snake oil much of a tonic for working people. The United Auto Workers, guardians of the flame of CIO populism, poured enormous resources into a campaign against him in 1968, reminding their members of how very little racism had achieved for working people in Wallace's Alabama. His economic concern for the little guy, they pointed out, was a total fraud. The union campaign succeeded, beating back what had at first appeared to be a powerful Wallace surge in the industrial districts of the North.[32]

But the p-word stuck as a description for working-class reaction. And while it is perhaps an exaggeration to say that Wallace's sneering, upside-down populism defeated the hopeful, traditional version, it is undoubtedly true that the Alabama governor's characteristic set of grievances became a kind of checklist for generations of resentful politicians of the Right. And it was in this way that the optimistic, liberal sixties ceded the stage to an angry counter-sixties of the Right, a pseudo-populism that honored ordinary, put-upon Americans who were fed up with all the protests and the revolution-talk and longed merely for law, order, and a little respect for Old Glory.

• • •

ONE OF THE earliest converts to this new sensibility was none other than Richard Hofstadter, the historian who had spent his career assailing the original Populists—and constructing the definition that scholars and journalists use today.

The particular ivied fortress from which Hofstadter had lobbed his missiles at populism was Columbia University in New York, an institution that he liked to idealize in the noblest terms. He had been shocked and deeply antagonized by the student protests there in April 1968, and when he spoke at Columbia's graduation ceremony that year, many of the students in the audience stood up and walked out on him.

Two years later Hofstadter paid them back in kind. In an interview with *Newsweek* magazine published a few months before his untimely death in 1970, he referred to the sixties as "the Age of Rubbish" and criticized left-wing college students for an "elitism" that was "based on moral indignation against most of the rest of us." When he referred to the vast numbers of Americans who "intensely dislike young people—college students mainly," Hofstadter was describing what he saw in society, but as he talked on it was clear that he was referring to himself. He resented students for their precious radicalism and for their "moral indignation" against the society that had raised them, and he cast this resentment in stark, class-based terms.

> The activist young operate from elitist premises which they
> themselves aren't aware of, but which working people are
> acutely aware of. The kids ask for two weeks off for con-
> ducting political activities, or to go on a pass-fail basis at
> the end of the term because so few of them have completed

their work. People who work in offices and on assembly lines can't negotiate such arrangements, but if they could, they'd certainly have to sacrifice their salaries. The kids implicitly assume a certain kind of indulgence that other types of people in this society don't get. This is intensely resented. The kids dislike the idea that they're thinking and acting as an elite, but they are.[33]

As the larger world came to embrace Hofstadter's suspicion of mass movements, Hofstadter himself became a populist, of exactly the embittered kind he had spent his career analyzing.

7

The Money Changers
Burn the Temple

In the early seventies a fog of grievance settled over the land. Never have Americans hated authorities like they did after the Vietnam War turned sour; after Watergate taught us the incorrigible venality of our elected leaders. Big government seemed omnipotent and yet incompetent; it possessed the world's greatest military machine but it couldn't do anything right. In the long list of groups it aimed to serve, We the People always seemed to come last. This snarling mood of disillusionment was the characteristic sensibility of the decade: the "wellsprings of trust" had been "poisoned," two self-designated populist authors wrote back in 1972.[1] They are still poisoned today.

The whole country was mad as hell, to use a favorite catchphrase, and the discontent seemed to go in every direction at once. It was economic, it was political; it was racial, it was cultural; it was liberal, it was conservative. Americans despised the CIA and also the Soviet Union. We cheered for Clint Eastwood as a rule-breaking cop who blasted lowlifes even when the lawyers told him to stop . . . and then we cheered for Burt Reynolds as a "bandit" in a black Trans Am, the roads behind him littered with the smoking remains of the Arkansas, Mississippi, Alabama, and Georgia highway patrols.

Responding to the new sensibility, our politicians tried to impress us with their humility. They courted us with soft southern accents, with tales of peanut farms and pork rinds. They posed as defenders of the people, the forgotten man, the silent majority, the great overtaxed middle, the "normal" Americans suffering the contempt of shadowy TV network elites. To list the leaders who were identified by the press in the 1970s as "populists" would be to include virtually the entire roster of prominent statesmen: both Richard Nixon and his opponent, George McGovern, were tagged with the p-word. So were Jimmy Carter, Ted Kennedy, and the hawkish Democratic senator Henry Jackson; so were big-city mayors Frank Rizzo and John Lindsay; so was West Virginia politician Jay Rockefeller, a great-grandson of the biggest Populist devil-figure of them all.[2]

Jim Hightower, the legendary Texas activist, relates the following tale from the seventies populism craze. One day a friend of his who worked for the Congressional Research Service received a request from the office of Senator Lloyd Bentsen, a man Hightower describes as an "aloof and patrician Texas Democrat who was known on Capitol Hill primarily as a faithful emissary for Wall Street interests." Bentsen was thinking of a presidential run, Hightower continues, and evidently he wanted a big idea with which to distinguish himself. And so: "*What is a populist?*" read the query. "*The senator thinks he might be one.*"[3]

And why not? Everyone else said they were one, and the pseudo-populist rebellions they led ultimately turned out to be great for Wall Street interests. What those years of revolt made possible was the opposite of populism: tax cuts, deregulation, deindustrialization, and the disempowerment of working-class people through the destruction of their unions.

By which I mean, the populist rhetoric invoked so abundantly in those years provided a perfect cover for the elitist politics we actually embraced. In the period I am describing, trade unions went from being a normal part of everyday life to a thing that had to be rooted out and crushed. America attacked inflation by embracing austerity. We gave up on the dream of economic equality—gave up on it so utterly that, in years to come, we would find it difficult even to recall what Reuther and Roosevelt meant when they used those words.

IT NEEDN'T HAVE happened that way. It was true that the old liberal order was having problems by the early 1970s, but the bonfire of public anger that consumed the country might have brought renewal to that system just as easily as right-wing backlash against it. Yes, Democratic leaders chose to turn away from the white working class and, yes, Republicans reached out successfully to that same group, but what that represented was not inevitability. It was liberal folly.

Bayard Rustin wrote one of the most perceptive takes on this situation back in 1971—so perceptive that it might have been written in 1980, or 2000, or yesterday:

> The potential for a Republican majority depends upon Nixon's success in attracting into the conservative fold lower-middle-class whites, the same group that the [liberal] New Politics has written off. *The question is not whether*

this group is conservative or liberal; for it is both, and how it acts will depend upon the way the issues are defined. If they are defined as race and dissent, then Nixon will win. But if, on the other hand, they are defined so as to appeal to the progressive economic interests of the lower middle class, then it becomes possible to build an alliance on the basis of common interest between this group and the black community.[4]

Might the white working class have joined a transracial movement taking America in a progressive direction rather than on into the decades of Reagan, Bush, and Trump? Unlikely though it sounds today, it was definitely possible.

After all, while some were angry with the liberal establishment because it was supposedly soft on crime and committed to racial integration, others were angry because it wasn't really liberal at all—because it had dumped the entire burden of the Vietnam War on their children; because it seemed only to care about the well-educated; because it was happily handing out subsidies to favorite corporate behemoths while their blue-collar lives still sucked.

Between these two alternative viewpoints lay the political choices of the decades to come. Would Americans choose some grand appeal to social solidarity, as they had in the past? Would we try tepid, managerial centrism? Or would we plunge head-long into the glamorous, self-pitying resentment of the culture wars?

The irony is that all three of these alternatives would be described with the same word: "populism."

• • •

LET ME REPEAT that a renewed populism of the Left was possible. Although almost nobody remembers it anymore, the early 1970s saw the biggest strike wave since World War II, with some 2.4 million workers walking out. Most of these were by-the-book work stoppages called by the leadership of still-mighty national unions, but a surprising number of them were wildcat actions that were authorized by nobody except ordinary workers themselves. On top of this came a series of grassroots efforts to replace the labor movement's aging and conservative and sometimes corrupt leadership—rank-and-file insurgencies in the Steelworkers, the Mineworkers, and the Teamsters, which were joined by a group of black union leaders drawn from across the movement. This new breed was nothing like Archie Bunker or the "hardhat" stereotype of those days: they were strong believers in workplace democracy; they were overwhelmingly anti-racist and anti-war; they were often non-white and non-male.[5]

Among the artifacts of this brief period of blue-collar possibility is a forgotten little book from 1972 called *A Populist Manifesto*, which proposed a grand plan for the seventies generation: a "pact between the have-nots." The manifesto's authors zeroed right in on the essential populist idea: "The key to building any new majority in American politics is a coalition of self-interest between blacks and low- and moderate-income whites," they declared. That was because "the real division in this country is not between generations or between races, but between the rich who have power and those blacks and whites who have neither power nor property." This was not a description of an existing movement, however; it was a blueprint for a new populism that might be called into being—"a platform for a movement that does not yet exist."[6]

There was a populist revival in academia to go along with this renewed spirit of working-class revolt. It focused, appropriately enough, on the People's Party of the 1890s. Instead of a cautionary tale about the paranoia and bigotry of working-class movements, the story of Populism was now remembered as a kind of golden moment for freedom itself. This was the teaching of *Democratic Promise*, Lawrence Goodwyn's landmark 1976 history. The book aimed to do nothing less than turn history's conventional understanding of progress upside down. The Pops, Goodwyn insisted, had a sense of democratic engagement that was better developed than our own; their movement, he wrote, made "the fragile hopes of participants in our own twentieth-century American society seem cramped by comparison."[7]

One working politician who tried to build the populist ideas of the era into something larger was the Oklahoma senator Fred Harris, who ran for president as a Democrat in 1976. Harris spent the sixties as a reliable supporter of Great Society programs, but in the seventies he looked out over a country where the traditional alliances of liberalism were crumbling—where the "Okies" he grew up among were voting for George Wallace and where the Right was on the ascendant. Liberal appeals were no longer convincing to anyone, and Harris went looking for the reason why. The answer was that liberalism had developed a massive contradiction. As Harris wrote in 1973, "You can't appeal to black people and poor people . . . on the basis of their own self-interest, and to everybody else"—meaning the vast, undifferentiated middle class—"on the basis of morality. That kind of an appeal is the luxury of the intellectual elite—for people who are, themselves, socially and economically secure."[8]

How to resolve this? The answer, Harris wrote, was to appeal to just about everyone except the wealthy on the basis of self-interest, by taking on "concentrated wealth and corporate power." By declaring war against oil companies, big banks, agribusiness, and so on, Harris proposed to build a transracial alliance of all non-rich people, white as well as black. His "New Populism," he wrote, "seeks to put America back together again—across the lines of race, age, sex, and region. Those in the coalition don't have to love each other. I wish they would. But all they have to do is recognize their common interests."[9]

"The issue is privilege" was the remarkable slogan under which Harris ran for the presidency in 1976. He promised to break up General Motors, big oil, and other gigantic agglomerations of economic power. He routinely quoted Jesse Jackson, which was then regarded as a daring move for an ambitious politician.[10]

The innovation for which Harris will always be remembered, however, was his spectacular low-budget campaign— driving around the country in a camper, using his house as his headquarters, staying in the homes of supporters, carrying his own bags, making his calls on a pay phone at the local gas station. "This campaign will be a people's campaign, both in strategy and belief," Harris said on launching the effort. These populist strategies were meant to illustrate the populist beliefs, of course, but Harris also thought of his regular-guy run for the White House as a necessity: the only way someone with his views could possibly stand for high office was by doing it on a shoestring.[11]

THE COMMON THREAD among these populist revivalists was that all of them had some experience with civil rights and had thus learned the power of mass movements. Jack Newfield, a journalist who co-authored *A Populist Manifesto*, had been in the audience for Martin Luther King's Montgomery speech in 1965, while Lawrence Goodwyn had spent much of the sixties organizing working-class black and brown voters in Texas.[12] Fred Harris, for his part, called for and then served on the Kerner Commission, which investigated the causes of the urban riots of 1967.*

Another thing all of them did was reject the technocratic, elitist liberalism that was then emerging. The Democratic Party was making its fateful turn away from organized labor in those days; they were becoming a party of experts and technocrats, of white-collar professionals who admired fancy college degrees but had little interest in working-class solidarity.

"Elitist" was the word *A Populist Manifesto* used to describe emerging centrist liberalism; a stylish politics for people bedazzled by experts but contemptuous toward their blue-collar countrymen. Populism, as the authors imagined it, "mistrusts the technocrats from the RAND Corporation and the Harvard Business School." Lawrence Goodwyn, for his part, called "rule by experts" a "Leninist paradigm" that justifies itself by expressing its "impatience with mass human performance."[13]

"People are smart enough to govern themselves" is how Fred Harris put this fundamental article of faith. Also: "Experts are always wrong." Where they were most wrong, he continued, was on foreign policy questions, which had for decades been directed by elites from business and academia, and which Harris proposed to democratize: "you have to open that thing

---

* Fifty years later, as the commission's last surviving member, Harris often commented on its legacy. See, for example, the op-ed that he co-authored for the *New York Times*, "The Unmet Promise of Equality," February 28, 2018.

up, level with people, let them in on things." Harris said these words in 1975, by which time the disasters of Vietnam were familiar to all. He added: "when you do, you can no longer justify most of what's going on."[14]

IN THE LARGE field of Democrats running for the presidency in 1976, several other candidates imitated Harris's trademark humility while divorcing it completely from his call for a war on privilege. Populism as style became a runaway #1 smash hit; populism as multiracial economic democracy faded slowly into the sunset.

Here was the catchphrase that eventually captured the nation's heart that year: "My name is Jimmy Carter, and I'm running for president." With such humble and direct words did the jeans-wearing "antipolitician" from Georgia make himself the screen upon which Democrats projected their populist dreams—"populism" now meaning a sunny, upbeat people-ism.[15]

Hailing from far outside Washington power circles and taking on a platoon of more famous Democrats, Jimmy Carter proceeded to win the party's presidential nomination in a blurry but noble-sounding quest to restore people's faith in a political system that looked rotten and corrupted after Watergate and Vietnam.

Carter was certainly capable of speaking the old populist language. In his acceptance speech at the Democratic convention that summer, he denounced (in his soft-spoken way) the "political economic elite" who "never had to account for mistakes" regardless of how they screwed up. Lobbyists, the CIA, the income-tax system—all of them were offensive to the democratic spirit as Carter understood it. "It is time for the people to run the government," he announced, "and not the other way around."

When Carter used the word "populist," however, he meant to invoke comforting myths of the general will, not working-class solidarity. On the campaign trail, Carter encouraged journalists to use the term to describe him as a way of avoiding the conventional tags "liberal" and "conservative." What populism was all about, he said, was expressing the will of the people, embracing a politics that arose "directly from the concerns and the yearnings of the people themselves, which is my own definition of populism."[16]

There were other definitions floating around out there, but somehow Carter always managed to fit. In 1976, the liberal *New York Times* columnist Anthony Lewis watched Carter give an idealistic speech about how fine the American people were and decided right then and there that the man was a democratic hero:

> I thought: Jimmy Carter really does see himself fighting entrenched power, the status quo. He resents privilege, official arrogance, unfairness. He thinks of himself as one of the outsiders, those without power in society. In short, he is an authentic modern voice of that old American strain, Populism.[17]

Journalistic admiration of Carter's ordinariness hit a sort of crescendo with his inauguration in January 1977, when the new president showed his distaste for the trappings of power by walking the length of Pennsylvania Avenue instead of riding in his limousine. Carter's speech, according to one wire service account, struck a "populist tone" by calling for "humility, mercy, and justice." This is a definition worth remembering in a time when our public thinkers routinely describe "populism" as a philosophy of vanity, cruelty, and intolerance, plus a snickering disregard for the rights of others.[18]

Put Carter's humility aside and examine his actual deeds in the White House, however, and it becomes clear that his was the least populist administration since Herbert Hoover's.

The historian Jefferson Cowie calls the Carter years "The New Deal That Never Happened," and the phrase is apt: After years of working-class discontent and African American uprisings, Carter's victory was the great opportunity for Democrats to show what they could do for the vast majority of the population. Instead they did next to nothing.

Oh, they were able to get a big capital-gains tax cut passed, all right—and if you're looking for the roots of today's extreme inequality, it's a good place to start. Carter's Democrats deregulated airlines and trucking. They embraced austerity as inflation mounted higher and higher. They stood by indifferently as an employer counterattack squashed the decade's militant unionism. When it came to New Deal programs like a proposed full-employment scheme, they proved to be worse than useless.[19]

What the Carter team really cared about was fighting inflation and balancing the budget, anti-populist causes for which they were willing to accept spiraling unemployment. When his handpicked Fed chairman, Paul Volcker, chose to tackle inflation by jacking interest rates up to a now unthinkable 20 percent, he sent the economy into a sharp recession that, in turn, scorched Carter's hopes for a second term. As for the ordinary Americans who were hard hit by the shutting down of prosperity, Volcker had this winning admonition: "The standard of living of the average American has to decline."

A bland technocrat straight out of the consensus playbook, Jimmy Carter represented a new kind of Democrat—a post–New Deal centrist who campaigned with vague populist niceness but whose true affection was reserved for ultra-competent policy experts. This understanding of liberal leadership would far outlast Carter's political career: we would see it again in the presidencies of Bill Clinton and Barack Obama, two more true believers in meritocracy who also thought to present themselves as kindly reformers on the side of ordinary people.

In 1980 Carter led his Democrats into a sickening disaster. In a landslide, the country chose a new kind of Republican—Ronald Reagan, a man of ideology and moralistic rhetoric who *also* campaigned as a populist but who offered a far more forceful solution to the cynicism of the age.

ALL THROUGH THE 1970s, the Right had been sharpening its own populist appeal, coming up with all sorts of ways to express its outraged hostility to affectation and privilege—none of which, mirabile dictu, ever got in the way of their equally unrelenting efforts to roll back liberal economic achievements.

You know what I'm talking about, reader. The Right's war on the establishment has been the inescapable political soundtrack of the last forty years, playing at high volume from loudspeakers all around you. It has powered countless political careers. Thousands of fire-breathing right-wing best sellers have been printed so that they might clutter the attics of middle America. Conservative warriors too numerous to list have risen to celebrity status—radio, TV, journalism—burned briefly with rage against the establishment, and then settled back into obscurity.

What establishment, precisely, did this populist uprising

aim to confront? Well, there was the media, who supposedly poison our news and distort the truth. The intellectuals who hate our country; who instruct our kids in hating our country; who capitulate immediately to any kind of radical who hates our country. The pampered college kids who insult our soldiers and our cops. The activist judges who make the law rather than interpret it. In other words, the elite: the disdainful, contemptuous, East Coast, liberated, raised-consciousness elite.

Elites who longed to give away the Panama Canal. Elites who were soft on welfare, soft on crime, soft on school discipline, soft on communism—but who still wanted to make Americans wear seat belts and drive cars with airbags. Elites who failed to live up to basic moral standards of behavior when in the Oval Office. Elites who make endless excuses for Muslim terrorism.

What I am trying to describe with this hyperbole is a kind of inverted class war; a conflict that, as an early backlasher put it, "finds the upper classes rhetorically on the side of revolution in values and structure, and the lower classes rhetorically on the side of stability, slower evolution, and loyalty."[20]

But the war was also about race. Almost wherever you looked, the young Republican strategist Kevin Phillips wrote in a once-famous book, white voters were moving away from the Democratic Party because it had come to be identified with African American protest and achievement. "The principal force which broke up the Democratic (New Deal) coalition," Phillips wrote, "is the Negro socioeconomic revolution and liberal Democratic ideological inability to cope with it."[21] (Whatever that meant.)

In Phillips's understanding of the age, ideas counted for little. Demographics was all, and tribalism was the essential political impulse. In one supremely cynical passage, Phillips even seemed to encourage the Republicans to continue vigorous "civil rights enforcement" despite the preferences of the party's new, racist voters because securing African American voting rights would accelerate the ugly phenomenon of racial sorting. The more blacks entered the political process, Phillips predicted, the more they would "seize control" of the Southern Democratic Party, and the more the region's whites would come running to the GOP.[22]

The word that Phillips chose to describe what was going on with this new, majoritarian Republican Party was "populism." Those who hated or opposed the country's "establishment" or "privileged elite" were "populists," and the great shift under way was the transition of the Republican Party from one of these poles to the other—"from establishmentarianism to populism." As we know, biracial coordination was one of the things that defined 1890s Populism,* but for Phillips, "the new populist coalition includes very few Negroes." This form of populism encouraged one group of working people to despise another.[23]

THE GREAT OPPORTUNITY for this phony populism of the Right, in both its cultural and its racist flavors, arrived in the late seventies. Its embodiment was an actor, of course: sunny Ronald Reagan, who played the heroic Rooseveltian role, the man who would dispel the air of defeat and decline that hovered over the

---

* Oddly enough, Phillips seemed to be aware of this. In the course of his famous book, *The Emerging Republican Majority*, Phillips used "populist" both in the original sense, describing the destruction of the biracial People's Party at the hands of the southern elite, and also in the completely opposite sense, as a shorthand for racist southern demagogues—which is to say, the people who destroyed it.

United States. Reagan would save us from the great malaise of the Carter presidency; he would inspire us with talk about our "rendezvous with destiny"; he would lead us on "a great national crusade to make America great again."

That last phrase was one Reagan used in his 1980 acceptance speech to the Republican convention, and his theme that night, as with so many of FDR's speeches, was the problem of out-of-control elites sneering at the common man. It wasn't money changers in the temple that Reagan aimed to disperse, however; it was the temple itself that needed to be burned down. Reagan promised the assembled Republicans that he would do it in the name of the "working men and women" for whom the bureaucrat's pet programs were merely a "theft from their pocketbooks."

So perverse had the situation become, Reagan continued, that the government now heeded the advice of "a tiny minority opposed to economic growth" rather than the voices of the great majority; it was actively "betraying the trust and goodwill of the American workers who keep it going" with their taxes. But his administration would put things right, Reagan declared: it would put "an end to the notion that the American taxpayer exists to fund the Federal government. The Federal government exists to serve the American people."

At Reagan's feet the old-school Republicans celebrated their triumph—realtors and small-town bankers; insurance brokers and Buick dealers; pensioners and golfers-for-life. Dressed in the colorful blazers and whimsical hats of convention-goers circa 1980, they capered joyfully about the arena, screaming their approval. Now it was their turn to play rebel.

"We can build a new majority around social and economic populism," the conservative Republican congressman Jack

Kemp announced that same year. What he meant by that expression was simple: tax cuts, like the far-reaching one that President Reagan would sign into law the following year.[24]

Mad-as-hell businessmen were now the ultimate populist subject. Not farm women, or sharecroppers, or day laborers. Business people: they were zealots for reform wherever you turned. The burning idea behind their uprising was that to oppose capitalism or to scoff at the successful were acts of snobbery if not of outright bigotry. No one put it better than social theorist George Gilder, whose 1981 book *Wealth and Poverty* was widely hailed as the handbook of Reaganism: "The war against the rich," Gilder wrote, "is a campaign now led and inspired by the declining rich, to arouse the currently poor against the insurgently successful business classes." In a verbatim reversal of the old Populist formula, he announced that "hatred of producers of wealth," meaning capitalists, was "the racism of the intelligentsia."[25]

Reagan brought all the seething resentments of right-wing populism together. His adviser Jeffrey Bell tried to describe the coherence of Reagan's "Populist Agenda" for readers of the *Wall Street Journal* in 1981. The genial movie star, Bell wrote, was going on the offensive against elites and elitism in every policy area. Reagan was cracking down on judicial activism ("the epitome of elitist government"); he was cutting taxes (to the chagrin of "the economics profession"); he was slashing federal spending (thus fighting an "unelected Washington bureaucracy" wielding "unprecedented power"); and he might even return the country to the gold standard (which "puts him on the populist side," Bell absurdly declared, because going back on gold would strip power from "central bankers and economists").[26]

How did Ronald Reagan, the Hollywood dandy, come to hold such emancipatory views? Bell explained that the transformation had come about in "a radically populist way." During the 1950s, Reagan had been a spokesman for General Electric, hosting the giant corporation's weekly TV show and touring its factories to talk with its workers. It seems these visits to GE installations had been like a graduate seminar in the school of hard knocks. As Reagan met with workers on the shop floor, the suntanned Californian was forced to listen to their real-world grievances. Absorbing these long drafts of honest proletarian wisdom, according to Bell, he was eventually converted to his "populist" suspicion of government.[27]

Let me pause here to remind you of something everyone knows: the revolution Reagan would inaugurate as president would shift the wealth of the world upward in a history-altering way; it would smash the power of organized labor once and for all; it would deregulate the banks and crush the dreams of ordinary Americans in towns and cities across the country. But in the beginning the myth of Reagan as a man of the people seemed somehow plausible. When campaigning in 1980, the candidate deliberately avoided identifying with big business, preferring (as he put it) "all those people I shake hands with who have calluses on their hands."[28]

THE PSEUDOPOPULIST REVOLUTION of the early 1980s didn't spend a lot of time pondering the nature of democracy or weighing its place in the Jeffersonian tradition. This populism was about winning elections and then rewriting the tax code, not theorizing. This uprising had no Omaha Platform; no Lawrence Goodwyn; no Bayard Rustin.

To the extent that the right-wing revolt had a philosophy at all, it was that government was the real elite, with its outrageous taxes and its wasteful spending. Federal intervention of virtually any kind was elitist by definition because it removed power from individuals and handed it over to government workers in Washington, D.C. Therefore farm programs (so beloved of the original Populists) were elitist. So were public works. So was basically any effort to achieve economic equality. All of it was snobbery. As the conservative direct-mail guru Richard Viguerie put it in his contribution to the genre, "The elitists in Washington believe that a fair distribution of the nation's wealth can be brought about only if it is controlled by the government, that is, by the elitists in Washington."[29]

Two terms of the Reagan presidency curdled this upside-down populism into a grotesque self-parody. But on it went. In 1988, George H. W. Bush, a prince of the establishment blood and quite possibly the preppiest man in America, managed to get himself elected president by making what his campaign manager, Lee Atwater, called "an emotional, populist appeal to traditional values." By which Atwater meant chomping on pork rinds, visiting flag factories, frolicking about the Midwest with country singers—and promising to get tough with criminals, meaning African Americans. [30]

For observers of populism-as-fraud, 1988 was a year of wonders, a zenith of fakery. Not only had populism become an almost exclusively right-wing phenomenon, but everyone who followed politics understood it to be a put-on. Even a born member of the nation's aristocracy could pull it off, given a sufficiently oblivious opponent.

The Democrats supplied that opponent: Massachusetts governor Michael Dukakis, a budget-balancing technocrat who took care to distance himself from his party's egalitarian traditions. It was all about "competence," Dukakis said, not "ideology." Not surprisingly, the public chose flag-factory jingoism over tepid, complacent centrism.

The disgust I felt that Election Day made me physically ill, and so I hope you will excuse me if I skip over all the preposterous variations on the populist theme worked in the years since then by such flag-waving champions of the working man as Oliver North, Newt Gingrich, Rush Limbaugh, Bill O'Reilly, Glenn Beck, Sarah Palin; or by George Bush's son Dubya; or by the NRA, or by Fox News, or by Rick Santelli and the Tea Party movement. I am sick of them all.

Still, let us genuflect before the superhuman perversity of the thing. Tax cuts, union busting, and deregulation—the historic achievements of right-wing populism—have led us straight back to the massively skewed economic arrangements of the 1890s. It takes a kind of hallucinatory bravado to call yourself a populist while cracking down on workers and ignoring antitrust laws, which the Reagan administration and its successors did. It's like a banker calling himself a freedom fighter because he likes Basque cuisine. It's like a slumlord signing his eviction notices, "Yours in solidarity."

THE CAREER OF one particular right-wing warrior holds special significance for our story: Patrick J. Buchanan, who has worked variously as a newspaper columnist, a speechwriter for Richard Nixon, communications director for Ronald Reagan, a TV pundit, and who also ran three insurgent campaigns for the presidency. Along the way, he did as much as anyone to reorient our understanding of populism. It was Buchanan who coined

Nixon's famous phrase "silent majority," and who urged him to cast himself as the embodiment of a middle-American uprising against elites; it was Buchanan who roared, in a speech at the 1992 Republican convention, that the libs had launched a "cultural war" against ordinary Americans.

Buchanan enthusiastically embraced the term "populist" during his presidential campaigns, seeming to understand that it ennobled his neo-medieval views; to this day on his website he can be seen posing with a pitchfork to emphasize his kinship with the angry agrarians of old. Strictly speaking, however, his claim to the title is weak: Buchanan is a lifelong Washingtonian whose ugly insinuations about Jews and Nazis and the Holocaust are well known. Getting more people to vote, he has even claimed, is the diabolical method by which liberals are going to "dispossess" good, reputable citizens.[31]

Bigotry and suspiciousness are not unusual on the Far Right, of course. What distinguished Pat Buchanan from his fellow Republicans was the startling innovation he brought to their primary contests: ripping corporate America and his own party for betraying working-class people with international trade agreements. Among conservatives this sneak attack was considered shocking, since it came from a man who virtually worshipped Ronald Reagan, destroyer of working-class organizations and the ultimate author of those trade agreements.*

---

* Among other things, Buchanan's victory in the New Hampshire primary in 1996 triggered a remarkable anti-populist outburst from conservative intellectual Bill Kristol. Republicans, Kristol griped, had shown "almost too much concern and attention for, quote, the people—that is, the people's will, their prejudices and their foolish opinions. And in a certain sense, we're all paying the price for that now. . . . After all, we conservatives

Still, it made for good theater, and in the course of his offen-sives against his old friends, Buchanan could sometimes sound like a 1930s labor leader, blasting GOP warhorse Bob Dole as "the bellhop of the Business Roundtable" and standing outside a shuttered factory to speak on behalf of the "losers from these trade deals."[32]

Populism was "all an act with this Beltway Bozo," a Bos-ton newspaper columnist fumed, but nevertheless Buchanan succeeded in making the act seem noticeably more authen-tic.[33] Every Republican was denouncing elites back then, but Buchanan had gone from attacking the cultural elite for hat-ing the flag to attacking the corporate elite as well. He did it, even more significantly, just as the traditional party of labor was recasting itself as trade-friendly "New Democrats."

In the run-up to the 2000 elections, a New York real estate developer with appalling taste but high political ambitions, Donald Trump, vied against Buchanan for the top spot on a third-party ticket. In the course of this contest Trump called Buchanan a "neo-Nazi" and a "Hitler lover," deplored the way he picked on Jews, and wrote an op-ed for the *Los Angeles Times* depicting Buchanan as a busy little bigot who had a put-down for just about everyone. "On slow days, he attacks gays, immi-grants, welfare recipients, even Zulus."[34]

But by the time of his own presidential run in 2016, Trump had pretty much taken over Buchanan's old program, from the ecumenical bigotry right down to his 1992 campaign slogan, "America First." Trump had always been critical of America's trade practices, and now he seemed to understand that the real

are on the side of the lords and barons." Quoted in Lloyd Grove, "The Castle Storms Back," *Washington Post*, February 23, 1996, p. C1.

audience for such a critique was not his fellow business leaders but American workers, abandoned by the increasingly upper-class Democratic Party.[35]

Buchanan, for his part, chortled with delight to behold the Trump phenomenon, which he described as "the future." Trump had "hard proof these trade deals have de-industrialized America," Buchanan told the *Washington Post*: "From 2000 to 2010, the U.S. lost 55,000 factories and 6 million manufacturing jobs." When the *Post* asked him how Trump should proceed with his presidential campaign, Buchanan came back with a reply that should have rung every alarm bell in Washington: "After securing the party base, go for victory in Pennsylvania, Ohio, Michigan and Wisconsin, by campaigning against the Clinton trade policies . . . and on a new Trump trade agenda to re-industrialize America."[36] Those remarks were published in January 2016, a year before Trump would be sworn in as president after taking exactly those four states.

Buchanan provided the model but it took a political entrepreneur named Steve Bannon to mold Donald Trump's loud-mouthed opportunism into the full-blown thing the world has come to know as "populism." Class was central to the insurgency Bannon believed he summoned up as Trump's chief campaign executive. Although Bannon once worked as an executive at Goldman Sachs, he is the product of what one profile called a "blue-collar, union and Democratic family" and was said to feel "an unreconstructed sense of class awareness, or bitterness—or betrayal." Betrayal, specifically, by the two main political parties, which promised such fine things to "the workingman" and yet always chose the elite when the going got tough.[37]

Betrayal, more specifically, by Wall Street. It seems that Bannon's dad, a salt-of-the-earth type, got badly played during the 2008 financial crisis, persuaded to panic by a financial huckster on TV and to sell—at almost the exact bottom, of course—his little hoard of shares in AT&T, the company where he spent his working life. "The only net worth my father had beside his tiny little house was that AT&T stock," Bannon seethed shortly after the 2016 election. "And nobody is held accountable? All these firms get bailed out. There's no equity taken from anybody. There's no one in jail. These companies are all overleveraged, and everyone looked the other way."[38]

As Buchanan had done with trade deals, so Bannon did with the bank bailouts: he swiped the outrage that should have belonged to the Left. Democratic officeholders never really contested his grab for it, of course: their energy was all going into claiming that everything was OK, that the problem had been solved, that there was no reason for the economic grievances expressed by people like Elizabeth Warren or Bernie Sanders.

So the Right stepped in, claiming leadership of this generation's revolt against the financial establishment. For Steve Bannon, the financial crisis and the bailouts were the "inciting incident" for the global populist rebellion he wanted to lead.

The movement in the United States—and the one that I am associated with worldwide—is anti-elite. We believe that what I call the "Party [of] Davos"—this kind of scientific, engineering, managerial, financial, cultural elite—has taken the world in the wrong direction, buying into globalization to the detriment of the "little guy." And so this is really a representation of anti-elitism, and really about having the little guy get a piece of the action.[39]

Republicans had been performing indignation against a shadowy "liberal elite" for decades, but now Bannon came close to identifying society's true dominant class. In the process, he swiped some of the classic formulations of the American Left. "We have socialism in the United States for the very wealthy, and the very poor, and a brutal form of Darwinian capitalism for everybody else," Bannon said on one occasion.[40] He has spoken often of his dream of turning the GOP, that mighty fortress of bankers and billionaires, of fat cats and war hawks, into a "workers' party," which is what the original Populists tried to build in 1892.* In his brief career in the West Wing, Bannon reportedly fantasized about inflicting an old-fashioned 44 percent marginal tax rate on high-earning individuals.

On the campaign trail, Donald Trump was playing a similar game. On the issue of trade, for example, he took an unusual stance for a Republican, constantly criticizing NAFTA and trade with China, the bêtes noires of organized labor, and reaching out to alienated, white, working-class voters, the rank and file of so many historical protest movements. He said he cared so very much about the people of the deindustrialized zones and their sufferings. He claimed to feel for the victims of the opioid epidemic.

The billionaire did his best to sound like a protest candidate, angry to see ordinary Americans abused by the mighty.

---

* Bannon expressed this idea to Robert Kuttner in an amazing interview published in the left-wing magazine the *American Prospect* on October 6, 2017. Bannon said it again to the *Guardian* in an interview published on December 17, 2019. Donald Trump himself has said almost exactly the same thing. See the story by Josh Green, "How to Get Trump Elected When He's Wrecking Everything You Built," *Bloomberg Businessweek*, May 26, 2016.

In his final TV commercial of the 2016 race, he tapped the zillion-volt themes of perfidious financial elites and the nobility of the common man. He denounced what he called "the establishment" as follows:

> It's a global power structure that is responsible for the economic decisions that have robbed our working class, stripped our country of its wealth, and put that money into the pockets of a handful of large corporations and political entities.
>
> The only thing that can stop this corrupt machine is you. The only force strong enough to save our country is us. The only people brave enough to vote out this corrupt establishment is you, the American people.

Let us pause here and acknowledge how strange this is: a conservative was assailing the "global power structure." A Republican was claiming deindustrialization as one of the great causes of the Right. And he was doing so in language that bordered on the idealistic. With a few changes, Trump's monologue might have been uttered by a Democrat of the old school—which was certainly his campaign's intention.[41]

The most forthright statement of Trumpian populism, if that's the name for it, was his inaugural address, which Trump took as another occasion to denounce "the establishment" in characteristically Bannonesque tones. An assemblage of one-line clichés, it saw the billionaire declaring that his rise to the presidency represented no mere trade-off between parties but rather a transfer of power "from Washington, D.C." to "you, the American people." He also declared, in a shout-out to the 1930s, that "the forgotten men and women of our country will be forgotten no longer" and described the landscape of deindustrialization as "rusted-out factories scattered like tombstones across the landscape of our nation."

And then . . . the working-class hero in the Oval Office delivered a landmark tax cut for the rich. Trump deregulated Wall Street banks, too. With his attacks on Obamacare, the president did his part to make our capitalist system just a little more brutal and Darwinian for ordinary people. He turned over the judiciary to the elites of the Federalist Society. He turned over the economy to the Chamber of Commerce. He turned the EPA over to polluters. He ran the U.S. government in a way designed to enrich and empower himself. The one leadership task to which Trump took with enthusiasm—rolling back the regulatory state—is essentially an attack on one of the few institutions in Washington designed to help working-class Americans. If this is populism, the word has truly come to mean nothing.

It is a commonplace of Trump theory to depict the forty-fifth president as utterly without precedent, a man whose every word is a falsehood and whose every move is a constitutional crisis. But as these gross betrayals of his base remind us, Trump is far more a culmination of long-term right-wing trends than he is a divergence from them. The ridiculous nickname his supporters applied to him in 2016, the "blue-collar billionaire," summarized perfectly the Reagan-era idea that tycoons are regular guys just like workers. Trump's war on the media is just an old melody from the Nixon era that he has chosen to play in a pounding fortissimo. Trump's broad, careless bigotry is just a slightly more open expression of the prejudice that has tickled the right-wing mind ever since George Wallace. Trump's fascination with tariffs—he is a "tariff man," he announced in 2018—is merely a return to the habits of William McKinley, who was known as the "Napoleon of Protection."

Nor is Steve Bannon's populism much more genuine. Listen to this brassy, assertive man talk for more than a few minutes and you start to realize that there's nothing beneath the surface froth. The whole right-wing populist revolt of 2016, you start to suspect, was little more than a clever conservative outreach program, an effort to gin up the fury of the disinherited without actually doing anything for them. Winning was not even necessarily Trump's goal. He and his Republicans prevailed by accident, and by the most un-populist of means: by the Electoral College; by gerrymandering; by vote-suppressing.

And, once again, by the dazzling folly of the other side. In 2016, Trump defeated a better-funded and far more competent opponent, a Democrat who was advised by the best consultants in the business and behind whom the nation's financial and cultural and media elites stood united. But in their revulsion against Trump's ugly rhetoric, the Democrats committed an elementary mistake, dismissing the anti-elitist impulse itself because the man who was thought to embody it was so manifestly a blowhard.

What they failed to understand is what centrist Democrats have persistently failed to understand since the 1970s: technocratic competence isn't enough, especially when that competence somehow never means improving the lives of working people. Just because the imbecile Trump denounced elites doesn't mean those elites are a legitimate ruling class. Just because the hypocrite Trump pretended to care about deindustrialization doesn't mean deindustrialization is of no concern. Just because the brute Trump mimicked the language of proletarian discontent doesn't mean working people are "deplorables."

8

Let Us Now Scold Uncouth Men

The long debate over populism that I have traced in this book has been, in part, a debate over image and rhetoric. But it has also been about something more solid: how liberals are to understand their relationship to the country they want to reform and the people they wish to lead. One liberal model—the elite paradigm—admires expertise and looks to highly educated professionals to make the right decisions on our behalf. The other—the populist model—looks to ordinary people as the ultimate repository of the democratic genius.

For many years, the Democratic Party followed the populist model; that's what many of its leaders thought democracy was all about. But beginning in the 1970s, liberalism began to change. Over the course of countless intra-party debates, the Democrats came to think of themselves not as the voice of working-class people at all but as a sort of coming together of the learned and the virtuous.

They came to this understanding, ironically, at the historical moment when populism, as a generalized hostility to the establishment, was sweeping the country. From Madison Avenue to the classic rock radio station in your sad hometown, Americans were imagining themselves to be rebels against rules and tradition and authority. Even conservatives were posturing as insurgents. The only group that seemed to have trouble embracing this new mood was the Democratic Party.

And so we come at last to the shabby synthesis to which this book's many competing strands have been leading us all along: As conservatives trumpeted their uprising, liberals turned against it all. They became anti-populists.

The dominant faction of the Democratic Party decided they wanted no part of any systematic criticism of big business or monopoly or the financial industry. They shied away from building or supporting mass movements. The idea of putting together a coalition of working-class people was one they came to regard with deep distaste.

Scorning ideology and passion, insisting that our problems were technical in nature—this was the shorthand version of what became the Democratic philosophy. The answer to the class-based onslaught of the Right, Democrats began to believe, was to surrender their own claims to the populist tradition and to get past ideology altogether.

When compared to the party's record in the New Deal era, this was not a particularly successful electoral strategy. Until very recently, however, none of the party's setbacks over the years caused their thought leaders to reconsider the decision to become the party of the white-collar elite. Instead they used what power they had to encourage investment banking and to secure trade agreements that were designed not to grow but to hollow out American industry. When challenged by constituents who found themselves on the receiving end of such policies, Democrats would roll out economists and political scientists to inform working people that what had happened to them was the consequence of inevitability, of economic progress itself.

"Populism" became a term of anathema for the party's thinkers. In a celebrated book from 1992, the fledgling pundit Mickey Kaus advised Democrats to abandon their traditional concern for economic equality and to resist the people he called "Money Liberal populists"; Dems had to stop listening to labor unions, he said, and visibly sever their ties with the black "underclass." Similar denunciations were a common thread in the publications of the Democratic Leadership Council, where you could see populists defined as those who "resist the changes stemming from a New Economy" and who longed pointlessly for "the glory days" when Americans had "stable jobs at big corporations."[1]

The "big corporations" line was an interesting twist, but the essence of the argument was the same as ever. Once again, populists were defined as people who foolishly refused the future, crying about their beloved toilers when everyone could see that the only ones that mattered were white-collar professionals—the "Learning Class," to use the name co-invented for them by political scientist William Galston. What the innovative dynamism of the Learning Class represented, declared a 1998 manifesto co-authored by Galston, was the power of higher ed and the way that "millions of Americans are surging into the ranks of the upper middle class and wealthy." Americans were getting smart, Americans were getting rich, and therefore the Democratic Party had to become the party of the smart and the rich, of the "better-educated upscale voters" who wanted private retirement accounts but weren't so keen on public schools.[2]

Post-ideological ideas like these soon became the common sense of the party's dominant faction. Democrats had put the New Deal behind them and remade themselves as leaders for an age of innovation and flexibility, affluence and sophistication, investment bankers and tech billionaires. When their turn in power came in 2008, new-style Democratic leaders declined to break up Wall Street banks. They delivered a version of national health insurance that, amazingly, did not inconvenience Big Pharma or private insurance companies. Silicon Valley executives, radiating futurific exuberance, swarmed through the Barack Obama White House and its would-be successor organization, the Hillary Clinton presidential campaign, helping usher the nation into a new golden age of cyber-transformation.

Right until the end, this post-ideological, Learning Class fantasy ambled high-mindedly along. A month before the 2016 election, President Obama hosted "South by South Lawn," a White House–specific version of the famous Texas innovation festival. Under a perfect October sky, Hollywood stars rubbed elbows with climate scientists while audience members (chosen in a merit-based admissions process) gazed at colorful conceptual art and heard about creative solutions for poverty and disease. The president expressed confidence, in that low-key way of his, that we would overcome global warming "because we happen to be the most innovative and dynamic business and entrepreneurial sector in the world." It was consensus liberalism's last moment of supreme self-assurance, and so unruffled was the performance that one journalistic fan was moved to dub Obama our "commander in cool."[3]

The Democratic presidential campaign, which expected to rotate Hillary Clinton smoothly into Obama's office a few months after that golden afternoon, exemplified this air of unflappable complacency. If "affinity among the elites" was the ultimate objective of modern politics, as Edward Shils said back in 1956, the Democrats achieved a state of nirvana that fall. Clinton's campaign not only promised consensus; it was itself an act of consensus, with seats at the table for representatives from Wall Street, Silicon Valley, and the national security apparatus. Every orthodoxy was included. For once the Democrat outraised and outspent her Republican rival. In the nation's college towns and affluent, Learning Class suburbs she was acclaimed as the embodiment of inevitability.

Just as in 1936, "affinity among the elites" included professional economists, 370 of whom signed an open letter urging people not to vote for Donald Trump. It also included the press, with journalists taking Clinton's side as a matter of Learning Class solidarity. In the newspaper endorsement race, she defeated Trump overwhelmingly, winning the editorial support of fifty-seven of the country's largest papers to Trump's two. Of the money donated by journalists to a presidential campaign, 96 percent of it went to Clinton. Nearly every media polling operation asserted that Clinton would win the election easily; in October 2016, the *New York Times* reported that Clinton was pushing her campaign into Republican states in order to enlarge her certain landslide over the racist Trump.[4]

And then on November 8 the unthinkable happened. The blowhard billionaire managed to win much of the declining industrial Midwest and with it the presidency. Shocked by the disaster, white-collar America descended into a full-blown Democracy Scare similar to the ones I have described in this book. Once again populism was identified as the culprit; it was the evil political spirit that made Trump possible and that haunted the nightmares of the affluent. That Trump had not, in fact, won the popular vote didn't slow this accelerating narrative; that his populism was a fraud was also unimportant: for the well-educated and the well-heeled, the old, familiar anti-populist tune became the inspirational anthem of the era.

LAWRENCE GOODWYN, THE great historian of mass democratic uprisings, once wrote that to build a movement like the People's Party of the 1890s or the labor movement of the 1930s, one must "connect with people *as they are in society*, that is to say, in a state that sophisticated modern observers are inclined to regard as one of 'inadequate consciousness.'"[5]

Goodwyn also warned against a politics of "individual righteousness," a tendency toward "celebrating the purity" of one's so-called radicalism. If you wish to democratize the country's economic structure, he argued, you must practice "ideological patience," a suspension of moral judgment of ordinary Americans.[6] Only then can you start to build a movement that is hopeful and powerful and that changes society forever.

If you're not interested in democratizing the country's economic structure, however, individual righteousness might be just the thing for you. This model deals with ordinary citizens by judging and purging; by canceling and scolding. It's not about building; it's about purity, about stainless moral virtue. Its favorite math is subtraction; its most cherished rhetorical form is denunciation; its goal is to bring the corps of the righteous into a tight orbit around the most righteous one of all.

What swept over huge parts of American liberalism after the disaster of November 8, 2016, was the opposite of Goodwyn's "ideological patience." It was a paroxysm of scolding, a furor for informing Trump voters what inadequate and indeed

rotten people they were. The elitist trend that had been building among liberals for decades hurried to its loud, carping con-
summation.

Where populism is optimistic about rank-and-file voters,
the variety of liberalism I have in mind regards them with a
combination of suspicion and disgust. It dreams not of organizing humanity but of policing it. It is a geyser of moral rebuke,
erupting against teenagers who have committed some act of
cultural appropriation, against the hiring of an actor for an
inappropriate role, against a public speech by someone with
unpopular views, against the wrongful dumping of household
trash, against inappropriate tree-pruning techniques spotted in
a nearby suburb. Its characteristic goal is not to get banks and
monopolies under control, as populism typically does, but to
set up a nonprofit, attract funding from banks and monopolies,
and then . . . to scold the world for its sins.

The Populists used to dream of what they called a "Cooperative Commonwealth," but today it's a vindictive commonwealth that inspires the reformer, a utopia of scolding in which
court is always in session and the righteous constantly hand
down the harshest of judgments on their economic and moral
inferiors.

WHY THE RULING class must continue to rule is always the
great theme of Democracy Scares, voiced by eminent economist
and newspaper editor alike. In our own time, even comedi-
ans have a role to play in the operation. *In Defense of Elitism*, a
2019 account of the Trump era by *Time* magazine humorist Joel
Stein, describes the essential divide between liberals and Trump
supporters like this: "Elites are people who think; populists are

people who believe." Populists are creatures of intuition and childlike impulse, people who think that facts "are indistinguishable from lies." Elites accept the expertise of experts; populism, however, is little more than "a primal scream for primordial masculinity." Just as in 1896, populism is supposed to represent the appetites and vulgar urges of the body, in revolt against the higher faculties of thought and reason.[7]

The idea of ordinary people having a say in matters of state is strictly a joke. In a precise replay of conservative humorists of 1896, the liberal humorist of 2019 laughs off the suggestion that farmers be represented on the sophisticated body that decides U.S. monetary policy: "Imagine if farmers" were involved in such decisions, Joel Stein guffaws, "trying to figure out how to establish central bank liquidity swap lines during a financial crisis." What our age urgently requires, he announces, is the opposite of that: a wide-ranging acknowledgment that elites are legitimate; that meritocracy is fair; that domination is rightful when the dominant group is made up of people who, like Stein and his friends, went to name-brand colleges. If ordinary people want things to change, I suppose, they must implore the brainy to change them. After all, democracy is, as he puts it, "a government of the nerds, by the nerds, and for the nerds."[8]

What is especially disheartening about this "defense of elitism" is the author's apparent unfamiliarity with liberalism's non-elitist past, of a time when liberalism was an expression of the democratic hopes of ordinary people. Disheartening . . . and yet utterly typical of the resistance culture of our time, where more and more one notices a frank acknowledgment of liberalism as the politics of a highly educated upper class.[9] After all, as Hillary Clinton herself put it a year after the election was over,

"I won the places that represent two-thirds of America's gross domestic product . . . the places that are optimistic, diverse, dynamic, moving forward."

What is missing from this vision of exuberant, future-minded liberalism is labor, the driving force of so many reform movements since the 1890s.

ONE STORY OF the Trump years that sticks with me was related to me by a high school student who went to a discussion of political issues with a group of progressive teenagers in an affluent part of the Washington, D.C., metro area. The group's leader went around the room asking the students what issues they considered significant and then getting a show of hands on the importance of each one. Racism was mentioned, and sexism, and LGBTQ issues, and gun control, and the environment. The student raised her hand and said, "Labor." It was, she told me, the only suggestion that drew no support at all.

That's a brief incident in a tiny corner of this country, and yet it brings us to a revealing political fact of our time: the disappearance of class from the mainstream liberal agenda. All genuine populist movements have aimed to bring working people together across barriers of race, religion, and ethnicity in order to reform capitalism. This is what defines the species; indeed, this has been one of the traditional objectives of left-wing movements since the nineteenth century.

The prophets of reproach who make up the modern Left aren't particularly interested in that, however. And once you start looking for this erasure—for this peculiar lacuna in the worldview of a certain type of liberal—you notice it everywhere. Social class is the glaring, zillion-watt absence, for example, in those anti-Trump yard signs that have become so popular in nice suburban neighborhoods and that strain for inclusiveness—

> In this house, we believe:
> Black lives matter
> Women's rights are human rights
> No human is illegal
> Science is real
> Love is love
> And kindness is everything

—but that say nothing about the right to organize or to earn a living wage.

Cataloging the history of American protest or disobedience has become something of a cultural set piece of the Trump era, only with one branch of that history always conspicuously left out.[10] Charles Blow, a solidly anti-Trump columnist for the *New York Times*, spent much of 2017 and '18 remembering different forms of historical resistance that modern-day liberals might look to for inspiration but almost never mentioned labor unions or strikes. He name-checked Selma, Stonewall, ACT UP, Occupy Wall Street, Black Lives Matter, and the 2016 protests at Standing Rock—but largely failed to notice the one form of resistance that is an ordinary element of economic life, that happens in cities and towns across America all the time.[11]

The work that really drove this home for me was "A Century of Protest," a 2018 video feature produced by the *New Yorker* magazine that was comprised of footage of protests throughout American history. When I watched the video—after sitting through an advertisement from Prada—I saw some fifty-eight different clips of historical footage covering everything from suffragette marches of 1913 to the big 1987 ACT UP protest, with a special emphasis on the civil rights movement, Vietnam War protests, and present-day Black Lives Matter confrontations. Communists and even the Ku Klux Klan were represented in this all-inclusive roll call of protest. But mainstream organized labor was not. In this version of history there is evidently no room for the AFL-CIO's enormous 1981 Solidarity Day rally on the National Mall, or for the Flint sit-down strike, or for the Memphis sanitation workers, or for red-shirted teachers in Arizona. The old WPA mural has been airbrushed over.*

One explanation for this omission, no doubt, is the much-commented-upon defection of white, working-class voters from the Democratic Party to Trump's Republicans. For a certain kind of Democratic partisan, this development has had the predictable consequence of rendering unsayable anything that smacks of traditional class grievances. Talk about the deindustrialization of vast parts of the country, the decimation of unions, the destruction of small towns by monopoly forces, and this kind of person hears "Trump voter." The enlightened liberal shuns such people. They are to be scolded, not championed.

Then there is the straightforward element of class. When affluent suburban lawns advertise a form of liberalism that has been cleansed of solidarity with workers, the self-interest of the gesture is obvious. When a history of protest is sponsored by a luxury fashion company, the results are, as they say in France, overdetermined.

---

* Of course, there were no motion-picture cameras on hand to record the get-togethers of the Populists, but other farmer protest movements (for example, the Farm Holiday strike of 1932 or the nationwide Tractorcade of 1979) were lavishly photographed, and yet they, too, are always overlooked in documentaries of this kind.

This pattern of erasure has muddled liberal conversation on economic issues for years. Take the critical matter of trade: On the campaign trail in 2016, Donald Trump made a point of loudly (if incoherently) criticizing the nation's trade agreements, deals that had been strongly opposed by labor unions but also happened to be the proud, defining achievement of the global-minded centrist wing of the Democratic Party. Trump was obviously using the issue to drive a wedge between the Democrats and one of their biggest constituent groups. At the time, however, liberal pundits pretty much ignored the matter.

Once Trump had won, a panicked punditburo swung into action, insisting in a crescendo of consensus that trade had little to do with the country's deindustrialization; that it was pretty much all due to technological factors; that what happened to manufacturing workers was therefore unavoidable. After the dust had settled, many commentators changed their mind on this question, quietly acknowledging the disastrous consequences of ill-crafted trade deals. But what matters for our purposes is the initial reaction, which was virtually unanimous and unfolded along the same lines as in 1896: the rationality of working-class grievances had to be denied.[12]

The outcome of the 2016 election, the same punditburo insisted, could not and must not be explained by reference to economic factors or to long-term, class-related trends. Yes, lots of Trump voters said they were motivated by economic concerns; yes, Trump talked about economic issues all the time; and yes, the economic stagnation of Trump-voting areas is obvious to anyone who has gone there. And also: every time our post-partisan liberal leaders deregulated banks and then turned around and told working-class people that their misfortunes were attributable to their poor education . . . every time they did this and then thought to themselves, "They have nowhere else to go" . . . they made the Trump disaster a little more likely.

But to acknowledge those plain facts was to come dangerously close to voicing the intolerable heresy that the D.C. opinion cartel dubbed the "economic anxiety" thesis—the idea that people voted for Trump out of understandable worries about wages or opioids or unemployment or deindustrialization. The reason this was intolerable, one suspects, is because it suggested that there was a rational element to certain groups' support for Trump and also that there was something less than A+ about the professional-class Camelot over which the Democrats presided for eight years. Just as in 1896, the rationality of certain low-class voters was ruled out from the start.

My point here is not to suggest that Trump is a "very stable genius," as he likes to say, or that he led a genuine populist insurgency; in my opinion, he isn't and he didn't. What I mean to show is that the message of anti-populism is the same as ever: the lower orders, it insists, are driven by irrationality, bigotry, authoritarianism, and hate; democracy is a problem because it gives such people a voice. The difference today is that enlightened liberals are the ones mouthing this age-old anti-populist catechism.

In 1966, AFTER losing a race for a California state senate seat, the political prankster Dick Tuck went on TV to concede and griped, "The people have spoken, the bastards."

Today the humor behind Tuck's legendary line is not so funny. Rebuking the people for delivering awkward election results became a serious, mainstream exercise after 2016. I mean by this something distinct from the social-science worries about populism that I discussed in the introduction: this was a red-hot moral rebuke of the millions. America was a wicked land and its people were bastards: racists, sexists, facilitators of evil who actually deserved the postindustrial and opioid-saturated bleakness of their red-state lives.*

It started with Hillary Clinton's disastrous decision, while campaigning in September 2016, to describe certain Trump supporters as "deplorables" and "irredeemables" because they were "racist, sexist, homophobic," and so on. Clinton, of course, was a practicing politician; she realized her blunder immediately and clarified that her dispute was with Trump himself and not the rank-and-file American.

Mainstream liberal commentators, on the other hand, never looked back. "Resentment is no excuse for bald-faced stupidity," was Garrison Keillor's assessment of the results, published in the *Washington Post* two days after the election. If working people were no longer moving upward in life, he continued, they had only themselves to blame. Maybe they should "encourage good habits" and make sure "the kids aren't plugged into electronics day and night" instead of "whooping it up for the candidate of cruelty and ignorance."

In an essay published a few days later, *Slate* columnist Jamelle Bouie suggested that it was "morally grotesque" to "insist Trump's backers are good people." The instantly famous title of his effort was, "There's No Such Thing as a Good Trump Voter"; his subtitle declared, "They Don't Deserve Your Empathy."

---

* Here is an actual headline of a *Daily Kos* story that ran about a month after the 2016 election: "Be happy for coal miners losing their health insurance. They're getting exactly what they voted for."

Writing in the *Boston Globe* a month later, NYU professor Charles Taylor insisted that Trump voters should feel "shame" for their ignorance. Republicans believed all manner of falsehoods, he thundered, "and still this imperviousness to fact pales next to the racism and xenophobia and misogyny—in other words, the moral ignorance—that Trump's supporters wallowed in."

As the ignominy of Trump's supporters expanded, the saintliness of his vanquished opponent gleamed ever brighter. Writing in the *Guardian* the week after the election, the literary scholar Sarah Churchwell insisted that what happened in November 2016 was in no way attributable to any shortcoming of Hillary Clinton. "It is time to stop suggesting . . . that Clinton failed us," she announced. "The truth is, we failed her." In not electing Clinton president, the people themselves had fallen short.

None of these were the views of radicals. Each of these statements—and I chose these from hundreds of similar expressions of moral disgust—was the product of a reputable writer or a high-ranking academic, published or broadcast by an established news outlet. It was our country's best-informed opinionators who were most determined to believe in the essential monstrousness of tens of millions of their fellow citizens.

Why did these liberals adopt this ferociously anti-populist line so quickly? There were many conventional explanations for Trump's catastrophic win other than the general wickedness of the American people. Surely some role was played by Trump's stand on trade and his rhetorical commitment to social-insurance programs, both highly unusual positions for a Republican, which might have made voters more willing to take a chance on him than they would have on, say, Mitt Romney.

There were his promises of populist-style reform, none of them sincere, but which sometimes sounded genuinely good. I mean, who doesn't despise the "power structure"? Who doesn't want to "drain the swamp" of Washington? Who doesn't want their mortgaged farm or their postindustrial town or their crumbling neighborhood to be made "great again"?[13]

But acknowledging that some Trump voters might be desperate and otherwise decent people became a thing unsayable in the small world of America's opinion class.* The total depravity of those people was the only acceptable explanation. Hillary Clinton had used the word "irredeemable" to describe some Trump voters, and her moralistic judgment far outlived her campaign. Trump's rise was not about politics, it was about sin, and it was the task of progressives to scold the unrighteous for their iniquity.

To scold . . . and conspicuously withhold forgiveness. In what was surely the strangest Trump-era fad of them all, various high-minded progressive commentators announced that they so hated the world that they were never, *ever* going to absolve those who had trespassed politically against them. Reasoning in 2019 that "conservatives spat in our face and elected an abusive, racist, misogynist criminal," the author and blogger Amanda Marcotte advised against forgiving rank-and-file Republican

---

* The exceptions to this tend to prove the rule. In early 2017, the liberal *New York Times* columnist Nicholas Kristof began urging his readers to show empathy toward certain kinds of Trump voters, specifically the marginal ones who were struggling with difficult economic situations. "Tolerance is a liberal value," Kristof reminded his audience. A few weeks later, the columnist recounted the outpouring of rage he had received since making this suggestion, writing that "Nothing I've written since the election has engendered more anger from people who usually agree with me than my periodic assertions that Trump voters are human, too."

voters. Should liberals just let matters slide as we had allegedly done with people who voted for George W. Bush, she asked rhetorically,

> Or should progressives impose social consequences, declining friendships and putting a chill on family relationships, in order to send the message that supporting Trump was not OK and will not be shrugged off as a harmless lark?

Blacklisting was one of the weapons to which this ferocious moral crusade inevitably turned. First, liberal thought leaders called upon private businesses to shun Trump administration employees when those worthies left government for the private sector; then, at almost exactly the same time, centrist Democrats tried to deploy this powerful new weapon against the party's left wing, with the Democratic Congressional Campaign Committee announcing that it would refuse to do business with any political consultancies that worked for challengers to Democratic incumbents.[14] Neither of these episodes, let us note, was an attempt to stop Washington's notorious "revolving door," only to prevent certain kinds of people from passing through it. To be sure, I have no sympathy for Trump officials who are prevented from cashing in after their "service" is completed. What I find shocking is how comfortable liberals have become with the weapons of the boss.

A minor yet telling illustration of this newfound comfort came up a few years ago when Lena Dunham—a much-celebrated TV star who spoke at the 2016 Democratic convention—happened to be delayed in an airport somewhere. While wandering the concourses, Dunham decided to contact corporate management and turn in some airline employees she thought she overheard making transphobic remarks—and doing all of it on social media, so the whole world could admire her as she snitched. "At this moment in history we should be teaching our employees about love and inclusivity," she tweeted. I was struck by that "our employees" line: not only did Dunham take for granted that her followers had employees but that employment is a relationship in which "love and inclusivity" are handed down by bosses to workers.

Needless to say, Dunham was applauded for her action; *Teen Vogue* opined that "it's important to recognize the importance of standing up to transphobia."[15]

Indeed it is. But might there have been a different way to go about it, a way that showed more ideological patience? I can't help but think that Dunham would have achieved a better result had she actually introduced herself to the transphobic people in person and talked it over with them.* Urging a boss to punish a worker for an overheard remark is the kind of officiousness that people sometimes resent.

Similarly, scolding people for having morally obtuse politics may be the very worst way to get them to change those politics. As of this writing, Trump voters have remained remarkably loyal to the man they chose in 2016, far more loyal than voters for other politicians who (like Trump) turned out to be incompetent or corrupt. One reason for this stubbornness, I suspect, is the constant hailstorm of rebuke and shame that has been directed against those voters from on high for the last

---

* A celebrated study published in 2016 showed that talking to someone about their prejudice against trans people was an effective method for reducing that prejudice. (See David Broockman and Joshua Kalla, "Durably Reducing Transphobia," *Science* 352, no. 6282 [April 8, 2016]: 220–24.)

four years. In other words, the scolding style may actually have served to confirm them in their dreadful choice rather than to persuade them to move away from it.[16]

What is certain is that the liberalism of scolding will never give rise to the kind of mass movement that this country needs. It is almost entirely a politics of individual righteousness, an angry refusal of Goodwyn's "ideological patience." Its appeal comes not from the prospect of democratizing the economy but from the psychic satisfaction of wagging a finger in some stupid proletarian's face, forever.

WHAT THESE EXAMPLES show us is a generation of centrist liberals collectively despairing over democracy itself. After turning their backs on working-class issues, traditionally one of the core concerns of left parties, Democrats stood by while right-wing demagoguery took root and thrived. Then, after the people absorbed a fifty-year blizzard of fake populist propaganda, Democrats turned against the idea of "the people" altogether.[17]

America was founded with the phrase "We the People," but William Galston, co-inventor of the concept of the Learning Class, urges us to get over our obsession with popular sovereignty. As he writes in *Anti-Pluralism*, his 2018 attack on populism, "We should set aside this narrow and complacent conviction; there are viable alternatives to the people as sources of legitimacy."[18]

There certainly are. In the pages of this book, we have seen anti-populists explain that they deserve to rule because they are better educated, or wealthier, or more rational, or harder working. The contemporary culture of constant moral scolding is in perfect accordance with this way of thinking; it is a new iteration of the old elitist fantasy.

The liberal establishment I am describing in this chapter is anti-populist not merely because it dislikes Donald Trump—who is in no way a genuine populist—but because it is populism's opposite in nearly every particular. Its political ambition for the people is not to bring them together in a reform movement but to scold them, to shame them, and to teach them to defer to their superiors. It doesn't seek to punish Wall Street or Silicon Valley; indeed, the same bunch that now rebukes and cancels and blacklists could not find a way to punish elite bankers after the global financial crisis back in 2009. This liberalism desires to merge with these institutions of private privilege, to enlist their power for what it imagines to be "good." The wealthy liberal neighborhoods of America have become utopias of scolding because scolding is how this kind of concentrated power relates to ordinary citizens. This isn't "working-class authoritarianism"; it's the opposite. Those people on top, this kind of liberalism says: They have more than you because they deserve to have more than you. Those fine people dominate you because they are better than you.

PERHAPS THE MOST lasting distinction between populism and its opposite is one of mood. Populism was and is relentlessly optimistic—about people, about political possibilities, about life, and about America in general.

Anti-populism is all about despair. Its attitude toward ordinary humans is bitter. Its hope for human redemption is nil. Its vision of the common good is bleak. Its dark mood gives us books with titles like *In Defense of Elitism* and *Against Democracy.*

Its darkest moments of all come when it contemplates

climate change. I have in mind a much-discussed op-ed the *New York Times* ran in December 2018, some two years after the election of Donald Trump shredded the tidy worldview of the Learning Class. The article I'm thinking of was not a political statement per se, but the philosophy professor who wrote it, Todd May, is a well-known anti-Trump activist on the campus where he teaches. To me, his essay's appearance on the nation's most prominent liberal op-ed page felt like a political act, like the final verdict of a dejected elite on a stubborn population that refuses to heed its admonitions . . . that revels in falsehoods and that persistently chooses ridiculous demagogues over responsible experts.

May's subject is human extinction—whether it should happen or whether it shouldn't. The professor phrases his indictment of mankind with a certain delicacy, but it's impossible to miss his point. We are a harmful species, he charges, "causing unimaginable suffering to many of the animals that inhabit" the earth. He names climate change and factory farming as the worst of our trespasses, and declares that "if this were all to the story there would be no tragedy. The elimination of the human species would be a good thing, full stop."

But there are other considerations, the professor admits. People do some worthwhile things. Also, it would be cruel "to demand of currently existing humans that they should end their lives." May's answer, ultimately, is to have it both ways: "It may well be, then, that the extinction of humanity would make the world better off and yet would be a tragedy."

This kind of highbrow pessimism, this barely concealed longing for the death of the species, is an attitude you come across all the time these days in enlightened liberal circles.[19] It is the inevitable flip side of the moralistic politics I have described in this chapter: the wages for our sins; the recompense for our irredeemable stupidity.

Every time I encounter sentiments like these in this abattoir of idealism known as Washington, my mind goes back to my old city of Chicago, to a noisy and rusty and callous place that no one is ever sentimental about but where I like to remember how ordinary Americans used to live their lives, concerned with work and play and maybe getting ahead someday.

I think of Carl Sandburg, the twentieth century's "Poet of the People," a man who saw no contradiction between human sin and human life. And I think of Sandburg's "Chicago," the greatest populist poem of them all, which acknowledges the town's vulgarity, all its tawdry sins—"They tell me you are wicked"; "they tell me you are crooked"; "they tell me you are brutal"—all charges that are as true today as they were in 1914.

But "Chicago" is not an anthem of scolding. It is a rejection of scolding. It's a song about loving life despite it all, loving the life of the people, even in the midst of all the grinding industrialized awfulness:

> Under the smoke, dust all over his mouth, laughing with white teeth,
> Under the terrible burden of destiny laughing as a young man laughs,
> Laughing even as an ignorant fighter laughs who has never lost a battle,
> Bragging and laughing that under his wrist is the pulse, and under his ribs the heart of the people,
>   Laughing!

The Question

The story of populism and anti-populism is a dialectic of hope and cynicism. We have seen how a party of democratic inclusion chose to remodel itself as the expression of an elite consensus, and how a party of concentrated private power started passing itself off as a down-home friend of ordinary Americans. This historic inversion—so bizarre when you step back and think about it—has had precisely the effects that you would expect it to have. The legatees of Thomas Jefferson, lukewarm in all things, no longer really believe their own founding philosophy; the hard-eyed heirs of the robber barons, meanwhile, have swiped the democratic vocabulary of their enemies; and between these two parties the greatest democracy in the world has become a paradise for the privileged.

But there is light at the bottom of this vortex. Today, both elite liberalism and right-wing demagoguery stand before us utterly discredited. The fraudulence of the Right's bait and switch is so plain it feels like a waste of space even to describe it. Instead of redeeming our communities and taking down the elites, as the Republicans promised, they found yet more ways to make the rich richer. Instead of draining the swamp, they have given us government-by-lobbyist; government-by-polluter; government-by-general. Under the stupid, swaggering leadership of our current commander in chief, it is not just the executive branch in Washington that has been corrupted; it is all of us. Lying is normal, Trump has taught us; it is natural for officeholders to line their pockets; incompetence at the top is the American way; justice is for the wealthy; bigotry is no big deal; money and power are the only things that matter.

The exhaustion of centrist, post-partisan liberalism is just as obvious. The disappointing experience of the Obama years made it clear that the ruling clique of the Democratic Party lacks the fortitude to confront the plutocratic onslaught of the last few decades. Even the most high-scoring meritocrats, we learned, will not take on the hierarchy to which they owe their exalted status.

The technocratic faction's other selling point—that they alone can check the rightward-charging Republicans—lies in a million pieces on the floor after 2016. Not even when the GOP backed the least competent and most unpopular presidential candidate of all time could the Democrats' consensus-minded leaders defeat him.

A joyless politics of reprimand is all that centrism has left: a politics of individual righteousness that regards the public not as a force to be organized but as a threat to be scolded and disciplined. Unfortunately, it is an ineffective politics in addition to an unhappy one. Plutocracy will go on even if we were to cleanse Twitter of every last problematic participant; health care will still be unaffordable even after the pundits manage to shame every last resentful Trump voter into silence. As a vehicle of reform this species of liberalism is useless.

There is another way, reader. As we have learned in these pages, there is a tradition that trusts in the people, that responds to their needs, that turns resentment into progress. That same populist tradition is and has always been at war with monopoly, with corporate authority, with billionaire privilege, with inequality. It insists and has always insisted that "too few people control too much of the money and power," as the modern-day Texas populist Jim Hightower described it to me.

Indeed, you can't really have the second part of the formula— the war on concentrated economic power—without the first part, a broad-minded acceptance of average people. That is because the only real answer to plutocracy is a mass movement of ordinary working people, hailing from all different backgrounds, brought together by a common desire to dismantle the forces that make their toil so profitless and to figure out how they might gain control over their lives.

The demand for economic democracy is how you build a mass movement of ordinary people. And a mass movement of ordinary people, in turn, is how you achieve economic democracy. Which is to say that the answer both to Trumpist fraud and to liberal elitism must come from us—from the democratic public itself.

As I write these words, under semi-quarantine due to the coronavirus pandemic, I can't help but think of the lives and livelihoods that a people-oriented healthcare system might have saved. As our endless wars drag on, I think of the road not taken—of what Bayard Rustin and his colleagues called the Freedom Budget, their proposal for a massive enlargement of the New Deal and the Great Society that would have ended unemployment while securing proper housing and health care for everyone. It was, in a sense, what all of the movements I have described here were ultimately after—the great unachieved goal of American populism. In his foreword to the 1967 booklet introducing the Freedom Budget, Martin Luther King wrote that "we shall eliminate slums for Negroes when we destroy ghettos and build new cities for *all*. We shall eliminate unemployment for Negroes when we demand full and fair employment for *all*. We shall produce an educated and skilled Negro mass when we achieve a twentieth century educational system for *all*."[1]

THIS IS NOT an idle dream. We know what genuine populism looks like; we have seen it crop up in the agrarian 1890s, in the New Deal 1930s, in the civil rights days of the 1960s.

Let me relate one final tale of democracy's promise. It's a story that starts with the *Appeal to Reason*, the legendary Kansas newspaper that began life as a supporter of the People's Party before transferring its allegiance to the Socialists. Years later, as Socialism followed Populism into oblivion, the remaining editor of the *Appeal to Reason*, a child of Jewish immigrants named Emanuel Haldeman-Julius,* cast about looking for ways to rescue the sinking publishing operation. The idea he eventually hit upon in 1919 owed much to the old Populist traditions of pamphleteering and mass popular education: left-wing essays, famous works of literature, and self-education tracts printed up in pocket-sized form and priced so low—five cents—that virtually anyone could afford them.

The People's Pocket Series, he called them, before eventually

---

* He was born Emanuel Julius but in 1916, when he married Marcet Haldeman, also a writer of note, they merged their surnames.

changing the name to the Little Blue Books. You could buy them from vending machines in railroad stations. You could get twenty titles for a dollar, postpaid from Girard, Kansas. They were great books for the common man, a bridge between the agrarian radicalism of the 1890s and the labor radicalism of the 1930s.

The Little Blue Books, Haldeman-Julius once wrote, represented "a democracy of literature" in which the highest of highbrow culture was made available to anyone who wanted it. They were not meant to be showy: their covers were unpretentious; their paper was coarse and uneven. Yet this flatly proletarian business model was an overwhelming success. Ten years after launching his cheapskate publishing empire, Haldeman-Julius had sold a hundred million of the little books. By 1951, the year he died, there were some twenty-five hundred different titles in his warehouse in Kansas; the grand total of Little Blue Books sold came to five hundred million.[2]

The books themselves are relics of an age when tramps read Zola and dirt farmers wanted to know about Goethe and every village had an atheist who could quote Tom Paine or Robert Ingersoll. Scan the biographical literature on Haldeman-Julius and you will find testimonials from people who read Little Blue Books while on strike or while in prison, people who read them on the subway train, people who passed them around in hospitals and at boardinghouses.

Haldeman-Julius's idea was not to reinforce hierarchies of taste but to demolish them—to "put all books on the same level," as he once wrote. "The door to learning and culture has been forced open," proclaimed one of his ads from the 1920s. The plain blue booklets were "not intended to decorate shelves but to enrich minds," announced another.[3]

The historian Christopher Lasch once famously declared that the professions "came into being by reducing the layman to incompetence." Haldeman-Julius's idea was to do the opposite—to undermine elites by making ordinary people capable. The Little Blue Books were emphatically about the intelligence of the "self-taught" American, about their ability to read Ibsen and Balzac on their own, about their power to undertake complicated projects by themselves: *How to Psycho-Analyze Your Neighbors; How to Be a Gate Crasher; Airplanes and How to Fly Them; How to Make Your Own Cosmetics; How to Acquire Good Taste; How to Be a Modern Mother; How to Become a Writer of Little Blue Books; How to Build Your Own Greenhouse*, and here, have a shot of Schopenhauer while you're building it.

The big idea behind the enterprise, Haldeman-Julius wrote, was to put an end to "cultural, intellectual, economic and political subservience and inferiority."

> There are men (rich and powerful) who shudder at the thought of a free world—free thinking, free living, sane behavior, mass health and happiness, individual freedom and social responsibility, the right to candid speech on any possible subject. They live on lies. I don't merely disapprove of them. I more than dislike them. I hate them with an implacable hatred.[4]

This form of populism was no "celebration of ignorance." It was a one-man campaign against the falsehoods of the mighty, against racism and intolerance, against organized religion, against superstition, against conventional interpretations of history, against orthodoxy of every kind.

For our purposes, though, it is Haldeman-Julius's campaign

against racism that means the most. Several Little Blue Books dealt with the Klan, which was generating great clouds of toxic nonsense in the twenties. In one of these, Haldeman-Julius described the Klan as a "viper," a "beast," a spreader of "poison," "bigotry," and "reaction."* In 1927 his wife, Marcet Haldeman-Julius, authored one of the most striking Little Blue Books of them all: an original account of a lynching in Little Rock, Arkansas, written so soon after the event that it reads like firsthand reportage. As the awful story unfolds, she interviews the people involved and describes the scenes in brutal detail: the cowardice of the city officials; the insane vindictiveness of the white population; the members of the mob who aren't ashamed of what they've done.[5]

The publisher was optimistic about the prospects for his campaign of enlightenment. Science, he believed, was slowly pushing back the "tyranny of bunk," loosening the grip of aristocracy and superstition. But there was an important caveat: for all his admiration of learning and science, Haldeman-Julius did not celebrate intellectual elites. One of Haldeman-Julius's titles might have been the motto for his entire operation: *The Dumbness of the Great.* What made our age of enlightenment so wonderful, he argued, was that it promised to "disseminate greatness among all the people." Experts may insist on the incompetence of the layman, but this Kansan aimed for something more democratic. Freedom and inquiry and brilliance

---

* On a happier note, the Little Blue Book series also carried important contributions from W.E.B. DuBois and NAACP leader Walter F. White, whose 1928 study of the Harlem Renaissance was published under the title *The Negro's Contribution to American Culture: The Sudden Flowering of a Genius-Laden Artistic Movement.*

could not be the property of some tiny clique: "It is the common man who has, by revolution and by the broader evolution of a new kind of civilization, been endowed with the rights of personality."[6]

What Haldeman-Julius was fighting was a war that was simultaneously *against* elitism and *in favor of* science and culture. This is contrary to everything we have been told populism stands for; it's contrary to the way we believe civilization works. Science and culture are supposed to be about rank and prestige—they are the property of the "Learning Class." And here are these coarse-grain booklets from Girard, Kansas, telling us exactly the opposite: that everyone has the spark of the divine.

This is populism in its best form. I mean this not just politically, and not just in terms of Haldeman-Julius's forthright contempt for elites and racism and mob rule, but also in his simultaneous faith in the "common man," his love for learning, and his guileless praise for Voltaire and Paine and Debs and Darrow.[7]

THE LAST POINT I want to make is this: populism wins. Not only is populism the classic, all-American response to hierarchy and plutocracy, but it is also the naturally dominant rhetorical element in our political tradition.

I make this claim even though the Populists themselves didn't get what they were after for many decades, even though the labor movement in the thirties never organized the South, even though Martin Luther King never saw the Freedom Budget enacted into law.

Still, populism has a power that technocracy and liberal

scolding and Trumpist bullshit do not because populism is
deep in the grain of the democratic personality. Americans do
not defer to their social superiors: we are natural-born egalitar-
ians. Populism is the word that gets at our incurable itch to
deflate pretentiousness of every description.

In political contests in most parts of America, the candidate
who captures this refusal of deference is, more often than not,
the candidate who wins. This is a crude and sweeping simplifi-
cation, but nevertheless it is usually true. Understood the way
I have defined it, populist protest against the economic elite
is what made the Democrats the majority party for so many
decades.

Another reason we know that anti-elitism works is because
we have seen it working against us for fifty years. The Republican Party owes its successful hold on power to adopting—
you might say "stealing"—the anti-elitist themes I have
described. From the days of Nixon to those of Trump, the
conservative revolution happened not because Americans love
polluters and disease but because Republicans sold themselves
as a party of protest against the elite. Most of the time it was
the cultural elite that was the target: the prideful people who
make movies and write newspapers; who love blasphemy but
hate the flag.

The point is so easy and so obvious that it's hard to understand why it's been so difficult for Democratic politicians to get
it: Populism is the supreme rhetorical weapon in the arsenal of
American politics. On the other hand, the impulse to identify
your goals with the elite—with *any* elite, even a moral one—is
a kind of political death wish. In a democracy, a faction that
chooses to go about its business by admiring its own moral

goodness and scolding average voters as insensitive clods is a faction that is not interested in winning.

BUT WE ARE learning. Thanks to insurgent campaigns like the one mounted by Bernie Sanders for the presidency in 2016, we know fairly precisely what a modern-day populism looks like. It would focus, of course, on economic reforms—ambitious ones, not technocratic fine-tuning. It would aim to put those reforms on the national agenda not by the strength of one candidate's popularity but by bringing together a movement of working people, by mobilizing millions of people who don't vote and don't participate and don't ordinarily have a say. It would be financed almost entirely by small individual contributions, in the classic Fred Harris manner. And it would aim to enlist millions of embittered voters—Republican voters, even—with far-reaching proposals of the kind we haven't heard for many years: universal health care, no more grotesque student debt, banking reform, a war on monopolies, a reimagining of our trade policy.

This is not just a plan to win the presidency. As Sanders himself used to say, it is a blueprint for a "political revolution," a complete reversal of the direction in which the country has been traveling for decades. And the key to making it work is movement-building on a massive scale; enlisting millions of ordinary people who have lost their faith in democracy.

Another man who understands this is the Reverend William Barber II, the North Carolina pastor who is building a modern-day Poor People's Campaign designed to pick up where Martin Luther King's effort left off back in 1968. Barber's plan is to organize poor people from every imaginable background with an eye to pulling together another unstoppable mass movement. As with other populist efforts I have described, it is the people themselves who provide the leadership. As Barber himself puts it, "the impacted people, poor people, are at the center of the leadership. We're not doing some kind of social service for them. . . . They have to be a part of setting the policies. They have to be part of the critique. Therefore we build a stage for their voice, not for ours alone."

It is an idea whose time has obviously come, and the place it must come first is the Democratic Party. The party of technocrats and consultants—of calculating triangulators and fans of the smoke-filled rooms—must eventually give way to the populism that we must have. Thus will the Democratic Party learn once again to breathe hope into those who despair.

The populism I am describing is not formless anger that might lash out in any direction. It is not racism. It is not resentment. It is not demagoguery. It is, instead, to ask the most profound question of them all: "For whom does America exist?"

I take that question from the culture critic Gilbert Seldes, who saw it as the great unanswered demand of the 1890s Populist revolt. The question was raised again in 1936, the year when Seldes wrote those words. It came up again in the 1960s. And here we are, asking it again today.[8]

For whom *does* America exist? Its billionaires? Its celebrities? Its tech companies? Are we the people just a laboring, sweating instrument for the bonanza paydays of our betters? Are we just glorified security guards, obeying orders to protect their holdings? Are we nothing more than a vast test market to be tracked and probed and hopefully sold on airline tickets, fast food, or Hollywood movies featuring some awesome new animation technology?

Or is it the other way around—are they supposed to serve us?

Let us resolve to ask that far-reaching question again: *For whom does America exist?* This time around, there can be only one possible answer.

NOTES

INTRODUCTION: THE CURE FOR THE COMMON MAN

1. As far as I can tell, the term "Democracy Scare" was first used by Noam Chomsky in 1998 to describe the U.S. reaction to events in Haiti and Central America. See Chomsky, "Power in the Global Arena," *New Left Review,* July/August 1998, p. 8. Jonathan Rauch: "How American Politics Went Insane," *Atlantic,* July/August 2016.

2. The report was signed by Kenneth Roth, the organization's executive director. Read it at https://www.hrw.org/world-report/2017/country-chapters/dangerous-rise-of-populism.

3. Barry Eichengreen, *The Populist Temptation: Economic Grievance and Political Reaction in the Modern Era* (Oxford University Press, 2018), p. x.

4. Jan-Werner Müller, *What Is Populism?* (University of Pennsylvania Press, 2016), pp. 36, 77, 81.

5. Pippa Norris and Ronald Inglehart, *Cultural Backlash and the Rise of Populism: Trump, Brexit, and Authoritarian Populism* (Cambridge University Press, 2019), p. 5.

6. "Asking everyone to vote is like asking everyone to litter," Brennan writes. He calls his alternative system an "epistocracy," or "rule of the knowers." He suggests a number of ways such a system might

be constructed, some more subtle than others, but always with the ideal of getting voters to reflect professional academic economics and/or political science. See Jason Brennan, *Against Democracy* (Princeton University Press, 2016), chapter 8. The "dance of the dunces" comes up on p. viii.

7. "Because of the intimate relevance that populist themes have for intellectuals," wrote Margaret Canovan in 1981, "scholarly interpretations of populism have often been controversial to the point where one can hardly recognize the same movement in different accounts." Their understanding of populism has "been deeply influenced by the fears of some intellectuals who have dreaded the grass roots and the appalling things that might crawl out of them, and by the idealism of others who have exalted the common man and his simple virtues." Canovan, *Populism* (Harcourt Brace Jovanovich, 1981), p. 11.

8. It is generally agreed that the individual who actually made up the word was one David Overmyer, a Kansas Democratic politician, who happened to be on the Topeka train and who had some familiarity with Latin. Overmyer suggested it in the course of a conversation with one or more People's Party leaders. It was immediately accepted and it quickly took off.

Accounts of the word's invention are not entirely consistent. The version of the story I am relying on here comes from Robert C. McMath, *American Populism: A Social History, 1877–1898* (Hill & Wang, 1993), p. 146. A slightly different version appears in an article by W. P. Harrington called "The Populist Party in Kansas" in the 1925 volume of *Collections of the Kansas State Historical Society*, p. 418.

A detailed telling of the story appeared in the *Kansas City Times* in 1936. This account doesn't mention the Cincinnati gathering but gives the names of the five individuals who were privy to the conversation on the train: Overmyer, the Democrat; one Populist; one Republican; and two reporters, one of whom was still alive in 1936 to provide the details.

"It is seldom that a popular pseudonym sticks so well that many believe it to be the real name," the paper recalled. "That is exactly what happened in one of the tremendous political upheavals in the United States. There are probably a great many people who called themselves Populists in the early '90s who do not to this day know that Populist was never the real or official name for the party."

Cecil Howes, "Group of Kansans Traveling Together Gave the Populists Their Title," *Kansas City Times*, February 4, 1936 (clipping in the collections of the Kansas State Historical Society).

Interestingly, the *Kansas City Times* story also reports that Tom Watson, the once-idealistic Georgia politician whose later career as a vicious racist cemented Populism's association with bigotry in the public mind, disliked the word. He reportedly wanted the new party's adherents to be called "Populites."

9. The *American Nonconformist and Kansas Industrial Liberator*, to give its full name, was written, edited, and published by Henry and Leo Vincent, sons of an abolitionist from Iowa named James Vincent. The brothers advocated various other pro-labor causes in the course of their long careers, thus providing a link between the abolitionist tradition and Populism and the twentieth-century radicalism that lay ahead.

   There is no way to know with finality whether this was the very first use of the word in print, although it was the earliest instance I was able to find. The *Kansas City Star*, which is thought to have been a pioneer on the subject, actually got the word wrong when introducing it. In an item published on July 1, 1891, the paper declared that "the Rank and File of the People's Party" were to be called "Publicists."

10. All of these quotations are from the *American Nonconformist* for May 28, 1891, the same issue that announced the coining of the word "Populist." Yes, emphasis in original.

11. For example, see the *Emporia Daily Republican*, June 22, 1891, p. 2. After laughing at the reformers' new word, a neighboring Republican paper sneered: "When the calamity howlers cry that the rich are growing richer and the poor poorer, don't you believe it. The great men of the nation were poor boys and the future great men are poor boys now." *Chase County* (Kansas) *Republican*, June 25, 1891.

12. "The Third Party," *Kansas City Star*, May 21, 1891, p. 4.

13. "Third Party!," *Topeka Daily Capital*, May 19, 1891, p. 1.

14. Neville's speech came to my attention via Gene Clanton's book *Populism: The Humane Preference in America, 1890–1900* (Twayne,

1991). It can be found in the *Congressional Record*, 56th Congress, 1st Session, Volume XXXIII, p. 1589.

15. I am relying for my description on the famous essay by Jack Walker, "A Critique of the Elitist Theory of Democracy," *American Political Science Review* 60, no. 2 (June 1966): 285–95.

16. The example presented by William Galston in *Anti-Pluralism* is perhaps most egregious. The crumbling of the American dream over the last few decades, the political scientist tells us, was simply the result of impersonal forces, of "globalization" and "technological change" adjusting "the balance between labor and capital, setting in motion the slow erosion of the postwar middle class" (*Anti-Pluralism: The Populist Threat to Liberal Democracy* [Yale University Press, 2018], p. 84). Shit happens, you might say. Galston acknowledges that things *did* get a little hairy during the Great Recession, which leads him to pen this remarkable, passive-voice excuse for the failures of the Bush and Obama administrations: "established parties and institutions found it difficult to respond to rising public discontent."

1. WHAT WAS POPULISM?

1. John D. Hicks, *The Populist Revolt: A History of the Farmers' Alliance and the People's Party* (University of Nebraska Press, 1959 [1931]), pp. 56–57. On the price of corn in 1890 see *The Annals of Kansas: 1886–1925*, vol. 1, ed. Daniel W. Wilder (Kansas State Historical Society, 1954–56), p. 92.

2. Hicks, *The Populist Revolt*, p. 130; Charles Postel, *The Populist Vision* (Oxford University Press, 2007), chapter 2.

3. The quotation is from Elizabeth Higgins, *Out of the West* (Harper & Brothers, 1902), pp. 133, 136. As quoted in Hicks, *The Populist Revolt*, p. 132.

4. This is a quotation from the Omaha Platform of the People's Party, approved July 4, 1892, as reprinted in Hicks, p. 440.

5. Lawrence Goodwyn, *The Populist Moment: A Short History of the Agrarian Revolt in America* (Oxford University Press, 1978), p. 33.

6. Roscoe C. Martin, *The People's Party in Texas: A Study in Third Party Politics* (University of Texas, 1933), quoted in C. Vann Woodward, *Origins of the New South, 1877–1913* (Louisiana State University Press, 1951), p. 274.

7. British Labour Party: According to the historian Chester McArthur Destler, the remarkable effort to bring the squabbling labor unions of Illinois together under the Populist banner in 1894 involved writing a state platform that imitated the "political program of British labor." Chester McArthur Destler, *American Radicalism, 1865–1901* (Quadrangle, 1966 [1946]), p. 176. Australian Labor Party: David McKnight, *Populism Now!: The Case for Progressive Populism* (Newsouth, 2018), p. 15.

8. 1891: From a statement issued by the Kansas People's Party in 1891 and quoted in Hicks, p. 221. T. C. Jory, *What Is Populism?* (Ross E. Moores & Co., 1895).

9. The Populists made a bid for the votes of urban, industrial America that year, bringing together Chicago's squabbling labor unions under the People's Party banner for a local electoral campaign. But the strategy didn't work. Despite impressive public displays of solidarity, including a rally featuring Debs, his lawyer Clarence Darrow, and the old-time abolitionist Lyman Trumbull, the Populist-Labor coalition fizzled at the polls. See Destler, *American Radicalism*, chapters 8 and 9.

10. Postel, *The Populist Vision*, pp. 271–75.

11. "The Populist Contribution" is the final chapter of John D. Hicks's 1931 book, *The Populist Revolt*.

12. Parrington, *The Beginnings of Critical Realism in America*, vol. 3 of *Main Currents in American Thought* (Harcourt Brace, 1930), p. xxiv.

13. "Threat to liberal": This is, again, a quotation from the "About" page of the Stanford Global Populisms Project. "Almost inherently antidemocratic": Anna Grzymala-Busse, director of the Global Populisms Project, on a Stanford radio program on June 30, 2018, available at https://soundcloud.com/user-458541487/the-future -of-populism-political-movements-w-guest-anna-grzymala-busse. "All people of goodwill": Max Boot, a columnist for the *Washington Post*, in his 2018 book, *The Corrosion of Conservatism: Why I Left the Right* (Liveright, 2018), p. 212.

14. Obama, "The Way Ahead," *The Economist*, October 8, 2016.

15. The Populists' attitude toward progress is the subject of Charles Postel's important 2008 study of Populism, *The Populist Vision*. For an example of Populist optimism, see the 1893 inaugural address of Kansas governor Lorenzo Lewelling, in which he hails "the dawn of a new era in which the people shall reign." The speech is reprinted

in Norman Pollack, ed., *The Populist Mind* (Bobbs-Merrill, 1967), pp. 51–54.

16. Niall Ferguson, "Populism: Content and Form," a paper dated October 31, 2017, and presented at the Stanford "Global Populisms" conference (quoted with permission). Ferguson explicitly states that he is describing populism of the "late nineteenth century." Ferguson has made the same argument in other venues, such as a 2016 issue of *Horizons*, a magazine published by the Center for International Relations and Sustainable Development. William Galston, *Anti-Pluralism: The Populist Threat to Liberal Democracy* (Yale University Press, 2018), p. 126.

17. The remarks about the "existing heavy tariff tax" appeared in the Ocala Demands, approved by the Farmers' Alliance in December 1890 and reprinted in Hicks, *The Populist Revolt*, appendix B. The railroad to the Texas coast is described in R. Alton Lee, "The Populist Dream of a 'Wrong Way' Transcontinental," *Kansas History*, Summer 2012. Here is how the historian C. Vann Woodward describes the southern farmer's attitude toward the protective tariff on page 186 of *Origins of the New South*:

"Everywhere it was the pattern for poverty. As a producer and seller the farmer was subject to all the penalties of free trade, while as a consumer he was deprived of virtually all its benefits. It did not soften his resentment to reflect that out of his meager returns was extracted the tribute that built up the monopolies he hated."

18. The quotation is from Eichengreen, *The Populist Temptation*, p. 2. See also Mounk, pp. 63–66.

19. Frank Basil Tracy, "Rise and Doom of the Populist Party," *The Forum* 16, no. 2 (1893), p. 246.

20. Populists "weaken" democracies: See Levitsky's paper "Populism and Competitive Authoritarianism," which he presented at the Stanford "Global Populisms" conference (quoted with permission). "When populists win": This is from Levitsky's best-selling 2018 book, *How Democracies Die*, which he co-authored with Daniel Ziblatt, p. 22. In the latter we read: "What kind of candidates tend to test positive on a litmus test for authoritarianism? Very often, populist outsiders do. . . . Populists tend to deny the legitimacy of established parties, attacking them as undemocratic and even unpatriotic. They tell voters that the existing system is not really a

democracy but instead has been hijacked, corrupted, or rigged by the elite. And they promise to bury that elite and return power to 'the people'" (p. 22). See also Levitsky and James Loxton, "Populism and Competitive Authoritarianism in the Andes," *Democratization*, 20:1 (2013).

21. Cf. Seymour M. Lipset's famous 1959 paper, "Democracy and Working-Class Authoritarianism," which was included in his book *Political Man* and which I discuss further in chapter 5.

22. "Brutal demonstrations of machine politics": I am following the vivid description of Matthew Josephson, *The Politicos: 1865–1896* (Harcourt, Brace, 1938), chapter 19. Josephson estimates twenty or thirty to one on page 706. When we compare electoral price tags as a percentage of gross domestic product rather than in dollar amounts (even adjusted for inflation), it becomes apparent that the 1896 campaign absorbed a greater share of the country's net worth than any other, before or since. See Matthew O'Brien, "The Most Expensive Election Ever . . . 1896?," *Atlantic*, November 6, 2012, https://www.theatlantic.com/business/archive/2012/11/the-most -expensive-election-ever-1896/264649/.

23. Niall Ferguson tells us that "populism is a backlash against multi-culturalism." "When populists invoke the people," writes Yascha Mounk, "they are positing an in-group—united around a shared ethnicity, religion, social class, or political conviction—against an out-group whose interests can rightfully be disregarded." The economist Eichengreen insists that "the hostility of populist politicians to not just concentrated economic power but also immigrants and racial and religious minorities is intrinsic to the movement." For a comprehensive summary of this viewpoint, see Uri Friedman, "What Is a Populist?," *Atlantic*, February 27, 2017.

24. C. Vann Woodward, *Thinking Back: The Perils of Writing History* (Louisiana State University Press, 1986), p. 31.

25. Woodward, *Origins of the New South*, pp. 244, 252. This narrative was to become one of the themes of Woodward's career as a historian.

26. Ibid., p. 249.

27. Tom Watson, "The Negro Question in the South," in Norman Pollack, ed., *The Populist Mind* (Bobbs-Merrill, 1967), pp. 370, 371–72.

28. Coxey's Army: See Postel, *The Populist Vision*, p. 258.

29. Hamlin Garland, *A Spoil of Office* (D. Appleton and Company, 1897), p. 358.

30. See Omar H. Ali, *In the Lion's Mouth: Black Populism in the New South, 1886–1900* (University Press of Mississippi, 2010), p. 76.

31. The quotation is from Ali, *In the Lion's Mouth*, p. 80.

32. The two extremes are captured by Walter Nugent in *The Tolerant Populists: Kansas, Populism and Nativism* (University of Chicago Press, 1963) and Charles Postel in chapter 6 of *The Populist Vision*.

33. Woodward, *Origins of the New South*, p. 393.

34. Especially disturbing is the story of the white supremacy campaign in North Carolina in 1898, which not only destroyed Populism in that state but led to the armed overthrow of the municipal government of Wilmington. See Michael Perman, *Struggle for Mastery: Disfranchisement in the South, 1888–1908* (University of North Carolina Press, 2001), chapter 8; Woodward, *Origins of the New South*, pp. 277, 348, 372, etc.

35. "Or should we say bossess, bosserina, or bossy?" The *Kansas City Journal*, quoted in *Public Opinion: A Comprehensive Summary of the Press Throughout the World*, August 9, 1900, p. 166.

36. On the Populists' inclusion of the "pauper immigration" plank, see John Higham, *Strangers in the Land: Patterns of American Nativism, 1860–1925* (Atheneum, 1978), p. 346, note 13. The Populists' candidate in 1892 was James B. Weaver; the quote is drawn from his campaign memoir, *A Call to Action: An Interpretation of the Great Uprising, Its Source and Causes* (Iowa Printing Company, 1892), p. 281. From the Democratic Platform of 1892: "We heartily approve all legitimate efforts to prevent the United States from being used as the dumping ground for the known criminals and professional paupers of Europe; and we demand the rigid enforcement of the laws against Chinese immigration and the importation of foreign workmen under contract," etc. From the Republican Platform of 1892: "We favor the enactment of more stringent laws and regulations for the restriction of criminal, pauper and contract immigration." The parties' platforms can be found at the website of the American Presidency Project, www.presidency.ucsb.edu.

37. Walter Nugent, *The Tolerant Populists: Kansas Populism and Nativism* (University of Chicago Press, 1963).

38. The anti-APA resolution is quoted on page 163 of Walter Nugent, *The Tolerant Populists*.

39. Neil Swidey, "If the Elites Go Down, We're All in Trouble," *Boston Globe Magazine*, October 5, 2017. David Brooks, "The Rise of the Resentniks and the Populist War on Excellence," *New York Times*, November 15, 2018. Tom Nichols, "How America Lost Faith in Expertise," *Foreign Affairs*, February 13, 2017. To his credit, Nichols acknowledges in this essay that experts often make mistakes. To his discredit, he quotes Richard Hofstadter as an expert on populism without acknowledging the overthrow of Hofstadter's views on that subject.

40. Rauch and Wittes, "More Professionalism, Less Populism," Brookings, May 2017. The final quote is from political scientist Bruce Cain.

41. See Postel, *The Populist Vision*, chapter 2; "progress through education" occurs on page 48. Lawrence Goodwyn estimates the number of Alliance lecturers at forty thousand in *The Populist Moment*, p. xxi. The university founded by a Populist leader was North Carolina State; the Populist in question was Leonidas L. Polk.

42. The *Appeal*'s list of books, in their issue for December 14, 1895, included titles by Karl Marx, Henry George, William Morris, Henry Demarest Lloyd, and the economist Richard T. Ely, in addition to the usual Populist favorites.

43. Postel, *The Populist Vision*, p. 281.

44. T. C. Jory, *What Is Populism?*, p. 4.

45. Postel, *The Populist Vision*, p. 286.

2. "BECAUSE RIGHT IS RIGHT AND GOD IS GOD"

1. These and many other amusing details of the 1896 campaign are found in Karl Rove's account, *The Triumph of William McKinley: Why the Election of 1896 Still Matters* (Simon & Schuster, 2015), pp. 330, 339.

2. *Sun* (New York), July 10, 1896, p. 6.

3. "The Duty of Democrats," *Sun* (New York), July 12, 1896, p. 6. John Hay, *The Platform of Anarchy* (N.P., 1896), p. 8

4. "A Few Points," *Sun* (New York), July 14, 1896, p. 6. Godkin: Untitled editorial item, *Nation*, October 8, 1896, p. 259. On the unanimity of the press, Godkin gloated: "There never was a Presidential campaign in which one of the two great parties received so little support from the press of the country" as that of 1896.

"Every independent journal in the United States was opposed to Bryan, and throughout the East all the old established and influential Democratic newspapers were outspoken against him. In the Western metropolis he got as little backing from the press as in the Eastern, not one Chicago journal of the first class advocating free coinage, and hardly any of the lower classes." Unsigned editorial, *Nation*, November 5, 1896.

5. The Methodist bishop was John P. Newman. See "Political Incident at Asbury Park," *New York Times*, July 27, 1896, p. 1. The "incident" made nationwide headlines. As the *Times* continued the story, "Instantly a man in the rear of the hall jumped up and shouted: 'Bryan is a good American.' The man tried to propose three cheers for the Democrat-Populist candidate for President, but his voice was drowned by the music of the choir."

The last two examples are both taken from Bryan's own account of the 1896 campaign, *The First Battle*, pages 471 and 474. The society preacher was Robert S. McArthur; the second was none other than Thomas Dixon Jr., who was later the author of *The Clansman*.

6. Fifteen university presidents: *Nation*, October 8, 1896, p. 259. White's pamphlet, titled *An Open Letter to Sundry Democrats*, was extensively quoted in the *New York Times* for July 16, 1896, p. 1. Here is the amazing headline that the *Times* applied to its account of his intervention: "Duty Now of Democrats / Andrew D. White Advises Voting for Mr. McKinley. / The Chicago Convention, He Says, Was Made Up Not of Democrats but of Anarchists, Socialists, Populists, Speculators, and Sectionalists—Outlines Further Steps in the Policy of Confiscation and Spoliation." White was also the author of the libertarian favorite *Fiat Money in France: How It Came, What It Brought and How It Ended* (D. Appleton and Company, 1896), which was reissued in 1896 with a new introduction denouncing "so-called 'Democrats,'" "their candidate and his Populist supporters." White later became McKinley's ambassador to Germany.

7. Josephson, *The Politicos*, p. 693.

8. Ibid., p. 698.

9. Ibid., p. 705. Karl Rove, in *The Triumph of William McKinley*, asserts that all rumors of economic coercion were false. However, there is plenty of evidence that coercion or something like it took

place. In his biography of Bryan, *A Godly Hero* (Alfred A. Knopf, 2006), Michael Kazin shows that coercive threats were widespread and commonplace. Examples are easy enough to find in published documents from the era. In an article in *Sound Currency* for September 1, 1896, Louis Ehrich (a supporter of the gold standard) reports that "within this very week two prominent bankers of Colorado have assured me that they would at once loan out 25 per cent more of their deposits if they were absolutely sure of Bryan's defeat." The cover of *Judge* for September 26, 1896, describes a "Free Silver Scare" that was threatening to close down factories with "thousands thrown out of employment." Matthew Josephson, in *The Politicos*, gives many more examples of threats and other inducements to workers and farmers as they were reported in the press of the day. "'Men, vote as you please,' the head of the Steinway piano works is reported to have said, in terms which were repeated throughout the country, 'but if Bryan is elected tomorrow the whistle will not blow Wednesday morning'" (p. 704).

10. "Good Riddance," *New-York Tribune*, November 4, 1896, p. 4.

11. *The Platform of Anarchy* is dated October 6, 1896, and claims to record "An Address to the Students of Western Reserve University," but according to one of Hay's biographers, no speech ever took place. Hay believed "address" could include a pamphlet printed for the occasion. See Tyler Dennett, *John Hay: From Poetry to Politics* (Dodd, Mead, 1933), pp. 178–79.

12. This verdict is delivered in the course of a profile of Tom Watson, the Populists' choice for the vice presidency. Theodore Roosevelt, "The Three Vice-Presidential Candidates," *Review of Reviews*, September 1896.

13. The story is called "A Walking Delegate"; Kipling published it in the *Century* magazine in December 1894 and collected it in *The Day's Work* a few years later. My quotes are drawn from the latter version, published by Doubleday & McClure in 1898. That the story referred to Populism was clearly understood in those days; in 1894 Theodore Roosevelt wrote to a friend and asked him to tell Kipling how the story was urged—hilariously—on William Peffer, the Populist senator from Kansas, who apparently did not find it amusing. See Joseph Bucklin Bishop, *Theodore Roosevelt and His Time: Shown in His Own Letters* (Charles Scribner's Sons, 1920), vol. 1, p. 56.

14. *Puck*, September 2, 1896.

15. Sumner, "Cause and Cure of Hard Times," in *The Forgotten Man and Other Essays* (Yale University Press, 1919; originally published in *Leslie's Weekly*, September 3, 1896), p. 153.

16. "The Chief of Blatherskites," *New York Evening Post*, July 10, 1896, p. 4. This is just a few columns over from an editorial denouncing "the Populistic, anarchistic Chicago platform."

17. "Since [1860] the size of the buildings has been increasing pretty steadily, and as a consequence the deliberative character of the conventions has steadily decreased until the present point has been reached." *New York Evening Post*, July 11, 1896.

18. Bryan as leader of a pirate gang: *Life*, July 30, 1896, p. 79. (The captured Democratic ship is flying a skull-and-crossbones flag marked "Anarchy" and "Repudiation.") As Mephistopheles: October 1, 1896, p. 247. As simpleton: October 29, 1896, p. 327. As stage performer: ibid., p. 325.

19. New York *Sun*, October 1, 1896.

20. Choate later served as McKinley's ambassador to Great Britain. He is quoted in Charles Beard, *The Supreme Court and the Constitution* (Macmillan, 1912), p. 112.

21. Hay had written a bitterly anti-union novel in the 1880s in which he made these points. To quote Vernon Parrington's summary: "The proletariat is groping blindly for leadership; it is stirring uneasily; if the educated classes do not offer an enlightened leadership, the laborer will follow low cunning to immoral ends and blind leaders of the blind will bring irretrievable disaster upon civilization. Selfish appeal will kindle envy and hate; the rich and prosperous will go down before brute force; the rights of property will be destroyed; law, order, and obedience will give place to anarchy." *The Beginnings of Critical Realism in America: 1860–1920* (Harcourt, Brace and Company, 1930), p. 174.

22. The paper then observed that, "just as during the French Revolution one demagogue swiftly supplanted another in the affections of the mob and for a time held the supreme place of power, so the revolutionists and repudiators of the Chicago Assembly or Convention have with bewildering rapidity transferred their allegiance through a succession of Populist favorites." "It Is Bryan of Nebraska," New York *Sun*, July 11, p. 6.

23. Godkin: *Nation*, July 23, 1896, p. 60. "'Blowing' Himself Around

the Country" was the centerfold in *Puck* for September 16, 1896. It can be viewed on the Library of Congress website at https://www.loc.gov/resource/ppmsca.28841/.

24. *The Education of Henry Adams: An Autobiography* (Houghton Mifflin Company, 1918), p. 344.

25. Hay, *The Platform of Anarchy*, p. 10.

26. On the day after the Democrats had adopted what the *New York Evening Post* called "the Populistic, anarchistic Chicago platform," the paper informed its readers that the disease was everywhere:

> In almost every community now there is a small band of thinkers who go about muttering to themselves, haranguing their acquaintances, and occasionally publishing an article or making a speech in which they call the attention of the public to appalling facts and events which no one else perceives or has any knowledge of (*New York Evening Post*, July 10, 1896).

Similarly, the noted gold bug Louis Ehrich suggested that what ailed the Populists and their allies was "intellectual astigmatism, a condition of the mind which renders it impossible for the individual to see certain lines of thought and fact in their true relation." Louis R. Ehrich, "The Poison in Our Circulation," *Sound Currency*, September 1, 1896, p. 11. Ehrich's article seems to have originated as a speech delivered to the convention of a breakaway gold faction of the Democratic Party, which met in Indianapolis that month.

27. The "alienist's" letter ran in the *New York Times* for September 27, 1896. That same day, the *Times* ran an editorial titled "Is Bryan Crazy?" The controversy continued for at least a week. The original story is reprinted at http://historymatters.gmu.edu/d/5353/. Other installments in the series can be read on the website of the *New York Times*: "Is Mr. Bryan a Mattoid," September 29, 1896; "Bryan Under Criticism," October 2, 1896.

28. J. Laurence Laughlin, "Causes of Agricultural Unrest," *Atlantic Monthly*, November 1896, p. 577.

29. Ibid., pp. 584, 585.

30. "A Most Lamentable Comedy" was published in installments in the *Saturday Evening Post* in 1901. White collected it that same year in *Stratagems and Spoils: Stories of Love and Politics* (Charles Scribner's Sons, 1901), which is the version I am quoting from here. White mentions Roosevelt's enthusiasm for *Stratagems and Spoils* in his *Autobiography* (Macmillan, 1946), p. 320.

31. See Gustave Le Bon, *The Crowd: A Study of the Popular Mind* (Ernest Benn Limited, 1952 [1896]). White acknowledges reading it in his *Autobiography*, p. 271.

    So what happens in White's story of the Populist revolt? Well, the orator Dan Gregg is elected governor, whereupon he reveals himself to be utterly incompetent and makes a complete wreck of things, plus gets involved in an affair with a wealthy woman. The mind-clouding folly of Populism eventually receding, Gregg is defeated in his bid for reelection and returns to tragic, solitary crank-dom on his remote farm.

32. Peffer's scrapbooks, available on the website of the Kansas State Historical Society, contain two examples of such imagery, both from *Judge* magazine, one of them undated, the other dated July 20, 1895. *Leslie's Weekly*, September 3, 1896.

33. The Italian stereotype cartoon was the centerfold in *Judge* for August 15, 1896. "The American 'Boxer'" was the cover cartoon for *Judge* on June 30, 1900. These two plus the Bryan/Satan cartoon were all drawn by Grant Hamilton, one of the best-known cartoonists of the era.

34. Absorbing great drafts of the white-supremacy propaganda, "the Populist white man who had valued his farm above his race," as the historian Glenda Gilmore puts it, learned that by voting for the third party, "he had opened the gates of hell for some distant white woman." Gilmore, cited in Michael Honey, "Class, Race and Power in the New South," in Timothy Tyson and David S. Cecelski, eds., *Democracy Betrayed: The Wilmington Race Riot of 1898 and Its Legacy* (University of North Carolina Press, 1998), p. 172. On the local business class and the racist cartoons, see James M. Beeby, *Revolt of the Tar Heels: The North Carolina Populist Movement* (University Press of Mississippi, 2008), chapter 8.

35. I am quoting from "'Those Who Own the Property Should Rule,'" the closing editorial from the *People's Paper* of Charlotte, North Carolina (November 4, 1898), as reproduced on the helpful University of North Carolina website "The 1898 Election in North Carolina," https://exhibits.lib.unc.edu/exhibits/show/1898/history.

36. Honey, "Class, Race and Power in the New South," p. 170. See also the final report of the 1898 Wilmington Race Riot Commission, dated May 31, 2006 and published by the North Carolina Department of Cultural Resources.

37. Michael Perman, in *Struggle for Mastery: Disfranchisement in the South 1888–1908* (University of North Carolina Press, 2001), argues that suppressing Populism was not the rationale for disfranchisement in every single southern state; in many of them it happened after Populism had already died out. However, in every case it was intended to prevent another challenge to Democratic one-party rule. On the North Carolina case, see Beeby, *Revolt of the Tar Heels*, chapter 9.

38. Anonymous letter to William McKinley dated November 13, 1898, and cited in Glenda E. Gilmore, "Murder, Memory, and the Flight of the Incubus," in Tyson and Cecelski, eds., *Democracy Betrayed: The Wilmington Race Riot of 1898 and Its Legacy*, p. 88.

3. PEAK POPULISM IN THE PROLETARIAN DECADE

1. Irving Bernstein, *The Turbulent Years: A History of the American Worker, 1933–1940* (Haymarket Books, 2010), p. 15.

2. Floyd Olson, "My Political Creed: Why a New Party Must Challenge Capitalism," *Common Sense*, April 1935, p. 7.

3. On the ubiquity of fascist practices in the United States in those years, see Joseph Fronczak, "The Fascist Game: Transnational Political Transmission and the Genesis of the U.S. Modern Right," *Journal of American History* 105, no. 3 (December 2018): 563–88.

4. Bernstein, *The Turbulent Years*, p. 769.

5. "Recall the Days When Populists Had a Foothold: Agrarian Revolt of '92 Akin to Present Farmer Discontent," *Nebraska State Journal*, December 19, 1932. The story was a reprint from the Associated Press.

6. Henry W. Lawrence, "Farmers in Revolt—1893 and 1933," *Santa Cruz News*, April 29, 1933 (the article was reprinted from *Every Week* magazine). The text under the headline reads, "Forty years ago the disgruntled agriculturalists put their trust in a third party, the Populists; today they are trying direct action but though their methods differ their grievances are much the same." See also Frank Parker Stockbridge, "Revival of the Populists," *Brooklyn Eagle*, May 5, 1933.

7. White was not a supporter of FDR that year (he was a friend of the Republican nominee, Kansas governor Alf Landon), but he was not hostile to the president, either. He makes a fascinating comparison between a speech of Roosevelt's that he watches and Bryan's "Cross

of Gold" oration in 1896. See William Allen White, "40 Years: New Men, Old Issues," *New York Times*, August 9, 1936.

8. Historians: In his 1946 history of American radicalism, Chester McArthur Destler drew a clear line from Populism to the New Deal and its various regulatory agencies (*American Radicalism, 1865–1901*, p. 31). In 1959, C. Vann Woodward looked back on the similarities between the 1890s and the 1930s and declared, "From many points of view the New Deal was neo-Populism" (Woodward, "The Populist Heritage and the Intellectual," *American Scholar* 29, no. 1 [Winter 1959–60]: 55). Popular writers: See in particular Gilbert Seldes, *Mainland* (Charles Scribner's Sons, 1936), where the connection between the two is made more than once. In a February 1936 column, Walter Lippmann compared the Tennessee Valley Authority to the dreams of the Populists. In the *New York Times* in 1932, John Chamberlain described the career of the famous Supreme Court justice Louis Brandeis as a form of "Populism become disciplined," and in January 1938 syndicated columnist Drew Pearson tipped his readers to look for stiffer antitrust enforcement when President Roosevelt appointed a man to the Federal Trade Commission who had supposedly got his political start in the old People's Party.

9. Perkins's remarks are found in Frances Perkins and J. Paul St. Sure, *Two Views of American Labor* (UCLA Institute of Industrial Relations, 1965), p. 2.

10. Perkins, *The Roosevelt I Knew* (Viking Press, 1946), pp. 72–73.

11. The New Deal as the dawn of expertise-in-government is, for example, the favored interpretation of Richard Hofstadter. See chapter 7 of *The Age of Reform* (Alfred A. Knopf, 1955), in which he argues that the New Deal represented the triumph of managerialism and the rise of "reform-minded Americans" from the various professions. Hofstadter's larger point is that the New Deal owed little or nothing to Populism. Years later, in the heyday of the free-market faith, Daniel Yergin would use the same understanding as a way of dismissing the New Deal for its top-down, big-government hostility to market freedom. See Yergin, *The Commanding Heights* (Simon & Schuster, 1998), pp. 51–56.

12. This last phrase is often transcribed as "lured us from the old barricades," but according to FDR's actual text for the occasion, the word was "verities." See https://www.fdrlibrary.org/documents

/356632/390886/1932+DNC+Acceptance+Speech.pdf/066093f1
-bab8-48a8-81b5-65ed8c000f89.

13. George H. Mayer, *The Political Career of Floyd B. Olson* (University of Minnesota Press, 1951), p. 17.

14. Undated 1934 speech by Olson, reprinted in James M. Youngdale, *Third Party Footprints: An Anthology from Writings and Speeches of Midwest Radicals* (Ross & Haines, 1966), p. 255.

15. Warren Susman, *Culture as History: The Transformation of American Society in the Twentieth Century* (Pantheon, 1984), p. 212. In the pages to come I am following the lead of Susman's famous essays, "The Culture of the Thirties," "Culture and Commitment," and "The People's Fair," all of which were collected in *Culture as History*.

16. Stu Cohen, *The Likes of Us: America in the Eyes of the Farm Security Administration* (David R. Godine, 2008), p. xv. The populist implications of the FSA style are explained particularly well by historian Stuart Ewen in *PR!: A Social History of Spin* (Basic, 1996).

17. See Gerstle's fascinating account of a textile union in Woonsocket, Rhode Island, *Working-Class Americanism: The Politics of Labor in a Textile City, 1914–1960* (Cambridge University Press, 1989).

18. The pamphlet was issued by the CIO's famous Political Action Committee, the first PAC of them all. It is reprinted in Gaer, *The First Round*, p. 19.

19. Roosevelt speech delivered in Cleveland, Ohio, November 2, 1940, from a transcript of the speech on the website of the FDR Library, Marist College.

20. For still others, as the historian Warren Susman points out, this was the language of public relations. The worship of the common man happened at roughly the same time as the invention of scientific polling and with it the discovery of "the concept of the typical or the average," an idea that would eventually become as ubiquitous as "the people" itself.

21. The quotations in this paragraph and the two that follow come from Kenneth Burke, "Revolutionary Symbolism in America," in *American Writers' Congress*, ed. Henry Hart (International Publishers, 1935), pp. 87–94, emphasis in original. On the extreme hostility with which Burke's speech was received, see Michael Denning, *The Cultural Front* (Verso, 1996), p. 443.

22. This is a point of special emphasis in vice president Henry Wallace's intensely populist wartime speech, "The Century of the

Common Man," reprinted in the book of that same title (Reynal & Hitchcock, 1943), p. 16. Additionally, Gilbert Seldes wrote in *Mainland* (Charles Scribner's Sons, 1936), a book much concerned with the Populist legacy: "How to use the middle class is the great problem for demagogues—and how to save it is the problem for democrats." Similarly, Kenneth Burke, in the speech quoted above, urged his colleagues to adopt a populist stance because it would help them "combat the forces that hide their class prerogatives behind a communal ideology," which is to say, to combat demagogues of the nationalist, fascist, and anti-Semitic variety.

23. According to Benjamin Hufbauer, "How Trump's Favorite Movie Explains Him," *Politico*, June 6, 2016.

24. I am following the analysis here of historian Michael Denning, whose 1996 book *The Cultural Front* is one of the most comprehensive efforts to grapple with thirties-style populism. On Welles, see chapter 10, "The Politics of Magic: Orson Welles's Allegories of Anti-Fascism."

25. Wallace, *The Century of the Common Man*, p. 20.

26. Welles's speech was delivered at Arlington National Cemetery on May 30, 1942. It is reprinted in a pamphlet called *Toward New Horizons: The World Beyond the War* (Office of War Information, 1942), p. 9.

27. One place Morgenthau's speech can be found is in the collection of archival material on the European Union compiled by the University of Luxembourg: https://www.cvce.eu/content/publication/2003/12/12/b88b1fe7-8fec-4da6-ae22-fa33edd08ab6/publishable_en.pdf.

28. I am reiterating here the standard critique of Popular Front culture. It is answered persuasively by the historian Michael Denning in his authoritative cultural history of the era, *The Cultural Front*, in which he argues that the thirties marked not the end of modernism but merely a departure in a different direction.

29. John Kenneth Galbraith, "On the Economics of F.D.R.," *Commentary*, August 1, 1956, p. 173.

30. FDR on academic "jargon": As quoted in Arthur Schlesinger Jr., *The Politics of Upheaval*, vol. 3 (Houghton Mifflin, 1960), p. 650. "Whole community" / "if the ballot": from "The Uses of an Education," a speech FDR gave at Washington College in Chestertown, Maryland, on October 21, 1933. It is reprinted in *The Public Papers and Addresses of Franklin D. Roosevelt*, vol. 2 (Random House, 1938), p. 418.

31. Richard V. Gilbert et al., *An Economic Program for American Democracy* (The Vanguard Press, 1938), p. ix.

32. Thomas T. Spencer, "The Good Neighbor League Colored Committee and the 1936 Democratic Presidential Campaign," *Journal of Negro History* 63, no. 4 (1978): 307–8. The detail about the Cab Calloway concert is related in Donald R. McCoy, "The Good Neighbor League and the Presidential Campaign of 1936," *Western Political Quarterly* 13, no. 4 (1960): 1014.

33. Denning, *The Cultural Front*, p. 130. Denning describes this antiracist culture admirably and at some length. At times he uses the word "populist" to describe it, but he also takes pains to distinguish Popular Front populism from received definitions of populism, a point that he carries a bit too far, in my opinion. See in particular his account of historical Populism on page 125.

34. Here as in many other places in this chapter I am indebted to the trailblazing work of Michael Kazin, *The Populist Persuasion: An American History* (Basic Books, 1995), chapter 6.

35. CIO Political Action Committee, *The People's Program for 1944*, reprinted in Joseph Gaer, *The First Round: The Story of the CIO Political Action Committee* (Duell, Sloan and Pearce, 1944), pp. 188, 211.

36. CIO National Political Action Committee, *The Negro in 1944*, reprinted in Gaer, *The First Round*, p. 451.

37. Gerstle, *Working-Class Americanism*, p. 296.

38. Penelope Niven, *Carl Sandburg: A Biography* (Charles Scribner's Sons, 1991), p. 245.

4. "THE UPHEAVAL OF THE UNFIT"

1. "Moral and intellectual bankruptcy": attributed to the prominent journalist Nathaniel Peffer. "Political democracy is moribund": attributed to ACLU president Roger Baldwin (!). "Modern Western civilization is a failure": attributed to novelist Louise Maunsell Field. All of these as quoted in Arthur Schlesinger Jr., *The Politics of Upheaval*, vol. 3 (Houghton Mifflin, 1960), p. 646.

2. On these points see Jared Goldstein, "The American Liberty League and the Rise of Constitutional Nationalism," *Temple Law Review* 86, no. 2 (2014): 296. Also: "Liberty League Income Equals Major Parties," *Washington Post*, January 3, 1936, p. 9.

3. Schlesinger, *Politics of Upheaval*, p. 633; Frank Luther Mott, *American Journalism: A History: 1690–1960*, 3rd ed. (Macmillan, 1962), p. 719.

4. Richard S. Tedlow, "The National Association of Manufacturers and Public Relations During the New Deal," *Business History Review* 50, no. 1 (1976): 36. Tedlow regards this slogan as self-evidently ridiculous in the violent context of the Depression.

5. See "Industry Offers Plan of Recovery," *New York Times*, December 4, 1934.

6. Edward F. Hutton, "Let Business 'Gang Up,'" *Public Utilities Fortnightly* 16, no. 11 (November 21, 1935): 684, 686, 688. Incidentally, the particular bit of regulation that provoked Hutton's outraged call to gang up was the Public Utility Holding Company Act of 1935.

7. "The N.A.M. Declares War," *Business Week*, December 14, 1935; Arthur Krock, "In Washington," *New York Times*, December 6, 1935; "Industry Adopts Political Planks for New Deal War," *New York Times*, December 6, 1935.

8. Professor: "Industry Adopts Political Planks," *New York Times*, December 6, 1935. Steelmaker: "Political Activity Urged on Industry," *New York Times*, December 6, 1935. Bardo: "Business Leaders to Enter Politics to End New Deal," *New York Times*, December 5, 1935.

9. The two correspondents were R. R. M. Carpenter and John J. Raskob. Their letters were published on page 2 of the *New York Times* on December 21, 1934, under the headline "The Carpenter and Raskob Letters." Page 1 of that day's issue carried a story in which Senator Gerald Nye of North Dakota announced, "These letters . . . bear all the earmarks of having been the birth-place and the birth-time of the Liberty League." See "Nye Sees in Letter by Raskob 'Birth' of Liberty League."

10. G. W. Dyer, *Regimenting the Farmers*, a speech given "over the Network of the Columbia Broadcasting System, May 5, 1935," American Liberty League pamphlet #33. Anonymous, *Economic Planning—Mistaken but Not New*, American Liberty League pamphlet #75, November 1935, p. 2. Anonymous, *The AAA and Our Form of Government*, American Liberty League pamphlet #80, December 1935.

11. Hoover, quoted in Schlesinger, *The Politics of Upheaval*, p. 544. Anonymous, *The Dual Form of Government and the New Deal: A Study*

of the Roosevelt Administration's Persistent Attempt to Destroy Local Self-Government in the United States and Substitute Therefor a Centralized, All-Powerful Federal Authority Similar to the Current Dictatorships in Several European Countries, American Liberty League pamphlet #134, September 1936, p. 22.

12. Smith's speech was covered with a huge page 1 headline in the Chicago Tribune for January 26, 1936: "NEW DEAL FRAUD: AL SMITH." The text I am using here is the version published by the American Liberty League itself as pamphlet #97, The Facts in the Case, pp. 13, 14.

13. The list of attendees was carried by the Tribune on page 6. The backfiring of the Al Smith broadcast is a staple of the historiography of the period. For example, see Goldstein, "The American Liberty League and the Rise of Constitutional Nationalism," pp. 312–16.

14. Captain William H. Stayton, Is the Constitution for Sale?, speech delivered "over the Network of the Columbia Broadcasting System," May 30, 1935, American Liberty League pamphlet #40, p. 3.

15. "Collectivism": Los Angeles Times, October 3, 1936; "Russia and Spain": Los Angeles Times, October 6, 1936.

16. All of these are from the Chicago Daily Tribune ("World's Greatest Newspaper"), October 20, October 22, and November 2, 1936.

17. Ralph M. Shaw, The New Deal: Its Unsound Theories and Irreconcilable Policies, American Liberty League pamphlet #39, 1935, p. 13.

18. Ibid., p. 11.

19. William R. Perkins, A Rising or a Setting Sun?: A Study in Government Contrasting Fundamental Principles with Present Policies in the Light of Authentic History, American Liberty League pamphlet #135, September 1936, p. 27.

20. Ibid., pp. 28, 30.

21. Thomas Nixon Carver, "Where We Need Planning the Most," Nation's Business, March 1935. This article was apparently an excerpt from Carver's pamphlet What Must We Do to Save Our Economic System?

22. Frederick H. Stinchfield, The American Constitution—Whose Heritage?: The Self-Reliant or Those Who Would Be Wards of Government?, American Liberty League pamphlet #90, January 1936, p. 6.

23. E. T. Weir, "'I Am What Mr. Roosevelt Calls an Economic Royalist,'" Fortune, October 1936, p. 198.

24. Edward Shils, *The Torment of Secrecy: The Background and Consequences of American Security Policies* (Free Press, 1956), p. 13. This is also Richard Hofstadter's understanding of the New Deal, as he described it in *The Age of Reform*.

25. The book was called *The Economics of the Recovery Program* and featured an essay by Joseph Schumpeter.

26. Walter E. Spahr, "The People's Money," part of a *Round Table Discussion of "The Constitution and the New Deal*," July 10, 1935, American Liberty League pamphlet #51, pp. 9, 11, 12. See also the article about Spahr in the *Chicago Tribune* for January 22, 1936, in which he attributed the "tragic" deeds of the New Deal to its "appalling mixture of ignorance and demagoguery."

27. *Professors and the New Deal: A Compendium of Quotations Demonstrating That a Great Majority of the Nation's Educators Believe in Sound Principles of Economics and Constitutional Theories of Government*, American Liberty League pamphlet #91, January 1936, p. 23.

28. "Real Experts on the Job," *Los Angeles Times*, April 11, 1936; *Professors and the New Deal*, American Liberty League pamphlet #91, January 1936, p. 23.

29. On the GOP brain trust, see "G.O.P. to Tell What New Deal Is Doing to U.S.: Group of 50 Experts Will Report on Record," *Chicago Tribune*, April 10, 1936, p. 13. On the popularity of this booklet among leading conservatives (including former president Herbert Hoover), see Luca Fiorito and Cosma Orsi, "'Survival Value and a Robust, Practical, Joyless Individualism': Thomas Nixon Carver, Social Justice, and Eugenics," *History of Political Economy* 49, no. 3 (2017): 487–89.

30. Thomas Nixon Carver ("as told to Kenneth Crist"), "Alms, the Man, and Prosperity," *Los Angeles Times*, May 19, 1935.

31. All quotations are from Carver's 1935 article, "Where We Need Planning the Most." The suggestion about marriage and cars is described in Fiorito and Orsi, "'Survival Value and a Robust, Practical, Joyless Individualism.'"

32. "Largely forgotten today, Thomas Nixon Carver was one of the prominent economists of the early twentieth century." His "renown as an economist came from his committed and eloquent defense of laissez-faire in books such as the *Distribution of Wealth* (1905), *Essays in Social Justice* (1915), and *The Revolution of American Economics* (1925)." Gregory T. Eow, "Fighting a New Deal: Intellectual

Origins of the Reagan Revolution, 1932–1952" (PhD dissertation, Rice University, 2007), p. 117.

33. See Fred Essary, "Politicians Scent Danger in Output of Professors," and the hilarious editorial, "New High in Brains," both in the *Baltimore Sun*, May 1, 1936. Also noteworthy, for our purposes, was the *Chicago Defender*'s take on Carver's booklet: "One of Prof. Carver's conclusions is that 'substantial people' must organize politically for two purposes: to end government regulation of business and to keep the underdog, white and Race members, cowed." *Chicago Defender*, May 23, 1936, p. 19.

34. Thomas Hart Benton, *An Artist in America*, 4th rev. ed. (University of Missouri, 1983 [1937]), pp. 190, 191.

35. Leuchtenburg describes the class-based voting pattern of 1936 in "When the People Spoke, What Did They Say?," *Yale Law Journal* 108, no. 8 (1999): 2109. The quotation is found on page 2111.

36. George Seldes, *Lords of the Press* (J. Messner, 1938), pp. 334, 332. Seldes attributes this last point to an analysis in *Christian Century*.

37. Schlesinger was writing specifically about events of 1934, but his remarks applied equally well to the years that followed. See Arthur M. Schlesinger Jr., *The Coming of the New Deal* (Houghton Mifflin Company, 1959), p. 496.

38. Jared Goldstein points out that the Democrats chose to make the Liberty League their main foil in 1936, rather than the Republican Party or the Supreme Court. "In countless speeches, advertisements, editorials, newspaper interviews, and even a well-publicized Senate investigation, the Roosevelt reelection team mocked the Liberty League as the voice of business tycoons who had long tyrannized the American people and whose power the New Deal was instituted to check." Goldstein, "The American Liberty League and the Rise of Constitutional Nationalism," *Temple Law Review* 86, no. 2 (2014): 307.

39. Thurman Arnold, *The Folklore of Capitalism* (Yale University Press, 1937), p. 81.

40. *The Public Papers and Addresses of Franklin D. Roosevelt, 1938 Volume* (Macmillan, 1941), p. xxix.

41. Roland Marchand, *Creating the Corporate Soul: The Rise of Public Relations and Corporate Imagery in American Big Business* (University of California Press, 1998), pp. 212, 220. See chapter 6 of Marchand's book for a fascinating discussion of the birth of corporate populism.

42. Herbert Hoover, "Uncommon Men," from a copy of the speech on the website of the National Archives, https://www.docsteach .org/documents/document/uncommon-man-speech-by-herbert -hoover.

5. CONSENSUS REDENSUS

1. Richard H. Pells, *The Liberal Mind in a Conservative Age: American Intellectuals in the 1940s and 1950s* (Harper & Row, 1985), p. 130.

2. Daniel Bell, "The Dispossessed," an essay dated 1962, published in his book *The Radical Right: The New American Right Expanded and Updated* (Doubleday, 1963), pp. 22, 32. Bell continues as follows: "A new profession, that of the 'military intellectual,' has emerged, and men like Kahn, Wohlstetter, Brodie, Hitch, Kissinger, Bowie and Schelling 'move freely through the corridors of the Pentagon and the State Department . . . rather as the Jesuits through the courts of Madrid and Vienna three centuries ago.'" (The quote is from an anonymous article in the *Times Literary Supplement* from 1961.)

3. Michael Paul Rogin, *The Intellectuals and McCarthy* (MIT Press, 1967), pp. 274–75.

4. Daniel Bell, *The End of Ideology: On the Exhaustion of Political Ideas in the Fifties* (Free Press, 1962), pp. 122, 123.

5. Hofstadter: Richard Hofstadter, *The Age of Reform: From Bryan to F.D.R.* (Alfred A. Knopf, 1955), p. 19. Lipset: Seymour Lipset, *Political Man: The Social Bases of Politics* (Anchor, 1963 [1959]), p. 170. Viereck: "The Revolt Against the Elite," in Bell, *The Radical Right*, p. 163, emphasis in original. Daniel Bell argued essentially the same thing in the 1956 essay quoted above.

6. Bell, *End of Ideology*, p. 114.

7. Hofstadter, *The Age of Reform,* pp. 62, 82, 85, 78.

8. Ibid., pp. 73, 78, 34.

9. 1953: Richard Hofstadter, "Democracy and Anti-intellectualism in America," *Michigan Alumnus Quarterly Review* 59, no. 21 (August 8, 1953): 288. Very first conference: Hofstadter, "North America," in Gita Ionescu and Ernest Gellner, *Populism: Its Meaning and National Characteristics* (Macmillan, 1969). This was Hofstadter's presentation to the first international academic conference on populism, held at the London School of Economics in 1967. He was

the sole authority at the conference on "North American populism." On the movement's simplicity of mind, see p. 17.

10. See the posthumous appreciation of Hofstadter by his protégé, Christopher Lasch, "On Richard Hofstadter," *New York Review of Books*, March 8, 1973. Lasch's feelings about Hofstadter would change later on.

11. Hofstadter explains his lifelong battle, in a typically indirect style, in chapter 12 of *The Progressive Historians: Turner, Beard, Parrington*, (Vintage, 1970). Hofstadter criticizes the Populists for their "simple social classification" and "delusive simplicity" in *The Age of Reform*, p. 65.

12. *The Age of Reform*, pp. 126–27.

13. Ibid., pp. 4, 5.

14. This is historian Alan Brinkley, as quoted in David S. Brown, *Richard Hofstadter: An Intellectual Biography* (University of Chicago Press, 2006), p. 99. Brinkley wrote this in 1985.

15. Edward Shils, *The Torment of Secrecy: The Background and Consequences of American Security Policies* (Ivan R. Dee, 1996 [1956]), p. 98.

16. Ibid., pp. 98–99.

17. Ibid., p. 100.

18. Ibid., p. 101.

19. Ibid., p. 104.

20. Ibid., p. 49.

21. Ibid., p. 227.

22. These quotations are from Lipset's famous book *Political Man*, p. 108.

23. Ibid., pp. 114–15, 123.

24. These arguments can be found in chapter 5 of *Political Man*, "'Fascism'—Left, Right, and Center," p. 169.

25. Ibid., p. 87. As far as I can tell, Lipset never acknowledges in this book the obvious similarity of his theories to those of the anti-democratic thinker Gustave Le Bon, which I described briefly in chapter 2.

26. A few of the main texts in the anti-Hofstadter canon are: Walter Nugent, *The Tolerant Populists* (University of Chicago Press, 1963); C. Vann Woodward, "The Populist Heritage and the Intellectual," *American Scholar* 29, no. 1 (Winter 1959–60): 55–72; Norman Pollack's various journal articles ("Hofstadter on Populism: A Critique of 'The Age of Reform'" [*Journal of Southern History* 26, no. 4 (November 1960): 478–500]; "The Myth of Populist Anti-Semitism" [*American Historical Review* 68, no. 1 (October 1962):

76–80]; "Fear of Man: Populism, Authoritarianism, and the Historian" [*Agricultural History* 39, no. 2 (April 1, 1965): 59–67]); and also his book *The Populist Response to Industrial America* (Norton, 1966); Michael Rogin, *The Intellectuals and McCarthy* (MIT Press, 1967), especially chapter 6; Lawrence Goodwyn, *Democratic Promise: The Populist Moment in America* (Oxford University Press, 1976); and Charles Postel, *The Populist Vision* (Oxford University Press, 2007). There are probably a hundred more.

27. Pollack, "The Myth of Populist Anti-Semitism." "What stands out about the People's Party in this history," writes Charles Postel, "was the relative absence of this type of political exploitation of religious prejudice."

   Charles Postel, "The American Populist and Anti-Populist Legacy," in *Transformations of Populism in Europe and the Americas: History and Recent Tendencies*, eds. John Abromeit, Bridget Maria Chesterton, Gary Marotta, and York Norman (Bloomsbury, 2016), p. 122.

28. See the argument of historian David Potter, summarized in David Brown, *Richard Hofstadter: An Intellectual Biography* (University of Chicago Press, 1996), p. 117. Here is Michael Rogin's take: "Populism was hardly a moralistic flight from an environment in which everyone else was concerned with facts. The movement made an effort to come to grips with the transformation of American society. Simply because Populism faced the changes America was undergoing while other groups in part denied or repressed them, it is not to blame for the more desperate political responses like McCarthyism." *The Intellectuals and McCarthy*, pp. 32–33.

29. According to his biographer, David S. Brown. See Brown, *Richard Hofstadter*, pp. 118–19.

30. Postel, "The American Populist and Anti-Populist Legacy," in Abromeit et al., *Transformations of Populism in Europe and the Americas*, p. 120. Christopher Lasch, *The True and Only Heaven: Progress and Its Critics* (Norton, 1991), p. 457.

31. Rogin, *The Intellectuals and McCarthy*, p. 275.

6. LIFT EVERY VOICE

1. King spoke on March 25, 1965. His understanding of Populism was explicitly drawn from C. Vann Woodward's famous 1955 book, *The Strange Career of Jim Crow* (Oxford University Press, 1955).

2. This passage is from King's speech to a Constitutional Convention of the AFL-CIO, December 11, 1961, as reprinted in Martin Luther King Jr., *"All Labor Has Dignity,"* ed. Michael K. Honey (Beacon Press, 2011), p. 38.

   King used variations on this theme many times over the years. Another example came in a speech to a gathering of a Retail, Wholesale and Department Store Union local on September 8, 1962: "It is refreshing indeed and encouraging to know that somebody still has the vision, the concern, the insight, and the moral commitment to realize that we are together, and that if the minority groups that are exploited and trampled over by the iron feet of oppression go up, labor will go up; and if we go down, labor will go down because the forces that are anti-Negro are anti-labor and vice versa. And therefore we must see that we are together in a struggle to make democracy a reality, and to make the American dream a reality in this day and this age." King, *"All Labor Has Dignity,"* p. 57.

3. From a speech King gave to the United Auto Workers Union, April 27, 1961, in King, *"All Labor Has Dignity,"* p. 29.

4. From speeches King gave in 1965 and 1963, respectively. See King, *"All Labor Has Dignity,"* pp. 105, 98.

5. From a speech King gave to the Shop Stewards of Local 815, Teamsters Union, May 2, 1967, in King, *"All Labor Has Dignity,"* pp. 125, 126, 129, 128.

6. On the proposed economic bill of rights, see King's posthumous essay, "We Need an Economic Bill of Rights," reprinted by the *Guardian* on April 4, 2018. On the strategy for the march, its debt to the Bonus Army, and the controversies that surrounded the project from start to finish, see Taylor Branch, *At Canaan's Edge: America in the King Years, 1965–68* (Simon & Schuster, 2006), chapters 36 and 37.

7. Speech to AFSCME members, March 18, 1968, in King, *"All Labor Has Dignity,"* pp. 175–76.

8. "The ballot . . . ": C. Vann Woodward, "Introduction" in Bayard Rustin, *Down the Line: The Collected Writings of Bayard Rustin* (Quadrangle, 1971), p. xv. See also Rustin's 1966 essay, "'Black Power' and Coalition Politics," reprinted in Rustin, *Down the Line,* pp. 154–65.

9. *Commentary* article: "From Protest to Politics: The Future of the Civil Rights Movement" (1965) reprinted in Rustin, *Down the Line*, emphasis in original.

10. Rustin continued: "Many people who marched in Selma are not prepared to support a bill for a two-dollar minimum wage, to say nothing of supporting a redefinition of work or a guaranteed annual income."

"Refashioning": "From Protest to Politics," Rustin, *Down the Line*, p. 118. "It is one thing": "'Black Power' and Coalition Politics," *Commentary*, September 1966, reprinted in Rustin, *Down the Line*, p. 164. Rustin hinted at the size of the expenditure he had in mind by pointing to the "$100 billion Freedom Budget recently proposed by A. Philip Randolph," which called for massive federal spending on jobs programs, housing, social insurance, health care, and education. Rustin, *Down the Line*, p. 163.

11. Rustin, *Down the Line*, p. 119, emphasis in original.

12. "The Blacks and the Unions" (1971), reprinted in Rustin, *Down the Line*, p. 346.

13. Ibid., p. 348.

14. The letter is reprinted in *I Must Resist: Bayard Rustin's Life in Letters* (City Lights, 2012), p. 202.

15. King, *"All Labor Has Dignity,"* p. 171.

16. Wesley C. Hogan, *Many Minds, One Heart: SNCC's Dream for a New America* (University of North Carolina Press, 2007), pp. 236, 235, 239. See also Clayborne Carson, *In Struggle: SNCC and the Black Awakening of the 1960s* (Harvard University Press, 1995), and Kevin R. Anderson, *Agitations: Ideologies and Strategies in African American Politics* (University of Arkansas Press, 2010), chapter 5.

17. Lewis's speech is reproduced many places online. Carmichael, quoted in Carson, *In Struggle*, p. 154.

18. According to James Miller, author of the authoritative history of the New Left, "Participatory democracy was a catchword. It became a cliché. It masked a theoretical muddle. It was a stick of conceptual dynamite. It pointed toward daring personal experiments and modest social reforms. It implied a political revolution." Miller, *Democracy Is in the Streets: From Port Huron to the Siege of Chicago* (Touchstone, 1987), p. 152.

19. Michael Kazin, *The Populist Persuasion: An American History*, p. 199.

20. See Barbara and John Ehrenreich, "The New Left: A Case Study in Professional-Managerial Class Radicalism," *Radical America* 11, no. 3 (May/June 1977): 7–22.

21. When the early SDS howled calamity, it often meant a calamity

of the middle-class soul: of the individual all stifled and isolated and alienated because of the conformist demands of mass society. "Loneliness, estrangement, isolation describe the vast distance between man and man today," declared the *Port Huron Statement*. "These dominant tendencies cannot be overcome by better personnel management, nor by improved gadgets, but only when a love of man overcomes the idolatrous worship of things by man." And so on.

22. Miller, *Democracy Is in the Streets*, pp. 23, 87. The man whose thoughts Miller describes in the first quote, Al Haber of the University of Michigan, went on to describe his conflict with SDS's union backers as follows: "They were within a trade-union model. . . . I was within a more free-form university model, a seminar model." Miller, *Democracy Is in the Streets*, p. 67.

23. Miller, *Democracy Is in the Streets*, p. 214.

24. Harold Jacobs, ed., *Weatherman* (Ramparts Books, 1970), p. 52.

25. What SDS "activists" aimed to do when they went to the segregated South, according to James Miller, was "to transform society, to transform their souls." Miller, *Democracy Is in the Streets*, pp. 59, 60. Christopher Lasch, *The Culture of Narcissism: American Life in an Age of Diminishing Expectations* (Norton, 1978), p. 83. See also Maurice Isserman and Michael Kazin, *America Divided: The Civil War of the 1960s* (Oxford University Press, 2000), p. 182.

26. "Excerpts from Walter Reuther's Address to the 1970 UAW Convention," on the website of the UAW's Region 8, http://www .uawregion8.net/UAW-History-Reuther.htm.

27. Charles A. Reich, *The Greening of America* (Bantam, 1971), pp. 305–6, 320.

28. This famous quote appears in Peter Biskind, *Easy Riders, Raging Bulls: How the Sex-Drugs-and-Rock 'n' Roll Generation Saved Hollywood* (Simon & Schuster, 1999), p. 68.

29. Jefferson Cowie, *Stayin' Alive: The 1970s and the Last Days of the Working Class* (New Press, 2010), p. 190.

30. The quotation is from Marshall Frady's classic biography *Wallace* (Random House, 1996 [1968]), p. 12. Frady describes Wallace as "the ultimate demagogue" but also notes his economic liberalism as governor. Frady is careful when applying the p-word to Wallace, but others would not be so finicky. For example, when Ted Kennedy visited Wallace in 1973, the *New York Times* described the

get-together as "Forming a Populist Front" (July 8, 1973). See also Stephan Lesher, *George Wallace: American Populist* (Da Capo, 1995). Dan Carter explicitly attributes the labeling of Wallace as a "populist" to the work of Richard Hofstadter. See *The Politics of Rage: George Wallace, the Origins of the New Conservatism, and the Transformation of American Politics* (Simon & Schuster, 1995), pp. 344–45.

31. Jim Folsom, an Alabama governor who preceded Wallace, was a racial moderate who clearly emerged from the Alabama populist tradition. On Wallace's failure to do much of anything for ordinary people, see Kenneth Reich, "George Wallace, Fake Populist," *Nation*, May 1, 1972. The most articulate rejection of the populist label for Wallace came from none other than C. Vann Woodward. See his review of Lesher's biography in the *New York Review of Books*, October 20, 1994.

32. On the UAW's war on Wallace, see Nelson Lichtenstein, *The Most Dangerous Man in Detroit: Walter Reuther and the Fate of American Labor* (Basic Books, 1995), pp. 428–29.

33. Richard Hofstadter, "The Age of Rubbish," *Newsweek*, July 4, 1970.

7. THE MONEY CHANGERS BURN THE TEMPLE

1. Here is how the passage continues: " 'The rich get richer and the poor get poorer.' " So 62 percent of white America tell the Harris Poll. A quarter of the American people abandoned their trust in our government between 1964 and 1970; by the start of this decade, two-thirds of us believed we had lost our national sense of direction; half of us thought we were on the verge of a national breakdown." Jack Newfield and Jeff Greenfield, *A Populist Manifesto: The Making of a New Majority* (Warner Paperback, 1972), p. 16.

2. Writing in 1972, C. Vann Woodward furnished a list of politicians identified in those days as "populists." See "The Ghost of Populism Walks Again," *New York Times*, June 4, 1972. The historian Eric Goldman did the same in "Just Plain Folks," *American Heritage* 23, no. 4 (June 1972). An even more comprehensive list is given by George B. Tindall in the important essay "Populism: A Semantic Identity Crisis," *Virginia Quarterly Review* 48, no. 4 (Autumn 1972): 501–18.

3. *The Hightower Lowdown*, May 2009, p. 1. Emphasis in original.

4. Bayard Rustin, "The Blacks and the Unions," in *Down the Line: The Collected Writings of Bayard Rustin* (Quadrangle, 1971), p. 349, my emphasis.

5. The 2.4 million strike participants as reported by Jefferson Cowie in *Stayin' Alive: The 1970s and the Last Days of the Working Class* (New Press, 2010). Cowie provides a good description of the insurgencies in the various unions, but the classic account is Thomas Geoghegan, *Which Side Are You On?: Trying to Be for Labor When It's Flat on Its Back* (Farrar, Straus and Giroux, 1991). "Non-white and non-male": See Lane Windham, *Knocking on Labor's Door: Union Organizing in the 1970s and the Roots of a New Economic Divide* (University of North Carolina Press, 2017).

6. Newfield and Greenfield, *A Populist Manifesto*, pp. 20, 9.

7. Lawrence Goodwyn, *Democratic Promise: The Populist Moment in America* (Oxford University Press, 1976), p. xiii.

8. Fred Harris, *The New Populism* (Thorp Springs Press, 1973), p. 8.

9. Ibid., p. 13.

10. Charles Mohr, "Harris Regards Key Issue as Need to Fight Privilege," *New York Times*, December 27, 1975; see also Tom Hayden, "Fred Harris: A Populist with a Prayer," *Rolling Stone*, May 8, 1975.

11. See Christopher Lydon, "Fred Harris Seeks Presidency," *New York Times*, January 12, 1975, and Richard Linnett, "What the 'Godfather of Populism' Thinks of Donald Trump," *Politico*, December 31, 2016.

12. Newfield: See his memoir, *Somebody's Gotta Tell It: The Upbeat Memoir of a Working-Class Journalist* (St. Martin's Press, 2002). Goodwyn's role in the Texas arm of the civil rights movement is described by Max Krochmal in *Blue Texas: The Making of a Multiracial Democratic Coalition in the Civil Rights Era* (University of North Carolina Press, 2016). Goodwyn himself wrote a considerable amount on the subject, mainly in the *Texas Observer*. See his articles "'Hey-You' in Huntsville," *Texas Observer*, August 6, 1965; "The Caste System and the Righteousness Barrier," *Texas Observer*, December 31, 1965; "Anarchy in St. Augustine," *Harper's Magazine*, January 1965.

13. Newfield and Greenfield, *A Populist Manifesto*, pp. 25, 26, 23. Goodwyn outlined his theories of democracy in issue number one of *Democracy*, January 1981, pp. 47, 51.

14. "People are smart enough": The line appears in Lydon, "Fred Harris Seeks Presidency," and also in Fred Harris, *Does People Do It?* (University of Oklahoma Press, 2008), p. 181; "Experts," "open that thing up": Hayden, "Fred Harris: A Populist with a Prayer."

15. "Antipolitician" is a description applied to Carter by Rick Perlstein in *The Invisible Bridge: The Fall of Nixon and the Rise of Reagan* (Simon & Schuster, 2014), p. 581. I am indebted to Perlstein's description of Carter in the passages that follow.

16. Robert S. Boyd, "Jimmy Carter Adopts a New Tag—Populist," *Philadelphia Inquirer*, July 18, 1976.

17. Anthony Lewis, "In Search of Jimmy Carter," *New York Times*, May 31, 1976.

18. See the UPI account as printed in the *Salina Journal*, January 20, 1977. For more on this theme, see the *New York Times* editorial from December 16, 1976, titled "Keeping in Touch," in which we learn that, "having been elected as a populist, Jimmy Carter is naturally perplexed as to how he can restore easier access and a more informal atmosphere to help him keep in touch with ordinary people."

19. On the employer counterattack and the Carter administration's failure, see Lane Windham, *Knocking on Labor's Door*, pp. 76–81. The full-employment scheme to which I refer was the Humphrey-Hawkins bill, a proposal that would have altered the basic nature of the American economy. The bill was a cause célèbre for the labor movement and also for the Congressional Black Caucus; it would have consummated the populist vision of so many of the figures I have described in these pages; and for a time it seemed to be the long-awaited answer to the discontent of the sixties and seventies. But the Democrats in the Carter administration pulled its teeth and turned it into an empty symbol that would bring no real effects. See Cowie, *Stayin' Alive*, chapter 6.

20. Michael Novak, *The Rise of the Unmeltable Ethnics: Politics and Culture in the Seventies* (Macmillan, 1973), p. 20.

21. Kevin P. Phillips, *The Emerging Republican Majority* (Arlington House, 1969), p. 36.

22. Ibid., p. 464.

23. Ibid., p. 470.

24. Kemp, quoted in Albert R. Hunt, "Which Conservatism, Traditional or Populist, Will Reagan Stress?," *Wall Street Journal*, May 27, 1980, p. 1.

25. I am summarizing here my own book *One Market Under God*. The quotes are from George Gilder, *Wealth and Poverty* (Basic Books, 1981), pp. 101, 98.

26. Jeffrey Bell, "The Elites and Reagan's Populist Agenda," *Wall Street Journal*, May 4, 1981, p. 24. Bell would later write a book-length contribution to the genre, *Populism and Elitism: Politics in the Age of Equality* (Regnery Gateway, 1992).

27. Ibid. Biographers of Reagan often depict the GE stage of the future president's life as something resembling indoctrination, with GE management personnel instructing the callow actor in the teachings of the free-market philosophers.

28. Reagan quoted in Kim Phillips-Fein, *Invisible Hands: The Making of the Conservative Movement from the New Deal to Reagan* (Norton, 2009), p. 247.

29. Richard A. Viguerie, *The Establishment vs. The People: Is a New Populist Revolt on the Way?* (Regnery Gateway, 1983), p. 23.

30. See Howard Fineman, "Poppy the Populist: A Onetime Preppy Talks to 'the Folks,'" *Newsweek*, November 7, 1988. Interestingly enough, Fineman seemed to think that the original American populist—the man all would-be populists must try to emulate—was former Alabama governor George Wallace.

31. Patrick J. Buchanan, "How Middle America Is to Be Dispossessed," his column for March 12, 2019, at Buchanan.org. See also "After the Revolution," his column for March 11, 2011.

32. See James Bennet, "Buchanan Attacking All Fronts," *New York Times*, February 29, 1996, and also Michael Lind, *Up from Conservatism* (Free Press, 1997), pp. 2–3.

33. David Nyhan, "Pitchfork Populist's Blue-Collar Con," *Boston Globe*, February 23, 1996.

34. Yes, Trump once wrote an op-ed for a major newspaper. See Trump, "Buchanan Is Too Wrong to Correct," *Los Angeles Times*, October 31, 1999. On Hitler and the Nazis, see Steve Kornacki, "When Trump Ran Against Trump-ism: The 1990s and the Birth of Political Tribalism in America," NBC News "Think," October 2, 2018, https://www.nbcnews.com/think/opinion /when-trump-ran-against-trump-ism-story-2000-election -ncna915651.

35. In a 1988 interview with Polly Toynbee of the *Guardian*, Trump denounces America's openness to foreign investment and trade for

reasons of national pride. The interview was reprinted in that paper on January 21, 2017.

36. Chris Cillizza, "Pat Buchanan Says Donald Trump Is the Future of the Republican Party," *Washington Post*, January 12, 2016.

37. Michael Wolff, "Ringside with Steve Bannon at Trump Tower," *Hollywood Reporter*, November 18, 2016. N.B.: "workingman" is Wolff's coinage, not Bannon's.

38. Michael C. Bender, "Bannon's Journey to Economic Nationalism—Trump Adviser Cites Father's 2008 Financial Trauma as a Turning Point," *Wall Street Journal*, March 15, 2017.

39. These lines are from an interview Bannon did with Rudyard Griffiths in 2018 before a debate in Toronto with David Frum on "The Rise of Populism." His remarks were published in *The Rise of Populism* (Anansi, 2019), p. 10, a transcript of the proceedings. See also the long critique of Wall Street and capitalism that Bannon unrolled in a 2014 talk to a group called the Human Dignity Institute. Read the transcript at https://www.buzzfeednews.com/article/lesterfeder/this-is-how-steve-bannon-sees-the-entire-world.

40. Bannon said this in his 2018 Toronto debate with David Frum.

41. On Bannon's (and hence Trump's) deliberate effort to appeal to the Left, see the remarkable interview/essay by Robert Kuttner, "Steve Bannon, Unleashed," in *American Prospect*, October 6, 2017.

8. LET US NOW SCOLD UNCOUTH MEN

1. Mickey Kaus, *The End of Equality* (Basic Books/A New Republic Book, 1992), p. 173. Robert D. Atkinson, "Who Will Lead in the New Economy?," *Blueprint*, June 2, 2000.

2. William A. Galston and Elaine C. Kamarck, "Five Realities That Will Shape 21st Century Politics," *Blueprint*, Fall 1998.

    "In the Industrial Age, the working class dominated the electorate," intoned Democratic grandee Al From in the course of one of his many denunciations of populism. "The new electorate of the Information Age is increasingly dominated by middle- and upper-middle-class voters who live in the suburbs, work in the New Economy, are culturally tolerant, and have moderate political views." From "Building a New Progressive Majority," *Blueprint*, January 24, 2001.

3. The "SXSL" festival took place on October 3, 2016. A description of its audience-selection process as well as the phrase "commander

in cool" appear in Erin Coulehan, "Commander in Cool," *Salon,*
September 26, 2016.

4. On journalists opposing Trump, see Jim Rutenberg, "Trump
Is Testing the Norms of Objectivity in Journalism," *New York
Times,* August 7, 2016; David Mindich, "For Journalists Covering
Trump, a Murrow Moment," *Columbia Journalism Review,* July 15,
2016. On journalists' campaign donations, remember that journalists rarely give to political campaigns because it is thought to
violate objectivity rules. See Dave Levinthal and Michael Beckel,
"Journalists Shower Hillary Clinton with Campaign Cash," *Columbia Journalism Review,* October 17, 2016. On Clinton campaigning
in Republican states, see Matt Flegenheimer and Jonathan Martin, "Showing Confidence, Hillary Clinton Pushes into Republican
Strongholds," *New York Times,* October 17, 2016. Also, see Nate
Silver, "There Really Was a Liberal Media Bubble," fivethirtyeight
.com, March 10, 2017.

5. See Lawrence Goodwyn, "Organizing Democracy: The Limits of
Theory and Practice," *Democracy* 1, no. 1 (1981): 51, 59. Emphasis in original. The idea was important to Goodwyn, and so he
repeated it a few pages later: an essential requirement of a mass
democratic movement, he wrote, is "an acceptance of human consciousness where it is."

6. "Individual righteousness," "celebrating the purity": Goodwyn,
The Populist Moment (Oxford University Press, 1978), p. 292.
Goodwyn used these phrases to explain the failure of the Socialist Party, which took over many of Populism's positions but got
nowhere electorally. "Ideological patience": Goodwyn, "Organizing Democracy." In *Many Minds, One Heart,* the historian Wesley
Hogan uses the phrase "democratic patience" to describe SNCC in
the 1960s.

7. Joel Stein, *In Defense of Elites: Why I'm Better Than You and You're
Better Than Someone Who Didn't Buy This Book* (Grand Central Publishing, 2019), pp. xvi, 161, 177.

8. Ibid., pp. 254, 239.

9. A study published in 2018 examined the demographics of seven
different political categories defined by their attitude toward
things like immigration, police brutality, and white privilege. It
found that the most liberal category, the group it called "Progressive Activists," was the wealthiest, the best-educated, and

the second-whitest category. ("Devoted Conservatives" were the absolute whitest group.) The study, titled *The Hidden Tribes of America*, was done by an anti-polarization group called "More in Common" and was published in October 2018. Read it at https:// hiddentribes.us.

10. See the graphic designer Bonnie Siegler's *Signs of Resistance: A Visual History of Protest in America* (Artisan Books, 2018), a full-color book that shows us protest artifacts of the Revolutionary period, the women's suffrage movement, the civil rights movement, the anti– Vietnam War movement, feminism, gay rights, opposition to the Gulf War, Black Lives Matter, and the opposition to Trump, but leaves labor out almost completely (participants in the 1968 Memphis sanitation strike are included under Civil Rights).

11. Blow did quote a famous 1946 poem by German cleric Martin Niemoller on July 27, 2017, which mentions Nazi persecution of "trade unionists." Labor unions here in the United States, however, are something Blow seems to view differently. One of the very few times Blow mentioned them during this period was in his *New York Times* column for August 31, 2017, when he accused Donald Trump of "cozy[ing] up to police unions and encourag[ing] police brutality."

12. Beginning in November of 2016, the American news media published dozens, probably hundreds, of articles blaming automation for the deindustrialization of America and specifically exonerating trade deals. It was one of the most remarkable displays of class-based herd thinking I have ever witnessed. Here is a sampling: "Don't Blame China for Taking U.S. Jobs," *Fortune*, November 8, 2016; "The real reason for disappearing jobs isn't trade—it's robots," CNBC, November 21, 2016; "Most US Manufacturing Jobs Lost to Technology, Not Trade," *Financial Times,* December 2, 2016; "The Long-Term Jobs Killer Is Not China. It's Automation," *New York Times*, December 21, 2016; Robert Samuelson's column on the matter, "Trump is obsessed with trade—but it's not a major cause of job loss," *Washington Post*, January 29, 2017; "Rise of the machines: Fear robots, not China or Mexico," *CNN Business*, January 30, 2017.

There were second thoughts on this matter, but generally speaking they were not published till much later. See the 2018 summary of the ups and downs of the pundit consensus by Gwynne

Guilford, "The Epic Mistake about Manufacturing That's Cost Americans Millions of Jobs," *Quartz*, May 3, 2018. See also the life work of the economist Dean Baker, who has written on trade and other class issues for years.

13. There is an enormous literature purporting to show the real reasons for Trump's unlikely victory; much of it finds a root cause to be rising income inequality in addition to factors such as race hatred. For a good summary of the inequality argument, see Rosalind Dixon and Julie Suk, "Liberal Constitutionalism and Economic Inequality," *University of Chicago Law Review*, March 2018.

A few notable studies that diverge from the "deplorables" hypothesis:

- Harris Beider, Stacy Harwood, and Kusminder Chahal, *"The Other America": White Working-Class Views on Belonging, Change, Identity, and Immigration* (Centre for Trust, Peace and Social Relations, 2017): A study of white working-class views that was conducted while the 2016 campaign was in progress; its finding was that white working-class Trump supporters "believed he could restore their sense of economic stability that has been taken away."

- Bob Davi and Jon Hilsenrath, "How the China Shock, Deep and Swift, Spurred the Rise of Trump," *Wall Street Journal*, August 11, 2016: Evaluated support for Trump in Republican primaries and noted the geographic correlation of Trump support with the economic effects from Chinese competition.

- J. S. Goodwin, Y. Kuo, D. Brown, D. Juurlink, and M. Raji, "Association of Chronic Opioid Use with Presidential Voting Patterns in US Counties in 2016," *Journal of the American Medical Association Network Open* 1, no. 2 (2018): e180450: Notes the remarkable correlation between support for Trump and "chronic opioid use" at the county level.

- Salena Zito and Brad Todd, *The Great Revolt: Inside the Populist Coalition Reshaping American Politics* (Crown Forum, 2018): A study of swing counties in the upper Midwest that attributes Trump's victory to, among other things, social media and the Democratic Party's supposed cultural radicalism.

14. Blacklisting Trump officials: See the petition and the "Open Letter to America's CEOs" circulated by the anti-Trump group Restore Public Trust (https://trumpadminseparation.restorepublictrust .org), and Michelle Goldberg's column approving of the operation in the *New York Times* for April 9, 2019, "Cancel Kirstjen Nielsen." DCCC blacklist: See Akela Lacy, "House Democratic Leadership Warns It Will Cut Off Any Firms That Challenge Incumbents," *Intercept*, March 22, 2019.

15. See Elizabeth Logan, "Lena Dunham Called Out American Airlines after Hearing Transphobic Talk from Two Employees," *Teen Vogue*, August 3, 2017.

16. See the thoughtful article on a closely related subject by German Lopez, "Research Says There Are Ways to Reduce Racial Bias. Calling People Racist Isn't One of Them," *Vox*, July 30, 2018.

17. A 2018 study of European and American voters by political scientist David Adler showed that centrists, rather than partisans of the left or right, were "the least supportive of democracy, the least committed to its institutions and the most supportive of authoritarianism." This fascinating challenge to the working-class authoritarianism thesis might seem counterintuitive, but it fits perfectly with what I am describing in this chapter as well as with the much-noted anti-democratic centrism of the European Union. See Adler, "Centrists Are the Most Hostile to Democracy, Not Extremists," *New York Times*, May 23, 2018.

18. William Galston, *Anti-Pluralism: The Populist Threat to Liberal Democracy* (Yale University Press, 2018), p. 22. Galston does not specifically endorse any of these "viable alternatives."

19. See the literature on the "Anthropocene."

CONCLUSION: THE QUESTION

1. Martin Luther King, "Foreword" in *A "Freedom Budget" for All Americans: A Summary* (A. Philip Randolph Institute, 1967), n.p. One place the Freedom Budget can be found online is https://www .crmvet.org/docs/6701_freedombudget.pdf.

2. "Democracy of literature": Emanuel Haldeman-Julius, *The First Hundred Million* (Simon & Schuster, 1928), p. 2. Statistics on H-J's lifetime achievement are from R. Alton Lee, *Publisher for the Masses: Emanuel Haldeman-Julius* (University of Nebraska Press, 2018), p. 202.

3. "Same level": Haldeman-Julius, *First Hundred Million*, p. 2. "The door to learning and culture": Haldeman-Julius advertisement quoted in Jonathan Freedman, *The Temple of Culture: Assimilation and Anti-Semitism in Literary Anglo-America* (Oxford University Press, 2000), p. 171. I am indebted to Freedman's book for the interpretation that follows. "They are not intended to decorate shelves": 1922 Haldeman-Julius advertisement quoted on www .haldeman-julius.org/haldeman-julius-resources/university-in -print.html.

4. E. Haldeman-Julius, *My First 25 Years: Instead of a Footnote: An Autobiography* (Haldeman-Julius, 1949), p. 6.

5. *KKK: The Kreed of the Klansmen: A Symposium*, 1924. Marcet Haldeman-Julius, *The Story of a Lynching: An Exploration of Southern Psychology* (1927). The story in question was the mob murder of John Carter, a savage incident that shocked the nation in May 1927. Two years later, Mr. and Mrs. Haldeman-Julius co-wrote *Violence* (Simon & Schuster, 1929), a novel describing a fictionalized version of the same horrible event.

6. *This Tyranny of Bunk* was the title of a Big Blue Book from 1927. *The Dumbness of the Great: A Survey of the Nonsense, Absurdities, Inconsistencies, Illogicalities, Inaccuracies, and Idiocies of the World's Outstanding Leaders* was a brutal attack on religiosity through history that was written by Joseph McCabe (one of H-J's favorite writers) and published by Haldeman-Julius in 1948 as Big Blue Book number 700.

   The other quotations are from H-J's *The Outline of Bunk* (Stratford, 1929), pp. 343, 448. Of the many secularist pamphlets published by Haldeman-Julius, probably the most famous are Bertrand Russell's *Why I Am Not a Christian* and Clarence Darrow's *Why I Am an Agnostic* (both 1929).

7. Haldeman-Julius's greatest hero seems to have been the Populist/ Socialist labor leader Eugene Debs, whom he describes in his autobiography as a kind of secular saint: "Debs was great. Debs was beautiful. Debs was noble. Debs was a son of the Socialist movement—a self-made, self-educated worker who, with the aid of his Socialist comrades, had disciplined himself as speaker, writer and leader." (Emanuel Haldeman-Julius, *My Second 25 Years: Instead of a Footnote: An Autobiography* [Haldeman-Julius, 1949], p. 59.)

   The former Populist Clarence Darrow was also a hero of the

Haldeman-Julius publications because of his well-known religious skepticism. Ironically, one of the hoariest set pieces of the anti-populist literature is the 1925 Scopes Trial over the teaching of evolution in the public schools, in which the by-then fundamentalist William Jennings Bryan clashed with the agnostic Darrow, thus supposedly revealing the ignorant fundamentalism of the Populist mind. But, as the historian Charles Postel points out, this cozy cliché only works when you omit the fact that Darrow had been an actual Populist leader while Bryan never stopped being a Democrat.

As long as we're on the subject, here is one last fun Populist detail: Mary Elizabeth Lease, the uber-Populist orator who coined the exhortation "less corn and more hell," was also a confirmed believer in the theory of evolution. In 1931 she told the *Kansas City Star* that "the Bible teaches birth control. And the Bible teaches evolution. I am a believer in inspired religion and I am a believer in scientific research." She went on to refer to Bryan as "a paid advocate of darkness" for his role in the Scopes Trial and to name her three "greatest teachers" as Moses, Jesus, and Albert Einstein, who "proved that the soul of man, co-operating with the mind of man, can understand everything."

8. Gilbert Seldes, *Mainland* (Charles Scribner's Sons, 1936), p. 151.

ACKNOWLEDGMENTS

In the 1980s I was passionate about Populism but gave up on the subject a few years into graduate school: going over a forgotten third party with a microscope somehow lost its appeal for me, and I moved on to other things. But the political panic of 2017 brought me back, as did the encouragement of my publisher, Sara Bershtel.

It's a challenge to return to a subject after neglecting it for so long, but the changes in research technology made it easier than one might expect. So did the people who helped me with the digging on this project: Zachary Davis, Charlie Goetzman, Grace Menninger, and Amelia Sorenson. Most of all I am indebted to Steve Richmond, who sank countless hours into this project in the late stages, unearthing many of this book's great finds, and without whom it would probably never have been completed.

The works of Michael Kazin served as models for this study; his 1995 book *The Populist Persuasion* had enormous significance for me when it first appeared. Another model was Christopher Lasch's *The True and Only Heaven*, a work and an author that will probably never get the serious attention they deserve.

For this project I interviewed the Reverend William Barber, Fred Harris, and Jim Hightower, three men who were enormously helpful in explaining the reform tradition and the power of mass movements. There are moments with all of them that I will never forget, but the one I am truly sorry I could not work into the text was when Hightower showed me a framed Texas poll tax receipt from 1964, a memento of a thankfully bygone era.

At Pittsburg State University in Kansas, a mandatory stop on the itinerary of anyone writing about the Little Blue Books, Steve Cox and Randy Roberts were especially helpful. The one who is most responsible for my fascination with this subject, however, is Bridget Cain, who picked up some Blue Books for me at a junk shop in Lawrence way back when.

Wesley Hogan helped me find my way through the civil rights journalism of Lawrence Goodwyn. Joe Vaccaro instructed me in the history of Minnesota radicalism. Matt Stoller furnished me with one of the best anecdotes in this entire enterprise. Liz and Matt Bruenig steered me toward probably a dozen more. Barry Lynn, who is as close to a populist as Washington, D.C., will allow, encouraged me throughout.

Thanks also to all the people who answered the seemingly random queries I posed: Lance Bennett, Joel Bleifuss, Taylor Branch, Fred Gardaphe, Jay Harris, Michael Honey, Michael Kazin (again), Steven Klein, Bob McChesney, Christopher Parker, Charles Postel, Gabriel Zucman, and the helpful staff at the Kansas State Historical Society.

Jim McNeill read the manuscript, as he has read all of my manuscripts over the last twenty years. Chris Lehmann took a crack at it, too, just like in the old days. Eric Klinenberg set me straight on a few things, and Kate Zaloom made valuable suggestions on a few others. Johann Hari's advice was consistently excellent. Rick Perlstein proved himself, once again, a man of remarkable insight both historical and contemporary.

Old Town Editions of Alexandria, Virginia, took pictures of cartoons from my 1896 copies of *Judge* magazine. The Newberry Library provided me with photographs of *Chicago Tribune* cartoons from 1936. Meg Handler helped me secure permission to reprint all the pictures I assembled.

Sara Bershtel and Riva Hocherman of Metropolitan Books steered this whole project brilliantly from start to finish. My agent, Joe Spieler, provided his usual shrewd counsel.

The mistakes and the blunders and the screwups are mine. I claim them all.

INDEX